Witch-hunting in Scotland

Between the late sixteenth and early eighteenth centuries Scottish courts prosecuted hundreds of women and men for the crime of witchcraft, an offence that involved the alleged practice of maleficent magic and the worship of the devil. Scottish witch-hunts claimed far more victims than the prosecutions that took place in the more heavily populated kingdom of England. *Witch-hunting in Scotland* presents a fresh perspective on the trial and execution of these people for inflicting harm on their neighbours and making pacts with the devil.

Brian P. Levack draws on law, politics and religion to explain the intensity of Scottish witch-hunting. Topics discussed include the distinctive features of the Scottish criminal justice system, the use of torture to extract confessions, the intersection of witch-hunting with local and national politics, the relationship between state-building and witch-hunting and the role of James VI. Scottish Calvinism and the determination of zealous Scottish clergy and magistrates to achieve a godly society are also examined as key factors.

This original survey combines broad interpretations of the rise and fall of Scottish witchcraft prosecutions with detailed case studies of specific witch-hunts. Throughout, extensive comparisons between Scottish witch-hunts and those that took place in England, New England and continental Europe are made. *Witch-hunting in Scotland* makes fascinating reading for anyone with an interest in witchcraft or in the political, legal and religious history of the early modern period.

Brian P. Levack is the John Green Regents Professor in History at the University of Texas at Austin. His publications on the history of witchcraft include *The Witch-hunt in Early Modern Europe* (third edition, 2006), *The Witchcraft Sourcebook* (2004) and *Witchcraft and Magic in Europe: The Eighteenth and Nineteenth Centuries* (1999).

Witch-hunting in Scotland

Law, politics and religion

Brian P. Levack

Routledge
Taylor & Francis Group

NEW YORK AND LONDON

First published 2008
by Routledge
270 Madison Ave, New York, NY 10016

Simultaneously published in the UK
by Routledge
2 Park Square, Milton Park, Abingdon, Oxon OX14 4RN

Routledge is an imprint of the Taylor & Francis Group, an informa business

Typeset in Garamond by
HWA Text and Data Management, Tunbridge Wells
Printed and bound in Great Britain by
TJ International Ltd, Padstow, Cornwall

British Library Cataloguing in Publication Data
A catalogue record for this book is available from the British Library

Library of Congress Cataloging-in-Publication Data
Levack, Brian, P.
  Witch-hunting in Scotland: law, politics, and religion / Brian P. Levack
    p. cm.
  Includes bibliographical references and index.
  1. Witchcraft–Scotland. 2. Witchcraft–Great Britain. I. Title.
  BF1581.L38 2007
  133.4'309411–dc22

                                                              2007013926

ISBN13: 978–0–415–39942–5 (hbk)
ISBN13: 978–0–415–39943–2 (pbk)

To Chris and Andy

Contents

Preface

This book has two main purposes. The first is to offer an interpretation of Scottish witch-hunting that emphasizes the influence of law, politics, and religion on Scottish witchcraft trials. The second is to explain why witch-hunting in Scotland was much more intense than in England. Chapter 1 identifies those differences, showing that they can best be understood in the context of the legal, political and religious history of the two kingdoms. The following three chapters address more specific questions. Chapter 2, a study of witchcraft and the law in Scotland, is explicitly comparative, emphasizing the way in which differences between the legal systems of the two kingdoms help to explain the striking disparity in the number of prosecutions and executions. Chapter 3 studies the role played by James VI of Scotland, who also reigned as James I of England, in the witchcraft prosecutions of his two kingdoms. Chapter 4 shows how the patterns of witch-hunting in Scotland and England began to resemble each other during the revolutionary years of the mid seventeenth century, when Scottish covenanters and English puritans both acquired political power. The remaining chapters deal mainly with Scottish witch-hunting but make frequent references to England as well as continental Europe.

Most of the chapters in this book originated as articles essays, papers, or lectures I have presented over the past twenty-five years. Because these items once stood by themselves, they sometimes repeat points made earlier in the text. In blending the chapters together I have eliminated some but not all of the repetition. I have tried to make it possible for individual chapters to be read by themselves with only minimal reference to what has gone before.

In quoting original sources I have modernized spelling and punctuation, except in the titles of books. I have made this decision reluctantly, since it has meant eliminating the distinctly Scottish spelling of English words. In the end, however, I chose to modernize these passages in the interests of readability. I have, however, maintained all Scottish words, giving their English equivalents in parentheses when necessary.

Acknowledgements

Preliminary versions of most of the chapters of this book were presented as lectures or papers at universities and libraries in many different locations. These include the University of Edinburgh, the University of Glasgow, the University of Exeter, the University of Texas at Austin, Fordham University, Washington and Lee University, Northwestern University, the Huntington Library, the Folger Shakespeare Library, the Essex Institute, the University of Melbourne, the University of Adelaide, the University of Queensland, the University of Hobart, the University of Oslo, and the University of Tampere. I have also read papers on the subject at meetings of the North American Conference on British Studies, the Sixteenth Century Studies Conference, the American Historical Association, and the American Society for Legal History. I wish to thank the scholars and students who attended these presentations for helping me refine my arguments and identify new sources.

Large portions of Chapter 8 were originally published in 'The decline and end of Scottish witch-hunting', in *The Scottish Witch-Hunt in Context* (Manchester, 2002) and are reprinted here with permission of the University of Manchester Press. Chapter 4 represents a revised version of my article, 'The Great Scottish Witch-hunt of 1661–1662', which was published in *The Journal of British Studies* 20 (1980). Some of the material in Chapter 3 regarding the possession of Anne Gunter first appeared in my article, 'Possession, witchcraft and the law in Jacobean England', *Washington and Lee Law Review* 52 (1996).

Because my work on this topic has spanned so many years, the debts I have incurred from scholars reach back just as far. During the early years of my research I benefited greatly from conversations with the late Christina Larner, whose premature death dealt a terrible blow to witchcraft scholarship. My debt to Richard Kieckhefer, who helped me teach my first seminar on witchcraft at the University of Texas, goes back even further. Richard and I have continued to share our ideas on witchcraft for more than thirty years. More recently I have benefited from conversations and correspondence with Julian Goodare, who shares with me a deep interest in Scottish witch-hunting. The work that he and his colleagues Lauren Martin, Joyce Miller, and Louise Yeoman did in producing the Survey of Scottish Witchcraft greatly facilitated the last few years of my research. Scholars and colleagues who have helped me in various ways include Ted Cowan, John Cairns, Hector MacQueen, David Sellar, John Langbein, Stuart Macdonald, Michael Wasser, Jenny Wormald, Stuart Clark, Malcolm Gaskill, Jim Sharpe, Cynthia Herrup, Erik Midelfort, Bill Monter, Owen Davies, Charles Zika, Sarah Ferber, Wilfrid Prest, Richard Golden, Johannes Dillinger, Alfred Soman, Rune Hagen, John Young, and Paula Hughes.

No one has spent as much time reading my drafts and listening to my ideas on witchcraft than my wife of forty years, Nancy Levack. An author and editor in her own right, she read an early draft of this manuscript and gave me much valuable advice for improving it. Our two adult sons, Chris and Andy, have not been so closely involved in the production of this book, but they have shared with Nancy and me many of the high and low points of my research on the subject. They have also acquired from me a love of Scotland and single malt whisky. As I complete this manuscript in the beautiful hill country of Texas, I thank them for their love and support, raise my glass, and dedicate this volume to them.

Utopia, Texas
February 2007

Abbreviations

APS	*Acts of the Parliaments of Scotland*, 12 vols, ed. T. Thomson and C. Innes, Edinburgh,1814–75
BL	British Library, London
CH2	Records of the church courts
CSPD	*Calendar of State Papers Domestic*
CSPS	*Calendar of State Papers Relating to Scotland and Mary, Queen of Scots, 1547–1603*, 13 vols, Edinburgh, 1898–1969
Daemonologie	James VI, *Daemonologie, in Forme of a Dialogue*, in J. Craigie (ed.). *Minor Prose Works of King James VI and I*, Edinburgh: Scottish Text Society, 1982
Larner, *Enemies*	C. Larner, *Enemies of God: The Witch-Hunt in Scotland*, Baltimore, MD: Johns Hopkins University Press, 1981
JC	Records of the justiciary court, National Archives of Scotland
Justiciary Cases	S.I. Gillon and J.I. Smith (eds), *Selected Justiciary Cases, 1624–1650*, 3 vols, Edinburgh: Stair Society, 1954–1974
Mackenzie, *Laws*	Sir George Mackenzie, *The Laws and Customes of Scotland in Matters Criminal*, Edinburgh, 1678
NAS	National Archives of Scotland, Edinburgh
NLS	National Library of Scotland, Edinburgh
PA	National Archives of Scotland, records of parliament
RPCS	*Registers of the Privy Council of Scotland*, 38 vols, Edinburgh 1877–
SHR	*Scottish Historical Review*
SHS	Scottish History Society
Source-book	Larner, C., Lee, C.H. and McLachlan, H.V., *A Source-book of Scottish Witchcraft*, Glasgow, 1977
SWHC	J. Goodare (ed.), *The Scottish Witch-Hunt in Context*, Manchester: Manchester University Press, 2002.
WEMS	Normand, L. and Roberts, G. (eds), *Witchcraft in Early Modern Scotland: James VI's* Demonology *and the North Berwick Witches*, Exeter: Exeter University Press, 2000.

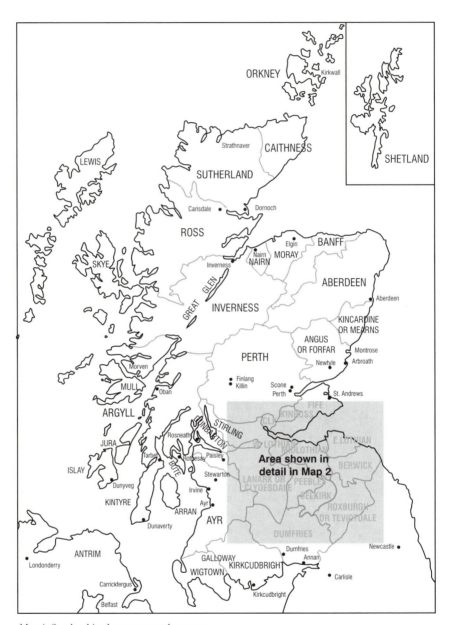

Map 1 Scotland in the seventeenth century

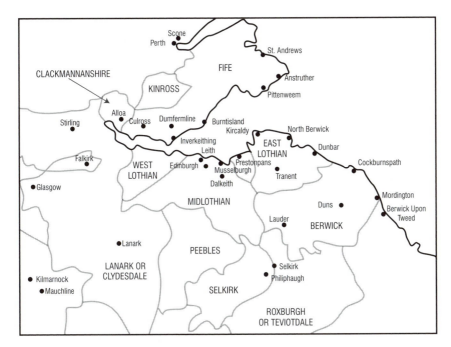

Map 2 Central Scotland in the seventeenth century

Map 3 Synods and presbyteries in the seventeenth century

1 Witch-hunting in Scotland and England

During the early modern period of European history, Scottish courts prosecuted hundreds of women and men for the crime of witchcraft. These people were accused of causing harm to other human beings or their domestic animals by means of some sort of mysterious, magical, or occult power. In many cases they were also accused of making pacts with the devil – the supernatural entity that was believed to be the source of their power – and worshipping him with other witches. We will never know how many Scots were prosecuted for this crime, but we do know that at least 3,800 of them were accused by their neighbours or named as accomplices by other witches.[1] The number of witches who were executed is even more difficult to determine; estimates range from about 1,000 to as many as 2,000 individuals.[2] Even if we use the lower figure, it represents a sizeable group, especially if we take into account the size of the Scottish population, which probably never reached 1 million people during the years when witches were being prosecuted. No wonder that in 1650 an English newspaper reported that Scotland was a 'country very fruitful of witches'.[3]

The intensity of Scottish witch-hunting, measured by the number of executions in proportion to the population, can be appreciated if we compare it to the intensity of witch-hunting in other lands. The most striking and instructive comparison lies with England, the southern British kingdom. The histories of Scotland and England were inextricably interlinked during this entire period, and not simply for reasons of geographical proximity. After indulging in centuries of mortal rivalry during the Middle Ages, the two countries became Protestant allies during the reign of Elizabeth I of England (r. 1558–1603). When James VI of Scotland (r. 1567–1625) inherited the crown of England upon the death of his childless cousin Elizabeth in 1603, the two kingdoms were joined in a regal or personal union. This union did not, however, bring about a union of the governments, churches or laws of the two kingdoms, and therefore each kingdom followed different policies in dealing with witches. English policy resulted in relatively few witchcraft executions. Once again, we don't know how many English witches were killed, since the records of the county assizes – where almost all English witchcraft trials were held – have not all survived. But it appears that England, with a population of about four million people in the middle of the seventeenth century, executed 500 witches between the passage of the Elizabethan witchcraft statute in 1563 and the last execution in 1685. This would mean that if we use the figure of 1,500 Scottish executions, witch-hunting in Scotland was twelve times more intense than in England. Expressed in personal terms, a Scottish woman in the seventeenth century was twelve times more likely than her English counterpart to be executed for witchcraft.

The intensity of Scottish witch-hunting can also be compared with that of other European countries.[4] It was not as intense as the brutal persecutions in the German ecclesiastical territories, such as Bamberg, Würzburg, and Ellwangen, or in the French-speaking duchy of Lorraine, where some 1,400 executions took place in a territory with a population half the size of Scotland's. But Scottish witch-hunting, when compared to that of most other kingdoms and states, did take a very high toll in human life. It was, as Christina Larner argued in her foundational work on Scottish witch-hunting, a major European witch-hunt.[5]

Law

How then do we explain this intensity of Scottish witch-hunting, especially when compared to that of England, which had only one brief period of intense witch-hunting in its history, between 1645 and 1647?[6] This book argues that there were three main explanations. The first and most fundamental lies in the differences between English and Scots law. There were, to be sure, many similarities between the two systems, which had grown up side by side in the Middle Ages. Much of medieval Scots law had been influenced by English law, so much so that when the regal union occurred in 1603 Thomas Craig of Riccarton thought they were entirely compatible. Nevertheless, significant differences had arisen between English law and Scots law, especially in the late fifteenth and sixteenth centuries. Some of these changes took place in private law, that is, the law that regulated relations between individuals engaged in disputes over property and like matters. These differences owed a great deal to the incorporation of certain elements of Roman and canon law into the body of Scots law – a reception achieved mainly by means of judicial decisions. The most significant changes, however, occurred in the area of criminal law, and in particular criminal procedure. These changes, which will be discussed in detail in Chapter 2, changed the ways in which criminal charges could be brought against a person and the way in which trials were conducted. These changes made it much easier for an accused witch to be brought to justice, even if the verdict was still entrusted, as in England, to a jury of lay people rather than professional judges.

Even more important than the conduct of criminal procedure was the way in which the entire system of Scottish criminal justice operated. For reasons that had a great deal to do with the small size of the Scottish judicial establishment in Edinburgh, the majority of witchcraft trials were conducted by local authorities who had no judicial training or experience. This situation contrasted markedly with that which prevailed in England, where judges from the central common law courts at Westminster presided at the county assizes, the venue for the overwhelming majority of witchcraft cases. This difference, perhaps more than any other, explains the higher rate of convictions and executions in Scotland than in England. When Scottish judges did go on circuit, most notably in the latter half of the seventeenth century, the percentage of Scottish witchcraft prosecutions that resulted in convictions and executions began to approximate the corresponding percentages in England.

Two other legal considerations had a bearing on the high intensity of Scottish witch-hunting. The first is that torture and other forms of judicial coercion were much more frequently employed in Scotland than in England. Torture was strictly prohibited in both countries unless approved by a special warrant from the privy council, but this prohibition was more easily evaded in the northern kingdom, especially in witchcraft cases, for reasons that will be discussed in Chapter 2. Torture does not explain why all witches confessed to crimes they had not committed, but there is a close correlation throughout Europe between the freedom courts had to torture people accused of a capital crime and the number of convictions in witchcraft cases.[7] There is no doubt that the strict prohibition of torture in England, where confessions were not needed for conviction in capital cases, explains why the conviction rate in witchcraft cases was lower than in almost all European countries. In Scotland, where local authorities usually needed a confession just to get permission to hold a trial, they used a variety of procedures, including torture, to extract admissions of guilt.

The second consideration is that the Scottish witchcraft act of 1563, which resembled the English witchcraft statute of the same year in some respects, did not allow for non-capital sentences. Convicted Scottish witches were supposed to be executed, even though some did in fact have their sentences commuted to banishment or other forms of non-capital punishment.[8] By the terms of the English statute of 1563 and that of 1604 that replaced it, certain charges of witchcraft merited only imprisonment for a period of years. In practice, moreover, English witches were usually executed only when their alleged misdeeds had resulted in the death of another human being.[9]

Politics

One of the most striking features of Scottish witchcraft, which set it apart from witchcraft in England and from all other European countries, was its close connection with national and local politics. The word politics covers a multitude of meanings, and I am using it here to identify all those considerations of governance that may have impelled central or local authorities to inaugurate or encourage witch-hunts, sustain them once they had begun or at least allow them to continue. James VI of Scotland was in large measure responsible for the politicization of Scottish witch-hunting. As will be discussed in Chapter 3, James came to believe in 1590 that a group of witches in league with his aristocratic rival, the fifth earl of Bothwell, was conspiring to kill him by means of magic and witchcraft. In his mind witchcraft was therefore associated with treason – not just treason against God, as many demonologists had argued, but treason against the king himself. James participated in the prosecution of these witches, helping to secure their conviction and execution. In 1597 he became involved in a major witch-hunt after he became convinced, once again, that witches wished to kill him. The king's traumatic experience with witchcraft in the 1590s also inspired him to write a witchcraft treatise, *Daemonologie* (1597), the only such work produced by a European monarch. This was in a certain sense a political treatise, in that it described an inversion of ideal kingship that was present in many of the king's other political works.[10]

Although James's treatise became well known in England, where he succeeded to the throne as James I in 1603, his work never had the long-standing influence that it retained in Scotland. Like his absolutist political ideas, *Daemonologie* did not fit in comfortably with the mainstream of English thinking. By 1653 its ideas regarding witchcraft had been rejected even by an English political philosopher who was sympathetic to James's brand of royal absolutism.[11] Nor was the king instrumental in politicizing English witch-hunting. The hexes and imprecations of witches never became a personal threat to James in England, and he took no part in the prosecution of English witches. Moreover, by 1605, two years into his English reign, he had become much more sceptical regarding the guilt of witches and had even begun to question whether they were capable of some of the powers attributed to them.

The structure of English criminal justice also worked against the politicization of English witch-hunting. The trial of English witches before common law judges from Westminster, travelling on circuit as part of their semi-annual visitations of the counties, meant that the decision to prosecute was relatively immune from national political considerations. The charges against the accused originated in the fears and tensions of village communities, and the decision to put them on trial was made by the grand jury assembled in the county. In Scotland, however, only a minority of cases were handled by the counterparts of these English central court justices, the justice general and his deputes sitting in Edinburgh. Occasionally one or more of the justice deputes was assigned to an area where witchcraft accusations were multiplying rapidly, and towards the end of this period these judges from Edinburgh occasionally handled cases on circuit. Most cases, however, were adjudicated by local authorities who petitioned the privy council or parliament for permission to hold the trials themselves. These local commissioners then assembled an assize (a jury) to determine innocence or guilt, which in most cases turned out to be the latter. This arrangement for authorizing witchcraft trials meant that central political institutions determined whether or not witches would be prosecuted. The decision whether to grant a commission to prosecute and, even more important, whom to name as members of these ad hoc bodies thus became part of the constant but ever shifting relationship between the centre and the periphery, which was one of the main dynamics of Scottish political life in the early modern period.

Political considerations in Scotland influenced witch-hunting at the local level as well as at the centre. Not only did members of burgh councils expend considerable energy to secure the commissions they needed from the privy council to prosecute witches by themselves,[12] but they also had to negotiate jurisdictional differences between themselves and the local clergy. Ministers and elders of parishes often summoned suspected witches to appear at the weekly meetings of the parish courts, known as the kirk sessions, and respond to reports that they had engaged in behaviour that was considered demonic. The presbyteries, which consisted of ministers from several parishes and occupied the next level of clerical jurisdiction, often conducted preliminary examinations of witches and then referred the cases to the secular magistrates. In most cases the local clergy cooperated with burgh elites in a joint enterprise, but at times the burghs had to rein in ministers who had exceeded the boundaries of their jurisdiction.[13] In the prosecution of Geillis Johnstone in 1614, the privy council found it necessary to reprimand the presbytery of Dalkeith for trying to adjudicate a case that fell within the jurisdiction of the regality of Dunfermline.[14]

Local politics also played a role in the identification of Scottish witches. Most Scottish witchcraft prosecutions originated at the local level rather than in Edinburgh. Even the women tried for attempting treason against James VI in 1590 and 1591 were apprehended and charged first by local municipal authorities; the king's suspicion arose only after they were accused of involvement in a political conspiracy. Explicit political motives did not figure in most Scottish witchcraft prosecutions, which were usually directed against poorer members of society. There was a sizeable group of Scottish witches, however, who were fairly well off, and political motives often figured in their identification and accusation.[15] In some of these cases the women accused were involved in factional disputes within their burgh councils, either directly or through their husbands. In 1649 accusations of witchcraft against the wives of the burgh magistrates of Inverkeithing led the minister and the presbytery of Dunfermline to ask parliament to launch an investigation after the magistrates themselves (understandably) refused to apprehend their spouses.[16] Cases of this sort were far less common in England, where the overwhelming majority of witches came from the lower levels of society.[17]

Witch-hunts throughout Europe tended to occur at times of political uncertainty or acute crisis.[18] Without minimizing the uncertainty of English political life throughout the early modern period, it would be safe to argue that Scotland experienced far more political instability than England during the decades of witch-hunting. The first large witch-hunt in Scotland's history in 1590–1 coincided with James's efforts to fend off a series of rebellions, while the unstable political and ecclesiastical situation in Scotland in 1597 set the stage for the large-scale panic of that year. In 1643–4 severe witch-hunting took place after those presbyterians known as covenanters assumed political and ecclesiastical power. In 1649–50 a much larger witch-hunt coincided with the efforts of those covenanters who had resisted accommodation with England in 1648 to consolidate their position within their communities. After a period in which English military forces had occupied the country and had greatly reduced the intensity of witch-hunting, local elites, eager to reassert their influence in church and state, returned to the mission of hunting witches. The restoration of Charles II and the displacement of the covenanters by royalists eager to establish their credentials as religious reformers in 1660 provided the backdrop to the large-scale prosecutions of 1661–2.

England had only one period of profound instability during the 1640s, when it too experienced a revolution in church and state. Episcopacy was abolished in England in 1646, just as it had been in Scotland eight years earlier. Not coincidentally, England's largest witch-hunt took place during those years, and the men responsible for it included religious radicals who had recently seized political and ecclesiastical power in the localities. During the 1640s, therefore, Scottish and English witch-hunting resembled each other more closely than at any other time in the seventeenth century. After 1650, however, English witch-hunting entered a period of decline while in Scotland it experienced a vigorous revival in the later years of the decade. Legal developments provide the main explanation why England gradually abandoned witch-hunting at this time, but the return to political stability during the protectorate and the restoration rendered it unnecessary for local elites to establish their credentials as defenders of public morality.

Once again, therefore, politics had a greater impact on Scottish witch-hunting than it did in the southern kingdom. In England the restoration did signal a surprising and vigorous revival of witchcraft theory, indicating a desire to establish the parameters of a genuinely Christian community. This demonological theory became part of English political discourse for the next fifty years.[19] This discourse, however, which emphasized the connection between witchcraft and rebellion, was conducted in the pages of political pamphlets. Only in that sense did English witchcraft become politicized. The theory of witchcraft that emerged during those years, which included elements of diabolism that had become prominent during the 1640s, made hardly any impact on the actual prosecution of witches. The few individual prosecutions that did take place in those years did not lead to large witch-hunts; juries began to acquit witches in significant numbers; and judges reprieved the few witches who were sentenced to death after 1685. Scotland did not experience a decline of witch-hunting comparable to that which had occurred in England until the early eighteenth century.

Religion

During the revolutionary decade of the 1640s, witch-hunting in England as well as in Scotland had a common religious justification: to establish the godly society that English puritans and Scottish covenanters considered to be the goal of the Protestant reformation. At other times, however, the religious inspiration of witch-hunting in Scotland was far more evident than in England, and this difference goes a long way towards explaining why witch-hunting was more intense in the northern kingdom. The impact that religion had on witch-hunting can be seen in the way that judicial authorities in the two kingdoms viewed the crime of witchcraft and the role that the clergy played in its prosecution.

Ever since the early fifteenth century, when the first witch-trials took place in continental Europe, the crime of witchcraft was considered to have had two components. The first was the prosecution of harmful magic, often identified as *maleficium*. This was the alleged use of some sort of mysterious, occult, or supernatural power to inflict physical harm on one's neighbours, their domestic animals, or their crops. The second component was diabolism or the worship of the devil. Witches allegedly made pacts with the devil and worshipped him collectively in nocturnal assemblies known as sabbaths. At these meetings witches allegedly engaged in a variety of amoral and often obscene activities, including naked dancing, sexual intercourse with the devil and other witches, the sacrifice of infants to the devil, and cannibalism. At some of these gatherings witches were also reported to have engaged in a mockery of Christian religious services.

The two components of the crime were linked by the belief that witches acquired their magical power from the devil. Nevertheless, the charges brought against witches often emphasized one dimension of the crime or the other. The religious concept of the crime, reflected mainly in the belief that witches made pacts with the devil and joined other witches at nocturnal assemblies, was far more prominent in Scottish witchcraft trials than in those that took place in England. In Scotland witchcraft was defined primarily in religious terms. Ever since the 1590s, when intense witch-hunting began, witches were routinely accused of having made pacts with the devil, of renouncing their baptism, and of swearing allegiance to their new demonic master. The most common method of discovering a witch was to search her body for the devil's mark, a spot that the devil allegedly gave to the witch as a sign of her allegiance. Witchcraft in Scotland was often described as a sin as well as a crime, a violation of God's law as well as the law of Scotland. Indeed, the reason why the Scottish witchcraft statute of 1563 prescribed death as the punishment for all convictions was that the men who drafted the statute subscribed to the biblical injunction in Exodus 22:18, 'Thou shalt not suffer a witch to live.'[20] The reason Scottish witches were burned at the stake (after being strangled) rather than hanged was that burning was traditionally the punishment reserved for heretics in all

European countries. If Scottish witches had been found guilty of a purely secular crime, they would have been hanged, just like murderers or thieves. Burning at the stake sent a message to the entire community that they had committed on offence against the Christian religion as well as the social and political order.

The absence of references to the devil in the trial records of many Scottish witches does not undermine the contention that Scottish officials viewed witchcraft as a religious offence.[21] Most Scottish witchcraft prosecutions, like the majority of cases throughout Europe, originated in charges that the witches had harmed their neighbours by magical means. These charges would not have been of interest to the church courts if they had not been viewed as offences against the reformed religion. The main reason that the devil was not mentioned in many records of witchcraft prosecutions is that the victims of these acts, who provided most of the incriminating testimony against the witches, were not concerned about the demonic dimension of the witches' crime; their only grievance was the misfortune they had suffered. The devil was often introduced into the trial record at a later stage of the proceedings by judicial officials who viewed the crime mainly in religious terms. This explains why in the Fife cases studied by Stuart Macdonald most of the references to the devil appear in central court records. These are the only sources that record the full proceedings against witches. If we had the records of the hundreds of trials conducted by commissioners of justiciary in the localities, a very different picture of the devil's role in witchcraft would doubtless present itself.

The trial of Jean Craig of Tranent in April 1649 illustrates the way in which references to the devil were introduced into the trial. Because this trial was conducted by justice deputes at Tranent, the full record of the prosecution, including the papers submitted to the committee of estates requesting a commission of justiciary, is included within the records of the justiciary court.[22] The original accusations against Craig, supported by depositions of witnesses, enumerate various malefices that she had allegedly committed, including the murder of at least five individuals and spreading lumps of raw flesh and blood all over the house of one John Parker. The devil, however, does not appear in any of these charges; the most demonic of these charges was the characterization of some of her words as 'devilish'.[23] From the formal record of the court's proceedings, however, which includes references to Craig's confessions, we learn that she had become the devil's servant, received his mark, had carnal copulation with him, and renounced her baptism. She also kept trysts and meetings with the devil, 'her lord and master with whom she was conversant at all times'. The court record leaves little doubt that the minister, burgh officials, and 'honest men of the town' before whom she confessed considered her crime as religious in nature. The order of the court that Craig be 'wired to a stake until she be dead and thereafter her body to be burnt in ashes' confirmed she had committed a religious offence.[24]

The responsibility for defining Scottish witchcraft in religious terms rests mainly with the clergy. This should not surprise us, since the clergy in all European countries, especially the Protestant clergy, tended to emphasize the religious or spiritual nature of the witch's crime.[25] In Scotland a group of Protestant ministers that included John Knox drafted the witchcraft act of 1563, which formed part of a broader clerical program to establish a Protestant discipline during the early years of the Reformation. The act sought to eliminate necromancy and other magical acts that Protestant reformers considered remnants of Catholic superstition.[26] In the 1640s the clergy attempted to extend the definition of witchcraft to include charming, the practices of white magic that were usually prosecuted in the church courts.[27] The reason for this clerical campaign against witchcraft was the church's determination to establish a godly society by punishing this and other violations of God's commandments.[28]

A sermon preached by Mr James Hutchison at Paisley in 1697 during a witch-hunt occasioned by the possession of a young girl named Christian Shaw shows that the clergy continued to view witchcraft almost exclusively in religious terms, even when the witches were accused only of *maleficia*. The convulsions and distortions of Christian's body had led to the accusation of seven people for having caused her affliction by witchcraft. If any accusation of witchcraft should have elicited a discussion of the witches' *maleficia*, it was this case of demonic possession, since the symptoms of magical harm were readily apparent in her behaviour. Yet Hutchison's sermon said nothing about the infliction of harm to this girl, only the witches' diabolism. He defined a witch as 'a person that hath immediate converse with the devil, that one way or another is under a compact with him acted and influenced by him to the producing such effects as cannot be produced by others without this compact'. In keeping with a long tradition of Protestant demonology, Hutchison claimed that the essence of witchcraft was the pact with the devil. He even discussed infanticide, which had a place in continental witch beliefs but had not been incorporated into the charges against the Paisley witches. The reason why these malefactors had to be punished, according to Hutchison, was because the law of God demanded it. The most remarkable aspect of this sermon was the claim that the biblical injunction to execute witches was 'given to the judges of the people of Israel, that was a national church, as having the power of the sword committed to them'.[29] Hutchison was claiming, contrary to the law of Scotland and long-standing judicial practice, that the kirk should be able to execute witches.

In England witchcraft was not defined in religious terms. The English witchcraft statute of 1563 did not appeal to the biblical injunction against magical practices in condemning magical practices. Nor did it call for the execution of witches on the basis of biblical authority. Not all English witches were executed, and when they were, they were hanged like other felons, not burned in the manner of heretics. English witchcraft trials yielded far fewer charges of making pacts with the devil and of gathering at the witches' sabbath. The overwhelming majority of the charges brought against English witches referred simply to the *maleficia* they had allegedly performed. In the county of Essex only 28 of 503 indictments for witchcraft between 1580 and 1680 involved contact with evil spirits.[30]

When accusations of diabolism did arise in English trials, which was mainly during the 1640s, they were restricted mainly to charges that the witch had nourished a demonic imp or familiar, who had in turn allegedly assisted her in performing her maleficent magic. There is some uncertainty whether this belief in demonic familiars originated in an English popular tradition that viewed animals as having magical powers or was a remnant of the belief that ritual magicians (who were accused of making face-to-face pacts with the devil as early as the thirteenth century) commanded a demonic imp to perform magic for them. The unique claim that English witches suckled their familiars supports the former interpretation, whereas the presence of imps in trials for performing ritual magic, such as that of John Walsh in 1566, suggests the latter.[31] In either case, however, the charge that witches gave liquid nourishment to their familiars represents a weak version of the standard continental European and Scottish depiction of the witch's face-to-face pact with the devil.

Even more striking than the absence of references to the demonic pact was the rarity of charges of collective devil worship in English witchcraft trials. The first mention of a witches' sabbath in England appears in a trial that took place in Lancashire in 1612, and after that date reports of such assemblies were few and far between.[32] Only in the trials of 1645 and 1646, which shall be discussed in Chapter 4, did they appear with any regularity in witchcraft indictments. English assemblies of witches, moreover, were exceptionally mild affairs, involving few or none of the heinous activities reported at German and other continental European assemblies. The only reports of sexual commerce with demons occurred during the trials of 1645.[33]

The appearance of these charges of diabolism in the English witchcraft trials of the 1640s suggests that a religious definition of the crime of witchcraft was hardly absent in England. Indeed, a large body of demonological literature, almost all of it written by English clerics, had presented ideas regarding the pact and the sabbath to an English audience in the late sixteenth and early seventeenth centuries.[34] These ideas, however, did not find their way into English witchcraft trials, except in the 1640s. This can be attributed, at least in part, to the English prohibition of torture. Unable to force suspected witches to confess to having made pacts with the devil or attended nocturnal assemblies with him, magistrates who harboured such demonological beliefs would have had great difficulty introducing them at any stage of the judicial process.

Differences in criminal procedure, however, cannot provide a full explanation for this striking difference between English and Scottish witch-hunting. Scottish authorities may have been able to torture accused witches with impunity, but they certainly did not employ these tactics in all the prosecutions that yielded accusations of diabolism. The main reason for the greater Scottish emphasis on the religious nature of witchcraft lies in differences between Scottish and English religious culture. Owing to the greater strength of Calvinist thought in the northern kingdom, the devil had a more commanding and therefore more frightening presence in Scotland than in England. The devil was not an insignificant figure in English culture,[35] but he did not dominate religious life the way he did in Scotland. One measure of that dominance was the frequency with which Scottish preachers discussed the devil's presence in the world and in human affairs. This emphasis on the devil's immanence meant that all the people involved in Scottish witchcraft prosecutions, including the witches themselves, were more likely than their counterparts in England to see the crime of witchcraft as essentially diabolical in nature.

The Scottish definition of witchcraft as a religious offence helps to explain the greater number of convictions and executions in the northern kingdom. Prosecuting and executing 'enemies of God', as John Knox referred to witches, especially when the Bible instructed them to do so, inspired magistrates to be more thorough in their work than if they were merely prosecuting maleficent magicians. Only if witchcraft was considered a sin as well as a crime could Scottish lay and clerical authorities think of witch-hunting as a means to establish a godly society, as they did throughout the seventeenth century. In England this motive for prosecuting witches was paramount only in the 1640s. The belief that witchcraft was a religious crime also explains why the Scottish church courts, unlike those in England, played a crucial role in its prosecution, as shall be discussed in Chapter 2.

Charges of diabolism, especially when practised collectively, also expanded the pool of potential witches.[36] Unlike maleficent magic, which was often performed individually or in very small groups, devil worship was believed to be a collective activity. A witch who made a pact with the devil was usually suspected of worshipping him with other witches. In Scotland such meetings were relatively tame, at least by continental standards, but they did involve significant numbers. In the witch-hunts of 1649–50 and 1661–2 witches were accused routinely of attending such meetings. Indeed, most of the witches whose names appear in the judicial records of those years were brought to the attention of judicial authorities only after a confessing witch had named them.

The Scottish clergy were also much more active than their English counterparts in trying to persuade suspected witches to confess. In a major witch-hunt in the presbytery of Irvine in 1649–50, for example, ministers were asked on several occasions to bring the witches to a greater sense of guilt than they had manifested so far.[37] The fact that they succeeded in getting witches to confess, often without physical coercion, testifies to the existence of a 'culture of confession' in Scotland that was very different from the tradition of private auricular confession in Roman Catholic countries. In

1704 Isobel Adam confessed her pact with the devil, the renunciation of her baptism, and her attendance at meetings with witches and devils 'before the magistrates and elders and before the said minister himself'. She then renewed her confession 'before many in prison, before the presbytery, and before thousands, and did it with tears'.[38] The Scottish church considered this type of public confession to be the only way a person could acquire an assurance of salvation. It also served the essential legal purpose of giving the privy council the grounds for granting a commission of justiciary.

England did not have the same culture of confession that prevailed in Scotland, nor did confession have the same legal importance in the southern kingdom. Cases in which a minister pressured a suspected witch to confess were relatively rare in England. Henry Goodcole, the minister at Edmonton in Middlesex, succeeded in getting Elizabeth Sawyer to confess to some of the charges against her in 1621, but the confession was never repeated publicly, and it came after, rather than before, her conviction by a jury.[39] Englishmen in Scotland during the Cromwellian occupation became aware of the extent of the cultural and legal gap between them and the Scots regarding confession. In 1652 William Clarke expressed amazement that the main proofs offered for religious crimes committed by Scots 'were their own confessions before the kirk, who are in this worse than the Romish religion, who do not make so ill an use of their auricular confession'.[40]

A final connection between religion and witch-hunting in Scotland was the high degree of religious intolerance in the northern kingdom. Religious toleration is usually discussed as a matter of state policy, that is, the degree of religious pluralism governments were willing to permit. Until the late seventeenth century such tolerance was in short supply throughout Europe; most governments were committed to a policy of religious uniformity and used legal means to enforce it. Nevertheless, some governments, such as Poland in the sixteenth century, the Dutch Republic in the seventeenth century, France between 1598 and 1685, and England during the 1650s, adopted policies of limited toleration. They did so mainly for practical political reasons, not because they had abandoned their belief in the superiority of the established religion or recognized an individual's right to worship as he or she pleased. These tolerant governments tended not to encourage witch-hunting, mainly because they had decided that a policy of persecution was harmful to the maintenance of public order. Conversely, religiously intolerant regimes were more likely to hunt witches for the simple reason that these religious deviants constituted a serious challenge to their goal of establishing a godly state.[41]

A case might be made that the Scottish government was more intolerant than the English government throughout the late sixteenth and seventeenth centuries. One measure of this relative intolerance was the fact that Scottish Protestant dissenters (mainly episcopalians) received toleration only in 1712 and only as the result of action by a parliament dominated by Englishmen, whereas the English parliament had granted English Protestant dissenters a begrudging toleration more than twenty years before. It would be difficult, however, to link that greater intolerance to a record of more intense witch-hunting, especially since the role of the Scottish central government in prosecuting witches was problematic to begin with.

A much closer correlation between religious intolerance and witch-hunting can be found in the intolerance of religious groups towards other confessions. Let us call this denominational as opposed to official intolerance. There was an element of this intolerance in all religious denominations during the early modern period, but there were some tendencies in Protestantism that encouraged a limited ecumenism. They can be seen in the publication of the Heidelberg catechism, the repeal of laws condemning heresy, and in the development of the belief in some Protestant denominations that salvation was available to all. Among Scottish presbyterians such sentiments were in short supply. Their notoriously intolerant position towards papists and episcopalians contrasted markedly with the large numbers of conforming English Protestants, who later became known as Anglicans, or late seventeenth-century English Latitudinarians, who were known for their tolerance of other religions. Only the English puritans, especially those who were presbyterians, displayed a comparable degree of intolerance. The tendency of presbyterians to see religious practice in terms of black or white, godly or corrupt, to demonize their religious rivals, and to enforce a severe moral discipline on their congregations led them to take a hard line against witches, whom they saw as the devil's confederates. Presbyterians took a leading role in arresting and investigating witches throughout the period of witch-hunting, even after the British parliament had declared that witchcraft was no longer a crime.

The argument of this book is that witch-hunting in Scotland was more intense than it was in England because of the differences in law, politics and religion outlined above. In emphasizing these three areas of difference it does not deny the importance of social and economic factors in causing witch-hunts. Such considerations were crucial in explaining the accusations of the witches' neighbours. Nor does it deny the importance of gender in the identification of witches. The reason the book does not focus on these factors is that they do not provide answers to the comparative questions that drive this investigation.

Differences between English and Scottish society, except on the Celtic fringe, where very few witches were executed, were not significant enough to produce huge differentials in the incidence of witch-hunting. Nor did the economic experiences of the two countries, despite Scotland's lower standard of living, differ enough to explain the great disparity in number of witches executed in the two kingdoms. Both countries experienced runaway inflation, a decline in the condition of the poor, and sporadic famine during the early modern period. It is no coincidence that during the 1590s, when all Britain experienced greater economic hardship than in any other decade of the early modern period, witch-hunting intensified in both countries. A terrible famine in 1597 provided the economic setting for Scotland's witchcraft panic of that year.[42] Similar correlations between dire economic conditions and intense witch-hunting took place on the European continent.[43] Nor were gender roles much different in the two countries, except perhaps in the Scottish Highlands. Any effort to link the greater intensity of Scottish witch-hunting with attitudes towards women confronts the uncomfortable fact that women formed a larger percentage of the total number of witches in England than in Scotland.[44]

We come back, therefore, to the significant differences between the two systems of criminal procedure, the political concerns of national and local elites, and the relative intolerance of ministers and laity alike. The legal differences were essentially structural, the political differences arose in responses to problems of governance, and the religious differences, in the final analysis, were reflections of cultural difference. The combination of all three proved deadly for some 1,500 Scottish witches.

2 Witchcraft and the law in early modern Scotland

In 1618 Margaret Barclay, wife of Archibald Dean, a burgess of the burgh of Irvine in Ayrshire, was tried, convicted, and executed for committing the crime of witchcraft. Except for the high social status and fairly young age of the accused, the trial was fairly typical of the hundreds of witchcraft trials that took place in Scotland in the late sixteenth and seventeenth centuries.[1] The trial had its origins in a conflict between Barclay and Janet Lyle, the wife of her husband's brother, John Dean. Barclay had brought an action of slander against Lyle in the parish ecclesiastical court known as the kirk session. Despite an apparent reconciliation at the command of the session, Barclay's anger against Lyle and her husband never abated, and she was heard cursing a ship, *The Gift of God*, on which Dean and the provost of the town, Andrew Tran, had embarked on a voyage to France. She was reported as having prayed: 'God, let never sea nor salt-water bear them above that had injured me, but that the partans [crabs] eat them in the bottom of the sea.'[2] When news that the ship had in fact sunk off the coast of England near Padstow, leaving only two survivors, Margaret became the prime suspect of having caused the shipwreck by magical means. The case against Margaret Barclay, like that of the many thousands of people accused of witchcraft in Scotland and throughout Europe, thus began with the suspicion that she had performed an act of harmful magic in order to wreak revenge on a person with whom she was quarrelling.

Suspicion of Barclay was confirmed when a vagabond named John Stewart, who had delivered the news of the disaster before the two surviving sailors reached Irvine, admitted under questioning (and probably under torture) that Barclay had come to him to learn how to practise the magical arts. More specifically, he had visited her house shortly after the ship set sail and had found her with two other women making clay figures, one of which represented Provost Tran. Stewart also claimed that the women were making a clay model of the ship that had sunk. At this time the devil, according to Stewart's confession, appeared in the room in the shape of a handsome lap-dog. Shortly thereafter, the entire group of witches, together with the devil, went to the seaside, where they threw the clay figures into the water. The sea roared and turned red. In this testimony Stewart introduced the figure of the devil for the first time, thus compounding Barclay's and the other women's crime with diabolism.[3]

After giving this confession, Stewart identified Isobel Inch as one of Barclay's accomplices. Inch denied the charges but she was nonetheless imprisoned in the belfry of the parish church. Then, in an astonishing development, Inch's daughter, Margaret Taylor, an 8-year-old child who lived with Barclay as her servant and cared for Barclay's child, confirmed Stewart's charges against her mother and her mistress, while also identifying a 14-year-old girl as the other female accomplice. Young Margaret confirmed Stewart's reference to the diabolical black dog but added that a black man had been present as well. She also claimed that the dog emitted flashes from its jaws and nostrils when the women threw the figures in the sea.[4]

Attention then turned to Isobel Inch, from whom the magistrates and ministers of Irvine tried to secure a confession. Just at the point when she gave signs that she was about to break under the pressure, she attempted to escape from the belfry, falling from the roof and sustaining injuries that led to her death five days later. Before she died she denied everything she had admitted under pressure before her accident.

At this point burgh authorities petitioned the privy council in Edinburgh for a commission to try Stewart and Barclay.[5] This was the way in which most Scottish witchcraft prosecutions commenced. Local authorities would send a petition to the privy council with evidence of the guilt of the accused obtained by means of pre-trial interrogation, asking for permission to try to witch in the burgh or county where she resided. The council would then, if it agreed, send a warrant to a group of local dignitaries to assemble an assize (a jury) of thirteen or fifteen people to try the accused, known in Scots law as the panel. In this case the burgh officials requested the earl of Eglinton, who lived within a mile of the burgh, to assist them in their work.

On the day of the trial John Stewart, despite being put on a suicide watch, managed to hang himself from the door of his cell with a string made of hemp taken from his cap or garter. He took his own life just as he was about to be confronted with another witch from the neighbouring burgh of Ayr, presumably to identify him as an accomplice. His suicide was made possible, according to the record of the trial, with the help of his master, the devil.[6] Stewart's departure from this life left Margaret Barclay as the sole defendant, and since she had not yet confessed, a decision was made, with the assistance of the earl of Eglinton, to subject her to torture. The method used, described as 'the most safe and gentle', consisted of laying a steadily increasing number of metal bars on her shins.[7] A gentle torture is of course an oxymoron, but it is true that Barclay was not subjected to the brutal torture of the *strappado* that was often used on the continent, or the Spanish boots used not only on the European continent but also in a few instances in Scotland.

The torture of Barclay led to her 'free' confession, in which she admitted causing the shipwreck in order to kill her brother-in-law and Provost Tran but not the other members of the crew. She also implicated another accomplice,

Isobel Crawford, who upon her arrest and interrogation admitted her guilt but placed the main blame on Barclay. Barclay's confession was made before the four commissioners, the earl of Eglinton, and four ministers from neighbouring parishes, including David Dickson, minister in Irvine. At this point Barclay's husband appeared in court with a lawyer, whereupon Barclay retracted her confession, claiming 'all that I have confessed was in torture'. She also rebuked her husband, saying: 'Ye have been over-long in coming.'[8]

Despite this retraction, the jury convicted Barclay, claiming that the confession could not be attributed to torture since the bars had been removed from her legs when she actually made her statement. She was therefore executed by being strangled at the stake and her body then burned, the punishment suffered by most Scottish witches.[9] Just before the execution Barclay confirmed her original confession, probably to secure the sympathy of the ministers and the public who attended the execution. The final episode in this long saga was the granting of yet another commission to try Isobel Crawford, who likewise confessed under the torture of iron bars weighing 420 lbs. In her confession she not only admitted all of the charges against the two women but also of having had sexual relations with the devil for several years. She too was sentenced to death. Like Barclay, Crawford retracted her confession, but unlike Barclay did not withdraw her retraction and confirm it at the stake, remaining unrepentant to the end and interrupting the minister on several occasions.[10]

The trials of Margaret Barclay and Isobel Crawford were in a certain sense isolated prosecutions. They did not take place as part of one of the larger, national witch-hunts in the kingdom, such as those that occurred in 1590–1, 1597, 1649–50, and 1661–2. The trials do, however, reveal some of the distinctive features of Scottish criminal justice in the prosecution of witchcraft. The two trials also show the ways in which Scottish criminal law differed from that of England. These differences relate mainly to the way in which prosecutions were initiated, the extent to which torture was used in the interrogation of witches, the role of central and local courts in the prosecution of the crime, and the part played by the clergy in the identification and interrogation of suspects.

The initiation of prosecutions

In 1605, shortly after the regal union of England and Scotland in the person of King James VI and I, the Scottish jurist Thomas Craig of Riccarton argued that English and Scottish criminal procedure, just like the substantive law of the two kingdoms, resembled each other closely.[11] In his treatise *De Unione regnorum Britanniae* (On the Union of the Kingdoms of Britain), Craig wrote that in criminal actions the same laws and procedures of the two kingdoms were used. Craig had an axe to grind, for he was one of the most forceful Scottish proponents of perfecting the dynastic union that had just come about by bringing the institutions of the two countries into closer conformity. It is not surprising, therefore, that Craig emphasized the most fundamental similarity between the two systems, which is that they both used trial juries to decide guilt or innocence.[12] The use of juries is one of the hallmarks of accusatorial procedure, the system of criminal justice in which individuals or the community rather than the courts take the leading role in the detection and prosecution of crime. England and Scotland were not the only countries in Europe that still adhered to accusatorial procedure; the Scandinavian kingdoms and Hungary did so as well. These kingdoms had resisted to different degrees the introduction of inquisitorial procedure, the mode of criminal prosecution in which officers of state – judges and their subordinates – conducted the entire criminal process *ex officio* (by virtue of their office) and assumed responsibility for both the investigation of the crime and the determination of guilt based upon rational proof. Inquisitorial procedure was adopted first by the ecclesiastical courts and then by the secular courts in France, Germany, the Netherlands, Spain, Portugal, and Italy between the thirteenth and the sixteenth centuries. As we shall see, Scotland adopted certain features of inquisitorial procedure, most notably the adherence to new, more demanding standards of proof in criminal trials, in the sixteenth and seventeenth centuries, but as long as lay juries decided guilt or innocence, it is misleading to classify either the English or the Scottish system of criminal procedure as inquisitorial.[13]

The problem with Craig's discussion of Scottish and English procedure was that his determination to identify similarities between Scottish and English practice led him to ignore significant differences in the way crime was prosecuted in the two British kingdoms. Most notably, Craig did not explain that Scotland, unlike England, did not have a grand jury, which was required to approve the trial of all felonies before an English trial could commence.[14] Originally English grand juries, which were also known as presenting juries, were expected to have knowledge of the crime, just like the trial or petty juries that decided the facts of the case and delivered the final verdict. It is true that by the time that the Elizabethan witchcraft statute was passed in 1563, the English grand jury had begun to decline in importance. The part that it had once played in the preliminary investigation of crime had begun to pass to the justices of the peace (from whom, in turn, it later passed to the police), while its decisions regarding draft indictments (known as bills) prepared by the clerks of the peace and of the assize had in many cases become a mere formality. Nevertheless, the grand jury, which reflected the persistence of an accusatorial system of criminal procedure in the southern kingdom, still ensured that neither the Crown nor its ministers could try a person for felony on their own initiative. As John Baker has written, 'in matters of life or limb there existed between the Crown and the subject a shield borne by his neighbours'.[15]

This shield provides one explanation why witch-hunting in England never reached epidemic proportions, even in the 1640s. English grand juries could and often did approve draft indictments of witches, allowing their cases to be heard before the county assizes, but the jury's approval of these indictments was never guaranteed, especially in the prosecution of a crime like witchcraft that quite understandably raised many questions of evidence. Even during the 1640s, at the height of England's largest witch-hunt, grand juries rejected some of the draft indictments for witchcraft submitted to them for their approval. Even more important, the requirement that the courts needed a 'true bill', that is, an indictment approved by the grand jury, before beginning a trial, meant that witch-hunts could never be initiated by officers of the court on the basis of rumour or any other means by which popular suspicions might have come to their attention.

The absence of grand juries in Scotland meant that prosecutions such as that of Margaret Barclay and Isobel Crawford were much more likely to proceed to their tragic conclusion. Although Scotland did have a mechanism by which groups of neighbours – prominent individuals from the shires and burghs – presented criminals to the justice clerk, this mechanism did not always work effectively, especially when the system of circuit courts with which it was associated broke down in the sixteenth century. When that happened, individuals or local officials who wished to prosecute a crime still had a number of options. The first was to petition the privy council to grant a commission of justiciary to local lairds or burgesses to try the witches in the localities on the basis of evidence they had gathered during pre-trial examinations of the accused. This was in fact the way in which the trials of Margaret Barclay and Isobel Crawford were initiated in 1618.

The second option was to ask the lord advocate, the chief judicial officer of the Crown (analogous to the attorney-general in England), to draft an indictment of the defendant and prosecute the person in the justiciary court, which was the central criminal court in Edinburgh. The powers of the lord advocate were greatly enhanced by the judicial reforms enacted during the reign of James VI in 1587. Until the passage of this act, all criminal prosecutions in Scotland were technically private, in the sense that all trials were initiated by a personal complaint or accusation by one person or his kin against another. The person who presented the charge in court was known as the pursuer, which meant that he was the actual prosecutor of the crime. The problem that the royal government faced was that many victims of crime were reluctant to bring actions against malefactors or they chose to settle their disputes by alternate means. In this way royal authority was being significantly challenged or diminished. The act of 1587 provided that the lord advocate not only concur in all private prosecutions but also that he could bring a criminal action against the malefactors by himself even when 'the parties be silent or would otherwise privately agree'.[16] He would do this by having his assistants draft the indictment and then actually prosecute the crime himself.

The provisions of the act of 1587 marked the introduction of an important element of inquisitorial procedure in Scotland. The hallmarks of inquisitorial procedure were the elimination of the replacement of the private accuser by an officer of the court (known variously as a public prosecutor or fiscal) and the prosecution of the crime by officials rather than individuals acting in a private capacity. Scotland clearly did not adopt all the features of inquisitorial procedure; trial by jury was maintained, and many cases were still initiated by accusations from private parties. But this new approach to prosecuting harm marked a significant modification of accusatorial procedure. It also amounted to a major difference between Scotland and England, which never allowed an attorney-general or any other officer of the court to start a prosecution by his own authority. It is significant that a paper prepared for English MPs in 1604 describing the way in which crimes were prosecuted in Scotland included the notice that 'the party pursuer is either the party wronged alone, such as the relict [widow] and children of any that is killed, against the party slayer, or his Majesty's attorney general [i.e. the lord advocate] for his Highness's interest, or else both conjointly'.[17] The statement makes clear the fact that accusatorial procedure still operated in Scotland, since cases could still be initiated and prosecuted by a private person, but a government official now could either join the private party in the suit or start the prosecution by himself.

A third option to private prosecution, which was not exercised frequently, was that the Scottish criminal judges retained the right to charge criminals on the basis of information they had obtained themselves.[18] This option, which was likewise characteristic of inquisitorial procedure, was not available in England. The southern kingdom experimented with such a system in 1496 and 1650 but on both occasions quickly rejected it in all felony prosecutions.[19] Only in the prosecution of misdemeanours, that is, crimes that were not felonies, was it possible to initiate a criminal prosecution by information. These misdemeanours were tried mainly in the Court of Star Chamber before its abolition in 1641, and after that year in the court of King's Bench, which inherited some of Star Chamber's jurisdiction. Ironically, the only cases connected with witchcraft initiated in this way were those in which the government prosecuted people who had made false or malicious charges against witches.

The first of these English cases was the prosecution of Anne and Brian Gunter in the Star Chamber in 1606 for conspiring to indict three women for witchcraft in Berkshire. The women had been acquitted of the charges at the Abingdon assizes. The information was exhibited by Sir Edward Coke, the attorney-general, who was a consistent opponent of the use of inquisitorial procedure in the common law courts (on the grounds that the procedure was un-English) but who had no reluctance to use it in this non-capital case to punish defendants who tried to corrupt the legal process.[20] The second case, also heard in the Star Chamber, was a charge of slander by John Lowes, the vicar of Brandeston, Suffolk, in 1615 against one of his parishioners, Jonas Cooke, who had accused him of witchcraft earlier that year. The grand jury had thrown out all but one of Cooke's charges, and Lowes was acquitted of the fourth charge at the assizes that year. The outcome of Lowes's slander suit in the Star Chamber is unknown.[21] Later in the century, however, during the witch-hunt conducted by Matthew Hopkins and John Stearne in East Anglia, Lowes was tried once again for witchcraft and was executed in 1645. The third case was the prosecution of Richard Hathaway in King's Bench in 1702 for falsely accusing Sarah Morduck of witchcraft and thus maliciously intending 'to bring [her] into the danger of losing her life'.[22]

The difference between Scottish and English procedure was noted when Andrew Laidlawe was tried on indictment in the Scottish justiciary court after being named by convicted witches in 1671. One of the articles against Laidlawe stated that he had been prosecuted for attending 'divers meetings with the devil and other witches' in the English time, that is, in the 1650s, but that the English would put no one to death for witchcraft 'without proven malefice against them and when nobody was insisting'.[23] In other words, the English judges presiding over Scottish criminal trials in the 1650s would not convict someone of witchcraft unless there was proof of *maleficium* (as opposed to devil worship) and unless there was an individual accuser or complainant who was willing to insist, that is, go through with the prosecution.[24]

With so many different procedural options it was much easier therefore to start a witchcraft prosecution in Scotland than in England, and this accounts for the far greater number of witchcraft trials in the northern kingdom when figured on a per capita basis. The ease with which the trials could be initiated, however, cannot explain the higher number of convictions.[25] Some of those convictions were made possible by the fact that Scottish juries, which had either thirteen or fifteen members, required only a plurality to convict, while English juries required unanimity.[26] There is no substantial evidence, however, that Scottish juries convicted significant numbers of witches on the basis of plurality verdicts.[27] The higher conviction rate in Scotland had much more to do with the fact that torture was used in many Scottish witchcraft trials and that most of those trials took place in local courts without the presence of judges from Edinburgh.

Torture

One of the most significant procedural differences between English and Scottish criminal procedure in the prosecution of witches was that Scottish judicial authorities, unlike their English counterparts, often used torture to extract confessions from the people accused of this crime. Contemporary awareness of Scottish practice in this regard was fostered by pamphlets that reported gruesome incidents of torture north of the Tweed[28] and by statements from Scots themselves defending the legality of the procedure.[29] In a debate in the English parliament regarding the legal ramifications of the union of England and Scotland in 1656, the MP John Lambert proposed 'eliminating several laws and customs in Scotland, as the racking and tormenting of people under the lash of their justice'.[30] Lambert's critique of Scottish practice was informed by the widespread knowledge that the common law, which Englishmen considered superior to laws of all other nations, prohibited the use of torture.[31] Exposing the brutality of Scots law, therefore, served indirectly to bolster claims of English superiority over a country that had come under the influence of Roman law.[32]

Englishmen such as Lambert who deplored the Scottish propensity to administer torture would have been surprised to learn that, when Scottish judicial authorities tortured witches or other criminals, they almost always did so illegally. Scottish courts had no authority to employ torture in criminal trials. Scottish authorities, like their English counterparts, could not use torture unless they received a special warrant from the privy council. Scottish warrants could also come from the Scottish parliament, during whose sessions the privy council did not sit. The privy councils of both countries issued warrants only in extraordinary circumstances, on an average of not more than once per year, usually when they considered information from the accused to be vital to the state.[33] For this reason the great majority of English and Scottish warrants dealt with crimes of a political nature: treason, rebellion, sedition, attacks on prominent statesmen, and religious subversion.

As far as witchcraft is concerned, the 81 English warrants granted between 1540 and 1640 confirm what is already widely known: torture simply was not used in English witchcraft prosecutions.[34] A survey of Scottish warrants, however, yields a more surprising result. Considering the large amount of information we have about the use of torture in Scottish witchcraft trials, one would expect to find a large number of warrants dealing with that crime. This is not the case. Between 1590 and 1689 the Scottish privy council issued only two warrants to torture suspected witches. The first warrant was granted in October 1591, the year of the large witch-hunt in which James VI took a personal part. Since this hunt, which will be discussed at length in Chapter 3, involved the crime of treason as well as witchcraft, the warrant was in no way exceptional. It authorized six specially named commissioners – two councillors, two ministers, and two Edinburgh burgesses – to investigate charges of witchcraft, using torture when necessary, and to report back to the king and council so that the suspects might be tried.[35] The second warrant was granted in 1610 to the earl of Mar in the case of six men accused of murder by poison, witchcraft, or some other 'devilish' practice.[36]

In all other Scottish witchcraft prosecutions in which torture was reportedly used the privy council did not grant the required warrants. For that reason these applications of torture were technically illegal. There was, for example, no legal justification for using the thumbscrews on Geillis Duncan in 1591,[37] for keeping Alison Balfour in a heated iron frame known as the caspicaws for 48 hours at Patrick Stewart's castle in Orkney in 1594;[38] for the apparent torture of Thomas Leys at Aberdeen in 1597;[39] for the brutal torture of Geillis Gray by the laird of Lathocker in 1598;[40] for placing heavy weights on the legs of Margaret Barclay and Isobel Crawford at Irvine in 1618; for hitting Janet Love with bow strings, stabbing her with pins and driving wedges into her shins in 1632;[41] for putting David Johnstone in a haircloth when he was apprehended, 'which made him confess' in 1661;[42]

for the hanging of witches by their thumbs so that they 'confessed whatever they were pleased to demand of them' at Comer in 1662;[43] and for the severe beating of Beatrix Laing and Janet Cornfoot at Pittenweem in 1704.[44] Nor was there any apparent foundation for the treatment of six Scottish witches who in 1652 were hanged by their thumbs with their hands behind their backs, while candles were put under the soles of their feet, in their mouths, and finally to their heads. Four of these six victims were reported to have died during the torture.[45]

In many instances witches were subjected to the torture of forced sleeplessness, the highly effective method of making a defendant delirious and compliant and therefore willing to confess.[46] Many other witches confessed after being pierced with long pins for the ostensible purpose of finding marks that the devil was believed to have imprinted on their bodies as signs of their allegiance to him.[au] Pricking the witch to find the devil's mark was based on the belief that it was insensitive to pain and could not bleed. In 1661 Margaret Carvie and Barbara Horninam, both of Falkland, claimed that they had endured 'a great deal of torture by one who takes upon the trial of witches by pricking'.[48] John Ramsay inflicted so much pain when he pricked Margaret Tait in the same year that she died immediately thereafter.[49] John Lay lost so much blood when John Dick subjected him to pricking in 1662 that he was 'confined to his death bed'.[50] In 1678 David Cowan, a drummer in Prestonpans, pricked Katherine Liddell 'in sundry places of her body and bled her and tortured her most cruelly'.[51] The privy council responded to this outrage by imprisoning Cowan and declaring that judges of lower courts 'might not use any torture by pricking or by withholding them from sleep, etc. but reserved all that to themselves and the justices'.[52] At Pittenweem in 1704 the pricking of witches with pins was considered a 'cruel usage' that made some of them confess.[53]

It is important to note once again that all this torture was administered illegally, without warrant from the privy council. Indeed, the council took action on more than one occasion to imprison or prosecute those who tortured witches.[54] The main difference, therefore, between the English and the Scottish use of torture is not that the laws of one country allowed its use, whereas the laws of the other did not, but that the central government of one country was generally able to enforce its own strict rules regarding the use of torture, whereas the government of the other could not.

Why were local officials so eager to secure confessions by means of torture? On the European continent, in jurisdictions that followed inquisitorial procedure, the reason for torture was simply that a witch or any other defendant accused of a capital crime could not be convicted without either the testimony of two eyewitnesses or a confession. Since witnesses to a secret or imagined crime were in short supply, continental European courts were forced to administer torture to secure the necessary confessions. In Scotland, however, juries could convict without a confession.[55] The reason why local lairds and bailies tortured witches in Scotland was that the privy council required a confession before it would grant a commission authorizing the trial. As the members of the Aberdeen town council wrote in 1669, 'the Lords will not grant a commission except we send over, under our hand or the ministers', their confession and malefices'.[56] Sir George Mackenzie made the same point in his book on Scottish criminal law.[57]

The illegal torture of Scottish witches helped to ensure that witch-hunting in Scotland would take a heavy toll. We know from numerous studies of witch-hunting throughout Europe that the administration of torture vastly increased the chances of securing convictions in witchcraft trials.[58] Torture was also essential in the effort to get witches to name their alleged accomplices. The differential in the number of executions in England and Scotland was in large part attributable to the fact that Scottish local authorities were able to torture suspected witches with impunity whereas their English counterparts could not.

Torture also provides an explanation for the higher diabolical content of Scottish witchcraft confessions. We know from the work of Richard Kieckhefer and many other studies that charges of diabolism rarely can be found in the initial accusations made by people against their neighbours.[59] They were almost always introduced into the prosecution at a later stage of the legal process, and the men responsible for their introduction were inquisitors or judges who had some familiarity with demonological theory. Admissions to having made pacts with the devil and having attended the witches' sabbath often had to be suggested to witches and extorted from them by judicial coercion. It is very telling that in the account of the prosecution of Barclay and Crawford discussed at the beginning of this chapter, the devil did not enter the story until after John Stewart and Isobel Crawford had been subjected to torture. Until that time all the testimony had focused on the shipwreck of *The Gift of God* by maleficent magic.

Central and local judicial power

The torture of Scottish witches usually took place after the witch had been arrested but before her trial. It was intended to produce a confession that would persuade the members of the privy council to grant a commission of justiciary. That document would authorize a number of noblemen, lairds, sheriffs, bailies, or other local officials to summon a jury and hold the trial. The fact that the majority of Scottish witchcraft trials took place on the basis of such commissions of justiciary raises the question what role the central Scottish government played in witchcraft prosecutions.

Before 1597 the privy council granted commissions to one or more men. Some of these commissions, known as general or standing commissions, authorized them to try any witches who might be brought to their attention. Particular commissions authorized them to try only the witches named in the document. As the witch-hunt of 1597 developed, it became clear that some of the commissions granted by the council had led to the convictions and execution of innocent persons. In August the council took the first step towards remedying these abuses by revoking all the commissions that it had previously granted to one or two individuals. If these commissioners wished to continue hunting witches, they would have to reapply to the council for new commissions, and those would be granted to no fewer than three men conjointly[60] This order of the council did not directly address the problem of standing commissions, which was the main reason why the witch-hunt of that year had spread like wild fire. Some of those standing commissions remained in effect through September and October. Once they had expired, however, the council did not grant any new ones. This unofficial policy of the council did not deter local officials and clergy from trying to obtain standing commissions periodically during the next century.[61]

The main effect of the procedures adopted by the privy council in the wake of the witchcraft panic of 1597 was to keep future witch-hunting in check. This was certainly the intention of the policy, even though some prosecutions continued in Aberdeen in September and October on the basis of some of the commissions that had not been revoked.[62] During the following 30 years, when the council was dominated by men who were apparently reluctant to support large-scale witch-hunting, there were no large witch-hunts in Scotland. Nor did any large hunts take place in the late seventeenth and early eighteenth centuries, when the council and the lord advocate made serious efforts to bring witch-hunting to an end.

The procedures adopted in 1597 were not capable, however, of preventing large witch-hunts from ever occurring again. The practice of granting individual commissions could still, if the lords of the council were so disposed, encourage witch-hunting. This appears to have been what happened in 1628–30, 1643–4, 1649–50, and 1661–2, when the council or parliament (acting in its place) issued scores of commissions routinely, without properly scrutinizing the materials submitted to them by local authorities. In this way the lords of the privy council facilitated, if they did not actually encourage, the witchcraft panics that occurred in those years.

The most misleading claim regarding the procedures adopted by the council after the 1597 panic is that they made witchcraft 'a centrally managed crime', allowing the government to coordinate local prosecutions and thus create national panics such as those that began in 1629 and 1661.[63] This situation, according to Christina Larner, stood in marked contrast to that which prevailed in England, where the privy council did not exercise comparable 'management' of the crime. English witch-hunting therefore remained a strictly local affair that could not easily spread from one location to another.[64]

There is little evidence that the Scottish privy council exercised this type of coordination of witchcraft prosecutions. It is important to recognize that all the commissions issued by the council represented responses to petitions from local communities. The real stimulus came from the localities, not the centre. The council could grant these local requests and thus allow witch-hunting to go forward, but it could not manage or coordinate witch-hunts or encourage their spread from one locality to another. The news of other prosecutions, the employment of professional witch-finders by more than one town, and the shared fears of local authorities from different areas during periods of high political and economic anxiety are sufficient to explain the growth of so-called national witch-hunts.

In any event, the main reason for the relatively high number of Scottish witchcraft convictions and executions is not that the central government managed prosecutions, but that it did not supervise local trials more carefully. The problem was not too much but too little management. When the trials took place in the justiciary court, the government did of course have a great deal of control, both through the judge and the lord advocate. When the privy council granted commissions of justiciary to local authorities, however, the central government lost all control over the trial.[65] It delegated its judicial power to groups of local magistrates and landowners who in most cases had no legal training. Unless the government could assign a justice depute to the area, as parliament did for Midlothian in 1661,[66] or unless it could send judges on circuit, as it did during the Cromwellian military occupation, local prosecutions for witchcraft took place in the absence of a judicial officer of the Crown.

The delegation of central judicial authority to local magistrates and landowners had a profound effect upon the prosecution of witches in Scotland. The limited evidence we have regarding the fate of witches tried in this way suggests that the conviction rate may have been as high as 96 per cent and the execution rate 91 per cent. By contrast the conviction rate in the justiciary court was 57 per cent and the execution rate 55 per cent. If we include in the totals for the justiciary court the results of those trials in which the justice deputes went on circuit, the figures drop to 45 per cent and 41 per cent respectively.[67] The differentials between the first set of statistics and the latter two assume even greater significance when we consider that 56 per cent of all Scottish witchcraft prosecutions began with conciliar or parliamentary commissions, while only 30 per cent took place in the justiciary or circuit courts. The remaining 14 per cent either occurred in local courts without specific commissions or for some other reason did not receive mention in the records of the central courts.[68]

These figures explain why local magistrates who wished to try witches in their communities expressed a clear preference for commissions of justiciary over trials in Edinburgh. If they wanted to rid themselves of witches in their midst, their best chances lay with a trial conducted locally by prominent members of society in the shires or burghs rather than in the distant capital, where the trial would be held before a legally trained judge who might very well have no ties with the local community. As Mackenzie, the lord advocate, wrote in 1678, 'scarce ever any who were accused before a country assize [i.e. a jury] of neighbours did escape that trial'.[69] This was clearly the reasoning that led the burgh council of Pittenweem in 1704 to lobby officials in Edinburgh to obtain a commission of justiciary to try a cluster of witches imprisoned in the tollbooth. The burgh council was profoundly disappointed when the privy council denied their request, insisting that the trial take place in Edinburgh.[70] In 1669 the burgh council of Aberdeen was likewise disappointed when the privy council refused to allow local magistrates to try suspected witches by themselves, insisting that 'some able persons' be included in any commission they would grant.[71]

The English central government never relinquished its control of local witchcraft trials in the way that the Scottish government often did. It is true that the English privy council did not authorize local witchcraft trials in the manner of the Scottish council. In that sense the English government did not 'manage' prosecutions for witchcraft or any other crimes. Nor did the central criminal courts in England, King's Bench and Star Chamber, take cognizance of very many witchcraft cases. But the English government did have a mechanism for ensuring central judicial supervision of local trials. Almost all English trials for witchcraft on the basis of the statutes of 1563 and 1604 took place at the assizes, county courts over which judges from the central law courts travelling on circuit (or serjeants-at-law acting as their surrogates) presided. The presence of such royal officials at the assizes did not necessarily improve a witch's chances for acquittal; some English judges actively encouraged convictions in witchcraft cases.[72] In most cases, however, the supervision of the judicial process by professional judges provided greater assurances that accused witches would receive the benefit of whatever procedural safeguards the law allowed than if the judicial process were left in the hands of local amateurs.

In England many of these procedural safeguards pertained to the admission of evidence.[73] As men knowledgeable of the proofs sufficient for conviction in witchcraft cases, professional judges could be expected, if they were impartial, to assist the jury on such matters when they summed up the evidence. And we do know that at least in the late seventeenth century judges were directly responsible for the dismissal of witchcraft cases. All in all, the assize judges should be given some of the credit for keeping the conviction and execution rates in English witchcraft trials at relatively low levels. At the Essex assizes the conviction rate was 46 per cent, while the execution rate was only 24 per cent.[74]

Scotland actually did possess a system of administering criminal justice in the provinces that resembled the English assizes. In the Middle Ages, Scottish judges responsible for maintaining the king's peace had periodically travelled through the country to try subjects who had been accused of various crimes. Once a central justiciary court was established at Edinburgh in the early sixteenth century, however, this traditional system of holding 'justice ayres' collapsed, and despite repeated attempts by the government to revive it, it rarely worked effectively. The most serious effort was made as part of the judicial reforms of James VI in 1587, which as we have seen also allowed the lord advocate to initiate cases by himself. Owing mainly to a lack of trained personnel, the central criminal court could not handle both a heavy caseload at Edinburgh and a regular annual or semi-annual circuit of the shires. The old system of justice ayres gave way, therefore, to the occasional appointment of justice deputes to particular areas and the granting of conciliar commissions to local magistrates from either the privy council or parliament, during whose sessions the privy council did not sit. Only in the late seventeenth century was a system for holding regular circuit courts established.

If the practice of allowing unsupervised local trials offers an explanation for the high number of convictions and executions in Scottish witchcraft cases, then one can interpret in a somewhat different light the two periods in which Scottish witch-hunting declined noticeably. The first of these periods was the 1650s, when Scotland was united to England and criminal justice was entrusted to English judges, the commissioners for the administration of justice. The dramatic decline in the number of executions during this decade is usually attributed to the English commissioners' refusal to allow the use of torture. There were, however, two reasons of equal or greater importance. One was the abolition of the Scottish privy council and parliament, the two institutions that issued commissions to local magistrates; the other was the decision of the commissioners to go on circuit. Indeed, one of the most celebrated decisions of the commissioners, the acquittal of 60 witches on the grounds of insufficient proof, occurred when the judges were on circuit.[75] The only change that took place in the pattern of prosecutions during the 1650s was that cases normally heard by local authorities either came before the commissioners on circuit or were funnelled into Edinburgh, where the number of prosecutions rose by more than 450 per cent. The total number of prosecutions did not actually change much at all between the 1640s and the 1650s.[76]

The second period stretches from 1662, the last year of the largest witch-hunt in Scottish history, to 1727, the year of the last execution. This period witnessed a gradual though somewhat uneven decline in convictions and executions. The decline occurred not so much because of the growth of a philosophical scepticism rooted in a new worldview, but because the Scottish government expressed a renewed determination to control the excesses of local witch-hunting. The privy council initiated this new period of judicial caution and restraint in 1662 by prohibiting local magistrates from arresting witches without proper warrant and using torture or any unlawful means to secure their confessions.[77] In a series of steps that will be discussed in Chapter 8, the central government tightened this control over the administration of local justice. The final step was the abandonment of the practice of granting commissions of justiciary and the implementation of a new circuit court system in 1708.

The direct relationship between the lack of central control over witchcraft prosecutions and the high incidence of convictions that is evident in Scotland also helps to explain the one great anomaly in the history of English witchcraft, the hunt conducted by Hopkins and Stearne in the 1640s.

That hunt began at a time when the central government could not provide adequate supervision of local justice. One of the reasons why Hopkins and Stearne were successful in prosecuting a large number of witches in 1645 and 1646 was that they operated with relative freedom from central governmental control. The absence of judicial supervision by the judges of the common law courts was most obvious in the trials at the Chelmsford assizes in 1645. Because of the disruptions caused by the civil war the justices of the assize, who presided over the trial of serious crimes, could not be present. The person who filled in for them was the earl of Warwick, a man who had neither legal training nor clear judicial status.[78] The trials were conducted by the Essex justices of the peace, most notably the zealous puritan magistrate Sir Harbottle Grimstone, arch-enemy of William Laud, the archbishop of Canterbury. As we shall see in Chapter 4, Grimstone had the same attitude towards witches like Elizabeth Clarke as local Scottish magistrates had towards the witches who were allegedly infesting their communities.[79]

The fact that central political authorities in England and Scotland did more to control than to promote witchcraft prosecutions should not surprise us. Most witchcraft prosecutions, even those that developed into large hunts or panics, were local or regional affairs in which the residents of the afflicted communities harboured the greatest fears. Judges, councillors, and other officials in London and Edinburgh were understandably concerned about the alleged practice of witchcraft in the localities, but they did not have to live with the witches themselves. It was they, moreover, not local magistrates, who bore the main responsibility for ensuring that the judicial system operated in accordance with established procedures.

The generally negative effect that central governments had on the process of witch-hunting was also apparent on the European continent, where the great majority of European witchcraft prosecutions took place. Now, there is no doubt that central authorities in many continental European countries were directly responsible for a number of witchcraft trials, especially in the late Middle Ages, when the charges against the accused often included activities of a political nature.[80] Central authorities also inaugurated a number of witch-hunts in the sixteenth and seventeenth centuries. In a very different spirit, however, the same central governments set down strict rules regarding the use of torture, overturned a number of convictions for witchcraft on appeal and, as is well known, assumed a leading role in bringing the great European witch-hunt to an end. Throughout Europe the main pressure for witchcraft prosecutions and convictions came from local communities, not central governments, and the relative intensity of witch-hunting in different regions and kingdoms had much to do with the success or failure of central governments in enforcing their own procedural rules.

The effects of tight central control are most apparent in Spain, where the Spanish Inquisition, a national institution under the effective control of the king, exercised jurisdiction over most prosecutions for witchcraft. The central council of this Inquisition in Madrid not only had the power to intervene in cases tried by regional tribunals, but also demanded that the inquisitors who staffed those tribunals adhere to fairly strict procedural rules. Even during the most famous witch-hunt in Spanish history, the prosecution of large numbers of Basque witches at Logroño in 1609 and 1610, the restraint imposed by those rules, especially with respect to torture, was quite apparent.[81] After the conclusion of this hunt, and a subsequent investigation by the sceptical inquisitor Alonso de Salazar Frías, the central council at Madrid adopted an even stricter set of rules regarding the prosecution of witches and thereby, for all intents and purposes, put an end to witchcraft executions by the Spanish Inquisition.[82]

In France the legal picture was complicated by the complexity of jurisdictional arrangements, but the highest and most central court in the kingdom, the parlement of Paris, which exercised an appellate jurisdiction over most of northern France and which had more prestige than any of the other provincial parlements, had an astonishing record of leniency in dealing with witchcraft. Of the death sentences appealed to it from subordinate tribunals between 1564 and 1640, the parlement confirmed a mere 24 per cent, while at the same time releasing 36 per cent of all appellants.[83] The reason for this leniency, as Alfred Soman has shown, was not a sceptical attitude towards witchcraft but an adherence to an extraordinarily rigid law of proof. Torture was permitted, but the rules governing its use were very strict, and a confession made as a result of it could not be used to justify a death sentence.[84]

Perhaps the best illustration of the importance of the absence of central control over the judicial process comes from the Holy Roman Empire, where the largest witch-hunts and more than half of all European executions took place. The Empire did have a criminal code, the Carolina of 1532, which defined witchcraft as a crime and, like other central codes, laid down rather strict rules governing the use of torture.[85] Without a strong central government, however, and without a large central judicial corps, the Empire was unable to enforce its own procedural rules, and the great German witch-hunts of the sixteenth and seventeenth centuries were partially the product of this failure.[86] Those jurisdictions that adhered to the code produced far fewer convictions and executions for witchcraft than those that did not.[87]

The role of the clergy

One of the most striking differences between Scottish and English witch-hunting was the active role the Scottish clergy played in witch-hunting. That role was most evident in the proceedings of the kirk sessions, the basic unit of ecclesiastical justice staffed by the minister and the lay elders of each parish, and the regional presbyteries, which consisted of clerical representatives from a small number of parishes. Each of these institutions exercised a disciplinary function over the laity within its jurisdiction, and that discipline extended to all moral crimes, such as fornication, adultery, Sabbath-breaking, and blasphemy. Since witchcraft was considered a sin as well as a crime, involving apostasy or the abandonment of one's Christian faith, it was also a matter of concern for these church courts. The same was true for the practice of magic, which was considered a form of superstition.

The problem for these church courts was that witchcraft, unlike most moral crimes, was a statutory offence, triable only in the secular courts. Faced with these limitations, the kirk sessions and presbyteries could only play a limited role in its prosecution.[88] The courts cited suspects on the basis of rumour, interrogated them before a panel of ministers and elders, administered punishments (however mild) by their own authority, and recorded their testimony in a written document known as a process, which could be referred to higher ecclesiastical or civil authorities. In the early stages of the prosecution of Margaret Barclay, for example, ministers from Irvine and the neighbouring parishes joined magistrates in taking her confession.[89] They also joined civil magistrates in submitting petitions for commissions of justiciary from the privy council or parliament, as at Dunfermline in 1649 and Pittenweem in 1704. In this way the Scottish clergy played an active, albeit limited, role in witch-hunting.

In England the clergy played a much less prominent and influential role than their brethren in Scotland in the discovery and prosecution of witches. To be sure, the courts of bishops and archdeacons in England exercised a criminal jurisdiction over moral offences as well as a civil jurisdiction over tithes, marriage, and wills. By virtue of their criminal jurisdiction, they also tried to enforce a moral discipline within their jurisdiction, although they never duplicated the success of the Scottish kirk sessions and presbyteries in that regard. This disciplinary function often involved the prosecution of magical activities, but only in a small percentage of cases could the offence be classified as maleficent witchcraft.[90] The punishments meted out for these infractions were usually quite mild: reading a declaration in church, performing public penance, or paying a fine to relieve the poor.[91]

English ecclesiastical courts also failed to refer many cases of witchcraft to the civil magistrates. Even when witches who had been cited in the church courts for practising magic were later tried at the assizes, there is no evidence that the church courts actually referred the cases to the civil magistrate. There was no established mechanism for informing the common law courts of such offences, and disputes over the jurisdictional boundaries between the church courts and the common law courts may have discouraged cooperation of this sort. The only known referrals of witchcraft cases to the assizes came from the quarter sessions, the common law courts held by justices of the peace four times a year.

The main reason for the more limited role of the English clergy in witchcraft prosecutions was that the English state had been more successful than the Scottish state in restricting clerical power and jurisdiction. Even in the church courts the English clergy played a smaller role than their counterparts in Scotland, since after the Reformation the judges of the English ecclesiastical courts were often laymen trained at Oxford and Cambridge in the civil law.[92] Only a handful of English clerics received appointments to the commissions of the peace, and in any case they always constituted a distinct minority on those commissions.[93] Their role at the county assizes was even more limited by the strict division of secular and ecclesiastical justice. Their role in witch-hunting was therefore confined to occasional efforts to coax confessions from the accused, testifying at the trials, giving sermons that warned of the dangers of witchcraft and stressed the diabolical nature of the crime, and writing witchcraft treatises.[94]

The place within the British Atlantic world where the English clergy played a role in witchcraft prosecutions similar to that played by the Scottish clergy was the puritan colony of Massachusetts in New England. Since Massachusetts was an English colony, governed by English law, the clergy encountered some of the same obstacles as their counterparts in England when they wished to see that witches were prosecuted. The courts that tried witches in New England, just like those in England, were secular tribunals over which lay judges presided. But Massachusetts, which was founded with the intention of creating a godly community, allowed the clergy a much more active role in the administration of justice than did the central government at Westminster. During the Salem witchcraft trials in 1692, for example, the Boston clergy participated actively in the interrogation of the witches and made recommendations regarding the conduct of the trials. The clergy were also responsible in large part for bringing the witch-hunt to an end.

The conduct of the trial

The differences between Scottish and English criminal procedure were most evident in the actual conduct of the trial. Scottish courts devoted much more time to the evaluation of written evidence than did English common law courts. In this regard Scottish practice reflected the influence of continental jurisprudence, which established rules for evaluating evidence on the basis of accepted standards of proof. Scottish courts never got to the point where judges decided cases on the basis of those standards and dispensing completely with juries, although Sir George Mackenzie recommended that course of action in the late seventeenth century.[95] But criminal trials, especially in the court of justiciary, often involved long debates regarding the relevance of the evidence to the libel, which was the statement of the rationale for the witch's guilt. These debates were conducted by lawyers, and their pleadings often filled many pages. It was these debates that led J. Irvine Smith to classify the system of Scottish criminal justice as inquisitorial.[96] As we have seen, that designation is misleading, mainly because judges were still unable to prevent juries from ignoring the arguments of advocates or the instructions they received from the judge. The law of evidence, which is essentially a law of jury control, was still in its infancy during the seventeenth century. It was even less developed in England, where judges and legal writers tried sometimes without success to establish formal standards of proof for convicting a witch, such as those followed by judges in continental witchcraft trials.[97] Even in the late seventeenth century, English judges could not always direct juries to return the verdicts supported by the evidence and had to resort to granting reprieves or commuting capital sentences to imprisonment. Despite this independence of trial juries in both countries, the debates on relevancy of the evidence to the libel in Scottish witchcraft trials reflect one of the ways in which the originally accusatorial system of justice in Scotland was gradually modified to include some of the features of criminal procedure that had become established on the European continent.

One might expect that the influence of this feature of continental jurisprudence in Scottish criminal trials would have facilitated the prosecution of all crime, including witchcraft. This does not appear to be the case. Inquisitorial procedure by itself, without the administration of torture that often accompanied it, did not necessarily make conviction any more likely than when juries decided the cases.[98] Demanding standards of proof could cut both ways in witchcraft cases. On the one hand, they could induce judges to torture the accused in order to secure a confession when the evidentiary standard of two eyewitnesses for conviction of a capital crime could not be satisfied. On the other hand, the same standard could lead one to despair that the evidence for conviction could never be produced. This was especially true when witchcraft was defined exclusively as making a pact with the devil, as it was in colonial New England, since obtaining evidence of that transgression from witnesses was manifestly impossible.[99] When that happened, the days of witchcraft prosecutions were numbered, as they were in Scotland by the closing decades of the seventeenth century.

The right of Scottish witches to have benefit of counsel, another feature of inquisitorial justice that was absent in England, also helped to bring an end to witchcraft trials.[100] Legal representation was decisive in winning a significant number of acquittals in witchcraft cases in the late seventeenth century. These acquittals, however, took place mainly in the justiciary court in Edinburgh, and in some cases accused witches were unable to secure representation in that venue either.[101] But it soon became known that hiring a lawyer offered the best hope for an accused witch. Certainly the acquittal of Geillis Johnstone in 1614 can be attributed in part to the three advocates who defended her against the charge of witchcraft.[102] Her success might explain Margaret Barclay's exasperated rebuke of her husband in 1618 for showing up at her trial with a lawyer far too late in the process to make a difference. Barclay's fate had already been sealed, because no one had examined the original charges against her, because she had been forced to confess under torture, because the burgh of Irvine had been successful in securing a local trial, and because the local clergy believed that she had not only caused harm by magical means but had also made a pact with the devil. All of these developments that facilitated her conviction were made possible by the distinctive features of the Scottish criminal justice system.

3   King James VI and witchcraft

King James VI of Scotland (r. 1567–1625) was a central figure in the history of Scottish witchcraft. He played a key role in the two large Scottish witch-hunts of the 1590s, and he wrote a demonological treatise in 1597 that affirmed the reality of the crime and gave specific recommendations for its prosecution. James had a less pronounced influence on witch-hunting in England, which became his residence after he acceded to the English throne as James I in 1603. His treatise did contribute to the reception by educated Englishmen of beliefs that emphasized the witch's relationship to the devil, and in 1604 he signed into law a witchcraft statute that made commerce with demons punishable in the common law courts. His recognition that some witches had been falsely and maliciously accused, however, made him much less eager to promote witch-hunting in his southern kingdom, and within five years of his accession he had begun to question some of the positions he had taken in his treatise. At the very least he had shed his reputation, gained in Scotland during the 1590s, as a zealous witch-hunter.

Although there is wide recognition that James was a major figure in the history of Scottish witch-hunting, the nature of his contribution to witch-hunting remains unclear. The extent of the king's involvement in the Scottish witch-hunts of the 1590s, the novelty and sources of his witch beliefs, the connection between his witch beliefs and his political thought, and the degree of scepticism that he manifested towards the powers of witches have all become matters of historical controversy.[1] This chapter will investigate the extent of the king's involvement in the witch-hunts of 1590–1 and 1597, analyze the text of his witchcraft treatise, *Daemonologie*, and document the change that took place in James's outlook as he became involved in a case of witchcraft and demonic possession in England in 1605.

King James and the witches of the 1590s

King James would never have become especially interested in witchcraft unless he had become genuinely frightened that some of his subjects were trying to kill him by magical means. His fear of politically inspired sorcery provides the best explanation for his personal participation in the trials of the North Berwick witches in 1590–1 as well as his involvement in the witch panic of 1597.

James had nothing to do with the *origin* of either witch-hunt. The prosecutions of 1590–1 began in November 1590 when David Seton, the bailie depute from the East Lothian town of Tranent, suspected his servant, Geillis Duncan, of being a witch. Duncan had cured people of various ailments and had performed 'many matters most miraculous', raising the suspicion that she had done these things by 'extraordinary and unlawful means'.[2] To confirm his suspicions Seton interrogated Duncan and reportedly used torture to secure her confession. He also extracted from her the names of several alleged accomplices. This group included Agnes Sampson, an elderly woman from a village outside the burgh of Haddington who was known mainly as a healer and a midwife, and one Dr Fian, alias John Cunningham, a schoolmaster from the nearby East Lothian town of Prestonpans. Duncan also named two women from the upper echelons of Edinburgh society: Euphame MacCalzean, the daughter of a wealthy Edinburgh advocate, and Barbara Napier, wife of Archibald Douglas, brother of the laird of Carschogill.

The king soon began to suspect that these witches had attempted to use magic to harm him or cause him misfortune. The chain of events that aroused the king's suspicions had begun in September 1589 when Anne, the younger daughter of King Frederick II of Denmark, whose marriage to James had been arranged in June of that year, set sail for Scotland. Storms at sea, however, and a leak in the flagship forced Anne's party to take refuge in Norway. A further mishap at sea occurred in September when a Scottish ship laden with gifts for the royal couple making the crossing from Burntisland in Fife to Leith was destroyed by yet another fierce storm, killing 40 passengers and sinking its cargo.[3] James therefore decided somewhat rashly to leave his kingdom in October to fetch his bride. He married Anne in person in Oslo that November (they had already been married by proxy earlier in the year), and the royal couple then travelled to Denmark, where they spent the winter and early spring. Upon their return to Scotland in April 1590, the royal party encountered another fierce storm.

These events took place at a time when James's hold on the Scottish throne was hardly secure. Like his mother, Mary Queen of Scots, who had abdicated in favour of her infant son in 1567, James had faced a series of rebellions and conspiracies. In 1582, four years after assuming the full powers of king, he had been seized during an attempted coup led by the earl of Gowrie, from whom he managed to escape. In 1589, just months before his trip to Norway and Denmark, he had faced a rebellion from the northern Catholic nobility, led by the earl of Huntly, whose forces the young king managed to fend off at Brig of Dee. At the same time James's cousin, Francis Stewart, the fifth earl of Bothwell, had led an uprising on the borders. Bothwell had been declared a traitor, but his sentence had been suspended, and when the government was entrusted to him and others during the king's absence from Scotland, he had acted as a responsible steward. James knew, however, that he could not trust Bothwell, and the earl was eventually implicated in the alleged conspiracy of witches to harm the king.

The suspicion that these witches were the cause of James's and Anne's misfortunes at sea grew when Danish authorities arrested, tried, and executed six witches in May 1590 for having allegedly caused the storm that had thwarted Anne's initial attempt to reach Scotland. It was not uncommon for people in Scandinavian countries to attribute storms at sea to the imprecations of witches, and in this case the action of Danish authorities apparently raised suspicions that Scottish witches were also involved in these efforts. These suspicions soon devolved on the witches whom Geillis Duncan had named in her confession.

The examination of Agnes Sampson and Geillis Duncan at an unspecified date in the autumn of 1590 yielded the first testimony that witches had something to do with the king's misfortunes. In that examination Sampson made the first reference to an assembly of witches at North Berwick in 1590 that would later became a central episode in the alleged plot against the king. She also made a brief reference to the raising of a storm 'for staying the queen's coming home'. This testimony certainly caught the king's attention, as did her report that the devil had told her that 'ministers would destroy the king and all Scotland' but that 'if he would use his counsel, he should destroy them'.[4]

Early in December Sampson made a more detailed confession to these events before the king at Holyroodhouse, the royal residence in Edinburgh, possibly after she had been subjected to torture.[5] Her confession shows how the judicial process, in this case reinforced by the presence of the king as an interrogator, turned Sampson, a healer, prognosticator, and midwife known as 'the wise wife of Haddington', into a witch. In addition to divulging some of her techniques as a healer, Sampson confessed to having met the devil in various shapes on several occasions, of having receiving his mark on her body, and of having attended meetings with him and other witches. One of these assemblies had taken place in the North Berwick kirk on All Hallows' Eve (31 Oct.) in 1590.[6] At this meeting the devil appeared as a man, addressed them from the pulpit, and received the homage of the witches in attendance, who called him master and kissed his buttocks.[7]

What was clearly missing from Sampson's confession and from her dittay at her trial a month later was any mention of her efforts and those of her confederates to kill the king. That would not be forthcoming from any of the witches until after Sampson's execution in January 1591. Sampson did, however, confess to having been on the ship *The Grace of God*, which perished off the coast at North Berwick, and she claimed further that the devil had sunk it.[8] At the same time she repeated an earlier confession that the devil had told her that the king would have difficulty returning home from Denmark and that the queen 'should never come except he fetched her with him'.[9] These admissions were sufficient to confirm James's suspicions that witches had been the cause of his maritime misadventures as well as those of the queen, and it impelled him to continue the investigation of the other witches named by Geillis Duncan.

Although James's suspicions had been raised by Sampson's confession, the king did not leap to the conclusion that these witches were guilty of causing the storms in the North Sea. His report in July 1591 that he had spent nine months investigating the matter suggests that he had proceeded deliberately in his investigation.[10] The pamphlet *Newes from Scotland*, published in late 1591 for the benefit of an English audience, claims that the king became completely credulous after Sampson confessed the full details of the witches' meetings and the various plots to kill him in early December 1590. The pamphlet also claims that his original scepticism regarding the truth of Sampson's confession evaporated when the woman repeated the very words that he and Anne had exchanged on their wedding night. It is highly implausible that a healer who had just been pressured to confess before the king would have spoken to him this way. It is equally implausible that James was so gullible that he believed her, even if the king's anxieties regarding his sexuality had made him vulnerable to such manipulation. The legal record suggests, moreover, that the king's suspicions and fears were not confirmed until May or June 1591, after the earl of Bothwell had been implicated and the pieces of the North Berwick witches' plot against him had been woven together into a persuasive narrative.

The implication of Bothwell took place on 15 April 1591 and led to his imprisonment by the privy council. Bothwell had connections with Napier and Macalzean, and Agnes Sampson's testimony that Bothwell would pay the witches gold and silver had aroused further suspicion.[11] The crucial testimony against Bothwell came from Ritchie Graham, a notorious magician whom Agnes Sampson had identified as an accomplice in her first examination in 1590.[12] In 1591 Graham's testimony was almost certainly obtained by members of the king's government. The specific charge raised against Bothwell was that Agnes Sampson, after having made a wax image of the king, wrapped it in a linen cloth, gave it to the devil and held it up to the witches assembled there, saying that 'this is King James the Sixth, ordained to be consumed at the instance of a nobleman, Francis, earl of Bothwell'.[13]

Even after Sampson had been linked to Bothwell in this manner, the charge that the North Berwick witches had committed treason against the king took time to materialize. It had appeared in a series of depositions taken before the king during the early months of 1591 and was introduced during the trial of the jurors who had tried Barbara Napier in May 1591.[14] Napier had been convicted of consulting with Agnes Sampson and Ritchie Graham, an offence that merited death on the basis of the witchcraft act of 1563, but she had been acquitted of the more serious charges of consulting with Graham to kill the earl of Angus and of being at the North Berwick assembly of witches. She was condemned to death only after the king demanded that sentence be passed. After she pleaded pregnancy, her execution was postponed.

The claim that Napier was involved in plots to harm the king did not emerge until four weeks after her trial. It was introduced not in a legal proceeding against Napier but in a trial of her assizers (jurors) for having erred in acquitting her on three counts. Since the charges against the assizers were contained in letters from the king, it is likely that James, who broke legal precedent by attending the trial in person, was primarily responsible for this proceeding. The letters claimed that when Napier consulted Graham regarding a prediction he had made, he had responded that Napier, MacCalzean, and Donald Robson, a highland witch, would harm the king. Napier was also accused of having attended a convention of witches at Acheson's Haven, the harbour at Prestonpans, on 31 July 1591. At this assembly Agnes Sampson was reported to have proposed the destruction of the king and to have given Napier and MacCalzean a wax image of the king that they were told to roast. At the same time the devil instructed the witches to kill the king by placing a substance infused with the venom of a toad near the king 'so that another [i.e. Bothwell] might have ruled in his Majesty's place'.[15]

The evidence presented at the trial of Napier's assizers leaves little doubt that that by this time the king was fully convinced that witches had been involved in a treasonous conspiracy against him and that the earl of Bothwell was involved in the plot.[16] Two days later Euphame MacCalzean was indicted for 'certain treasonable conspiracies, enterprised by witchcraft, to have destroyed our sovereign lord's person and bereft his Majesty of his life'.[17] More specifically she was accused of attending the witches' assembly at North Berwick, and 'there inquiring for the king's picture, given by Annie Sampson to the devil to be enchanted for the treasonable destruction of the king'.[18] According to *Newes from Scotland*, on this occasion the devil greatly inveighed against the king, and when the witches asked the devil why he bore such hatred against the king, he replied that 'the king was the greatest enemy he hath in the world'.[19]

At her trial MacCalzean was also charged with having consulted Agnes Sampson and other witches 'for the staying of the queen's homecoming by storm and wind, and raising storm to that effect, or else to have drowned her Majesty and her company by conjuring of cats and casting them in the sea at Leith and the back of Robert Grierson's house'.[20] This is the first reference in the legal record to the charge that the North Berwick witches caused the storms at sea that had threatened both king and queen. Sampson had never been accused of these treasonous activities, even though *Newes from Scotland* claimed that she had confessed to them in her examination before the king six months earlier.[21]

Of all the North Berwick witches, Euphame MacCalzean was the most susceptible to the charge of treason as well as witchcraft. She was in fact the only one of the group named by Geillis Duncan who had been suspected of performing *maleficia* for many years. The charge that she had attempted to kill her husband by magic was regarded in both Scotland and England as petty treason, punishable by being burned alive. As Lawrence Normand and Gareth Roberts have observed, in MacCalzean's dittay 'the story of conspiracy against the king is retold by analogy in the story of a witch who tries to kill her husband'.[22] Although MacCalzean was eventually acquitted of that attempted murder, she was convicted of the 'cruel murder and slaughter' of her husband's 17-year-old nephew by similar means. She had also consulted with Agnes Sampson to plot the killing of MacCalzean's father-in-law, John Moscrop. What is more, MacCalzean had the closest ties of all the North Berwick witches to the earl of Bothwell.

If we assume that James played a role in formulating the charges against the North Berwick witches, the question arises whether the king was thereby responsible for introducing 'continental' ideas of diabolism into Scotland.[23] The problem with this claim is that some continental witch beliefs, especially the belief that witches made pacts with the devil, were already present in Scotland before Sampson's confession on 4 December and therefore did not need to be imported. Belief in the demonic pact, which had arisen in the condemnation of the practice of ritual magic by scholastic theologians in the fourteenth century, was implicit in the condemnation of necromancy in the Scottish witchcraft statute of 1563.[24] Acquiring legal evidence of the pact by means of the devil's mark had also preceded James's interrogation of Agnes Sampson. Witches had been searched for the devil's mark in 1572, while at the beginning of this witch-hunt David Seton had confirmed his accusations of Geillis Duncan by finding the devil's mark on her throat.[25]

The confessions of the North Berwick witches that they had gathered in large numbers with the devil, however, were unprecedented in the history of Scottish witchcraft. The idea that witches gathered collectively at nocturnal assemblies, often referred to as sabbaths, had been an important part of the cumulative concept of witchcraft since the mid-fifteenth century. During the sixteenth century the description of these assemblies in the confessions of witches and in continental demonological treatises based upon those confessions had become increasingly elaborate and horrific. At these gatherings witches allegedly danced naked, engaged in promiscuous sexual intercourse with demons and witches of both sexes, sacrificed unbaptized infants to the devil, and then, in the most gruesome ritual of all, ate the dismembered parts of the infants' bodies. The testimony of the North Berwick witches never included any of these activities, which constituted a rejection of all standards of morality. The only elements of the standard continental view of the witches' sabbath that worked their way into the trials of 1591 were the witches' acknowledgement of the devil as their master and their ritualistic kissing him on his buttocks. The dates of the assemblies on Lammas Eve (31 July) and All Hallows' Eve (31 October) might also have been suggested by descriptions of the witches' sabbath in continental demonologies.[26] If James (or whoever suggested the details of the witches' confessions) was introducing continental notions of the witches' sabbath, he was being deliberately selective.

The descriptions of the assemblies at North Berwick and Prestonpans were a Scottish variation on a standard demonological theme.[27] The description of the devil as a large black man with a black beard being dressed in the costume of a Protestant minister wearing an ugly skull-bonnet and a ragged black gown, holding a black book addressing the witches from the pulpit, had a distinctly Scottish provenance.[28] The meeting at North Berwick kirk described in the witches' dittays was a parody of a Scottish religious service, just as the saying of a 'black mass' in some European countries was a mockery and inversion of the Roman Catholic service.

The main activity of the witches who had gathered at North Berwick kirk was the practice of maleficent magic. In continental descriptions of the witches' sabbath in the sixteenth century, harmful magic was only one of many activities that the witches allegedly engaged in. Sometimes the devil instructed his servants to use powders and unguents to cause unspecified misery in the world. In the engraving produced by the Polish artist Jan Ziarnkov to illustrate the second edition of Pierre de Lancre's witchcraft treatise in 1613, the witches in the foreground were depicted throwing toads into a cauldron for such purposes.[29] That engraving, however, also depicts naked dancing, the sacrifice of children to the devil, and the feasting of witches and demons on the limbs of those children. This depiction of the witches' gatherings was intended to illustrate the witches' rejection of all moral standards. The worst offence committed by the Scottish witches at Acheson's Haven and North Berwick, however, was their attempt to harm or kill the king. This focus on their magical activities, rather than cannibalism, naked dancing, and promiscuous sexual activities, reflects the incorporation of an older tradition of ritual magic that had been practised in the Middle Ages, often at royal courts, into the more current demonological stereotype of the witches' sabbath.

The implication of Bothwell as the ringleader of the North Berwick witches strengthened the equation James made between witchcraft and treason, since Bothwell had actually plotted against the king on other occasions. James repeatedly exploited this theme of witchcraft-cum-treason in his unremitting campaign against Bothwell. On 5 June 1591, the day that Euphame MacCalzean was burned alive for witchcraft, he issued a proclamation accusing Bothwell of using witchcraft for political purposes and conspiring with 'enemies of God' to achieve 'the subversion of the true religion' in a 'treasonable conspiracy against his Majesty's own person'.[30] Bothwell countered that the charge of witchcraft was an invention of the king's chancellor, John Maitland of Thirlestane, but Bothwell's attempted seizure of the king at Holyroodhouse on 27 December 1591 gave James further cause to link this act of treason with witchcraft. In a letter to his ambassador in England one week after this incident, James claimed that Bothwell's act of 'sorcery and witchcraft devised against our own person' was inspired by 'the bloody counsels of the enemies to God, the true religion and to all monarchies professing the same'. These acts of witchcraft and treason revealed how 'Satan has so far prevailed within the compass of our own age'.[31] Witchcraft was thus not only a religious crime but a political one as well.

This politicization of witchcraft was James's main contribution to Scottish witch-hunting. Instead of introducing an entire set of continental notions regarding the worship of the devil, James had fused the demonological fantasy of the witches' sabbath with the traditional idea of politically motivated sorcery, thus transforming witchcraft as defined in the late sixteenth century into a political as well as a religious crime, tantamount to treason. The French political theorist and demonologist Jean Bodin, whose writings on politics were a main source of James's absolutist ideas, had defined witchcraft as treason against God, but James went further by equating it with the civil crime of treason as well. The king later used this equation of the two crimes to classify witchcraft, like treason, as a *crimen exceptum*, a crime so heinous and dangerous that courts did not need to follow the normal rules of evidence in its prosecution. In particular, he recommended that the traditional bar against the testimony of women and children in criminal trials should not apply in witchcraft prosecutions, just as it did not apply in trials for treason.[32]

The king's recognition of the political dimension of witchcraft also explains why in the commission of 26 June 1591, discussed in Chapter 2, the privy council authorized the six commissioners to use all necessary means, including torture, to bring about their confessions.[33] The granting of this warrant, which gave the commissioners unprecedented latitude to interrogate and torture any individuals who might come under suspicion, can be explained only by its primary purpose of detecting traitors. The power was not extended to any commissioners subsequently appointed to investigate or try witches.

The witch-hunt of 1597, which should be considered as a separate operation rather than an extension of the prosecutions that had taken place in 1590–1, reveals remarkably similar patterns regarding James's involvement. Once again, the hunt began in response to local conditions, at least in Aberdeen, the only location where substantial documentation of this witch-hunt has survived. There some 80 people were caught up in a witchcraft panic that began in the spring of that year but had shown signs of winding down by the summer. The hunt suffered a nearly fatal blow with the exposure of Margaret Aitken, the great witch of Balwearie, as a fraud. Aitken had played a role comparable to that of Agnes Sampson in 1591 by implicating a large number of confederates (she claimed that there were 2,300 in all) and thereby expanding the number of accusations and prosecutions. Aitken was exposed for having named innocent people as witches while she was being brought around the country to identify them. The revelation of her fraud resulted in the decision by the government, discussed at length in the previous chapter, to withdraw some commissions upon which the trials of 1597 had been based. It is unknown what role the king played in this significant change in governmental policy. He did agree to establish a new form of procedure for trying witches, but he apparently did not rush to implement such measures.

Two years later the general assembly of the Church of Scotland complained that the new procedures had not yet been established and reminded the king of his commitment. The assembly also raised the question whether it was permissible to move witches from place to place, suggesting that this important concern had not yet been addressed.[34]

The most perplexing aspect of James's involvement in this witch-hunt is that it began very late, in the summer of 1597, after the main witch-trials in Aberdeen and the few we know about in Fife had already taken place. Even more remarkable, his promotion of witch-hunting in Aberdeen began after the privy council had issued its order of 12 August revoking the commissions that had been the proclaimed cause of such flagrant judicial abuse. The key to James's belated promotion of witch-hunting was the discovery during the examination of Malcolm Anderson that he and other witches had planned to use sorcery to drown the king when he was travelling to Dundee to attend the meeting of the general assembly in May.[35] In other words, James became an active promoter of witch-trials in 1597 only after he learned that the witches had conspired to do him harm, just as he had in 1590 when the North Berwick witches had allegedly conspired to drown him and his bride in the North Sea. As Julian Goodare has argued, '1597 was another North Berwick – a major panic over treasonable witchcraft that was thought to be directed against the king personally'.[36] In both witch-hunts the king was particularly alarmed by reports of large numbers of witches. The number believed to have been at North Berwick was as high as 200, while on 15 August 1597 Robert Bowes reported to Burghley that 'the king has been lately pestered and in many ways troubled in the examination of the witches, which swarm in exceeding numbers and (is credibly reported) in many thousands'.[37] The only difference between the two witch-hunts was that the king's intervention in 1597 came much later in the process and therefore probably had less of an impact on the total number of trials and executions.

Daemonologie

James VI's witchcraft treatise, *Daemonologie*, provides the clearest expression of James's witch beliefs in the 1590s. Although we have little direct evidence of the time of composition, references to the events of both 1590–1 and 1597 strongly suggest that the king began work on the treatise in the aftermath of the North Berwick trials. He resumed work on the project and arranged for its publication after the witch-hunt of 1597. The book thus serves as a statement of the king's thinking during this critical period of Scottish witch-hunting.

The treatise places an unprecedented emphasis on the demonic nature of the witch's crime, providing a foundation for all subsequent Scottish witch-hunting. He does this, however, not so much by importing descriptions of the crime formulated by continental European demonologists (with whose works he was familiar) but by comparing magicians with witches. In this process he not only established the differences between these two types of activities but also demonstrated that they shared a common source of their power by making a pact with the devil. In this way James helped to make the pact with the devil the central Scottish witch belief and the primary concern of those who sought to prosecute them.

The structure of the *Daemonologie* differs from most of the other witchcraft treatises published in the late sixteenth and early seventeenth centuries in that it discusses magic and witchcraft separately, assigning each crime a separate book in the treatise. Most other demonologies considered magic part and parcel of the crime of witchcraft, differing only over how important the witch's *maleficium* or harmful magic was in relation to her commerce with demons. James's decision to treat the crime of magic separately and, even more unusually, to give magic top billing in Book I reflected his own fear of ritual attacks by learned magicians or necromancers on his person.

The distinction he made between magic and witchcraft had validity in contemporary language and law. Most European languages (French excepted) made clear distinctions between the two crimes, the latter being a broader, more comprehensive category involving a variety of diabolical activities, including the pact with the devil. The distinction is crystal clear in English and in German, where *Zauberei* (magic) can be distinguished from the more diabolical *Hexerei* or witchcraft. European courts, moreover, still tried individuals for magic as a separate crime and, as one might suspect, the defendants were almost always better educated than witches.

In James's discussion of magic in Book I the king promises to discuss all the forbidden arts, but he restricts himself mainly to divination in its various forms, including astrology. The form of divination with which he is most concerned is necromancy, which involved summoning the devil in ceremonial or ritual magic. James regards the study of this type of magic as perilous and its practice diabolical. He also emphasizes the learning and high social status of the people (usually men) involved in this activity, and he establishes the political world these men inhabited when he refers to their patronage by princes, dukes, and kings. Here James's preoccupation with the practice of magic at his own court and Bothwell's patronage of Ritchie Graham provides further evidence that the king's apparently scholarly investigation into occult crimes was inspired by, and based upon, his own personal experiences.

James, however, was well aware of the conventional distinction made between necromancers who practised ritual magic and the witches who were being charged in the witchcraft trials of the 1590s. 'For they say', wrote James, 'that the witches are servants only, and slaves to the devil, but the necromancers are his masters and commanders.'[38] Both groups, however, had threatened the king personally, and therefore James needed to establish the common ground between them. This he found in their allegiance to the devil. 'Many points of their craft and practices are common betwixt the magicians and them, for they serve both one master, although in diverse fashions.'[39] Just like the magicians who summoned up the devil, witches made face-to-face pacts with him and therefore were guilty of rejecting their Christian faith. In this way James was following the lead of early fifteenth-century theologians and inquisitors when they had applied the charges previously levelled against ritual magicians, who had been the main object of inquisitorial concern in the fourteenth century, to the newly discovered groups of predominantly illiterate, female suspects who were practising a very different type of magic.

The king's determination to obliterate the moral distinction between necromancers and witches explains why he wrote more about the pact with the devil than about the witches' assemblies. Unlike the more sensational demonologies that were produced in the same the period from 1590 to 1620, most notably those by Henri Boguet, Martin Del Rio, Peter Binsfeld, and Pierre de Lancre, James's treatise devotes very little space to the activities that witches allegedly engaged in at the sabbath. The prurient reader expecting to find salacious details of naked dancing, promiscuous sex between demons and witches, child sacrifice, or cannibalism would be sorely disappointed. James's discussion of sexual intercourse between humans and demons appears in another part of the treatise.[40] His main concern in describing the sabbath was the way witches aped and mocked Christian services. James described the inversion of a Protestant service by drawing a contrast between the minister teaching how to serve God in spirit in truth and the devil teaching his disciples how to do mischief.[41] This corresponds to the narrative of the devil preaching from the pulpit at North Berwick kirk. Regardless whether James's treatise inspired or reflected Scottish witch beliefs, the witches' sabbath in Scotland was a very tame affair indeed.

Over the course of the next century charges against witches and their confessions followed the basic outlines of James's treatise. Scottish witches were routinely accused of making a pact with the devil, renouncing their baptism, receiving the devil's mark, and meeting with other witches, but those assemblies were never described as orgies or as occasions for reversing the basic moral law. In that sense Scotland never fully received 'continental' notions of witchcraft. The pact with the devil became a central Scottish witch belief, and in that respect the crime differed fundamentally from the English conception of the crime before 1645. But the full elaboration of the witch's crime – the composite notion of witchcraft that developed over the course of three centuries in the hands of theologians and inquisitors – never entered the mainstream of Scottish witch belief, and for that failure James was at least partially responsible.

James's preoccupation with the pact with the devil explains his advocacy of two techniques that he recommended for discovering witches. Both of them are predicated on the religious nature of the crime. The first was pricking the witch to see whether the devil had given her a special mark that was insensitive to pain and could not bleed.[42] The belief in the devil's mark was particularly strong in Scotland, as it was in many Protestant countries, since Protestants emphasized the pact as the essence of witchcraft.[43] James argued in *Daemonologie* that, just as God allowed only those 'marked with his seal, the sacrament of baptism' to worship him in church, so the devil demanded that all the witches who adored him be given his mark.[44] The devil's mark, therefore, was in his view one of the many inversions that took place in the conclusion of the pact with the devil and in the witches' worship of him. Evidence that the mark had been found on a witch's body was thus an empirical indication of supernatural intervention in the world. As we have seen, the practice of pricking the witch for the devil's mark was used in Scotland before James's intervention in the North Berwick trials. James's endorsement of the procedure, however, contributed to its widespread use throughout the seventeenth and into the eighteenth centuries. It was so common that professional prickers who specialized in locating the marks appeared during the revolutionary years and during the great Scottish witch-hunt of 1661–2.

By contrast, the second extra-judicial technique recommended by James, swimming the witch to see if she floated, never became a routine practice in Scotland. Its use in Aberdeen in 1597, which certainly explains its inclusion in the *Daemonologie*, remains the only recorded instance of its official use in the northern kingdom. Somewhat ironically, the procedure was used more frequently in England than in Scotland, mainly during the prosecutions of the 1640s.

Swimming was originally one of the ordeals used by medieval courts to ascertain the guilt of an accused criminal. The suspect was thrown into a body of water that had been blessed by a member of the clergy. Floating was taken as proof of guilt on the grounds that the blessed water rejected her. If the accused sank, she was innocent, although in many instances she drowned. The swimming test and all other forms of the medieval ordeal were banned by the Fourth Lateran Council in 1215 and were replaced by systems of criminal procedure that relied on the evaluation of evidence by human reason (either judges or jurors) rather than signs given by an immanent deity to determine guilt or innocence. After its prohibition, swimming persisted as a popular test used by communities to confirm their suspicions of a witch's guilt.

The swimming test had no standing in Scots or English law. No jurist or demonologist, including Bodin, accepted the results of the test as valid legal evidence. It seems incongruous therefore that James, who prided himself on his adherence to the law, would recommend a procedure that jurists dismissed as worthless. James's reference to both pricking and swimming as 'good helps that may be used for their trial', however, suggests that he viewed them as presumptions rather than legal proofs, that is, evidence upon which a trial could proceed rather than that which is sufficient to convict. In this extra-legal context James was able to find a place for assistance from the deity in identifying witches: '[S]o it appears that God hath appointed (for a supernatural sign of the monstrous impiety of the witches) that the water shall refuse to receive them in her bosom, that have shaken off them the sacred water of baptism and wilfully refused the benefit thereof.'[45] Swimming therefore, just like pricking, gained its legitimacy from the sacrament of baptism, which, like all sacraments, was viewed by Protestants as a sign rather than the effectual means of God's grace.

The tameness of James's beliefs regarding the witches' sabbath raises the issue whether *Daemonologie* can be considered a sceptical treatise. If we consider the treatise as a whole, there is little foundation for such a claim. The book was written as a response to the sceptical witchcraft treatises written by two Protestant demonologists: the Dutch humanist Johann Weyer and the English gentleman Reginald Scot. In the preface James states clearly that he wrote the book to prove that witches really did the devilish things they were accused of and therefore merited punishment. The king's position on the reality of the crime and the need for its vigorous placed him squarely in the company of a group of European demonologists who had also responded to Weyer in the closing years of the sixteenth century: the French political theorist Jean Bodin, the Catholic suffragan bishop of Trier Peter Binsfeld, and the Swiss physician and political theorist Thomas Erastus.

Daemonologie took the form of a dialogue between two fictional characters, Philomathes and Epistemon, but the role of Philomathes in the dialogue was simply to ask questions that prompted the answers of Epistemon, who insisted upon the reality and the unlawfulness of witchcraft. Occasionally Epistemon would present the sceptical arguments which he then refuted, in the manner of a scholastic disputation, but there was never any question regarding the identification of the royal author with Epistemon.

The only way that *Daemonologie* can be read as a sceptical work is based upon the recognition that early modern writers on witchcraft cannot be classified as simply believers or sceptics but that there were elements of credulity and doubt in all their works. The credulous demonologist Henri Boguet, for example, denied the reality of the witch's ability to transform herself into a beast, whereas the sceptic Johann Weyer fully accepted the power of Satan in the world. Instead of placing a demonologist in one camp or the other we should think of a spectrum of belief in which demonologists could be positioned in various midway locations rather than at one end or the other.

Any such classification would certainly place James on the credulous side of the spectrum, but he would probably lie closer to the centre of that scale than many other contemporary demonologists. The sceptical elements in *Daemonologie* are most unequivocal in his discussion of the transportation of witches. He insists that witches' flight could only be the result of demonic illusion.[46] James was not alone among demonologists on this point, but he clearly separated himself from Heinrich Kramer, who argued that witches could be transported bodily from place to place although they could also be transported in their imagination.[47] In keeping with the Protestant emphasis on the sovereignty of God, James insisted that only God, not the devil, could perform deeds that were otherwise impossible. The same Protestant emphasis on the sovereignty of God lies at the root of James's distinction between the miracles that God could perform and the mere wonders achieved by the devil's power.

The part of the treatise that manifested the greatest scepticism regarding particular witch beliefs was the third and final book, which dealt with evil spirits that trouble men and women. In this book James focused on those spirits who inhabited places, those who assaulted people outwardly, those who possessed them inwardly, and the spirits known as fairies. Although witchcraft could be considered the cause of the first three groups of spirits, James dealt here only with their independent operation. The king's treatment of these subjects included elements of belief and scepticism. He accepted the reality of *incubi* and *succubi* as demonic spirits and the possibility that the devil could use the semen of a dead man to have sexual intercourse with a woman, but denied that he could thereby conceive a child, since the semen was cold. (Demonologists argued that since the devil's body was not corporeal, without flesh and blood, his penis would be cold to the touch.) James accepted the reality of spirits that entered houses to trouble human beings. He also believed that spirits could haunt isolated places (as opposed to communities that functioned harmoniously in inhabited areas), but he denied the reality of werewolves as 'one sort of such spirits'. Werewolves were in James's view human beings affected by melancholy who, believing that they were beasts, imitated animal behaviour by doing things like crawling on all fours. In this way James indirectly challenged the belief that witches could transform themselves into beasts, although he never identified werewolves as witches.[48]

James manifested far less scepticism in his discussion of demonic possession. In Book III the king fully accepted the possibility that a kind of spirit 'outwardly troubles and follows some persons, or else inwardly possesses them'.[49] Concerning the latter group, he fully accepted the possibility that a demon could enter human bodies and control their movements and behaviour, demonstrating superhuman strength, making their limbs so stiff that they could not be bent, and causing them to speak in foreign tongues previously unknown to them. In keeping with his firm Protestant beliefs, he denied the validity of Roman Catholic exorcisms, 'which while the clergy invents for confirming of their rotten religion'. Nonetheless James admitted that Catholics might be able to dispossess demoniacs if they used the biblically sanctioned methods of prayer and fasting that Protestants employed.[50]

James based his views regarding possession mainly on scripture, but he did refer to the confession of a young woman 'known by experience' who was troubled by a spirit that promised to leave her body if she would blaspheme God. In an early draft of this passage in *Daemonologie*, James referred more specifically to 'a young lass troubled with spirits laid on her by witchcraft', suggesting that this incident might have arisen during the witchcraft prosecutions of 1591.[51] The only reference to possession in the trial records of 1591 was the accusation that John Fian had caused the 'witching and possessing' of William Hutson.[52]

Witchcraft and possession in England

During the early years of James's reign in England the king became more sceptical regarding the possibility of demonic possession than he had been when he wrote *Daemonologie*. This shift in his attitude towards demonic possession reduced his commitment to witch-hunting and also made him more sceptical regarding the reality of witchcraft. The episode that marked this turning point in James's views was the possession of Anne Gunter.

In 1604 Anne Gunter, the 18-year-old daughter of Brian Gunter, a lesser gentleman from North Moreton, Berkshire, manifested many of the symptoms that were widely interpreted as the effects of demonic possession. She experienced convulsive fits in which her body writhed, quivered, and shook; she acquired temporary deafness and blindness; her body became extraordinarily stiff; she sneezed up, voided, and vomited pins, sometimes numbering in the hundreds, while still more pins exuded from her breasts and fingers; she foamed at the mouth; her pulse was temporarily interrupted; and she went as many as 12 days without eating. She physically assaulted those around her, throwing her sisters against the walls of their house. Her shoes, stockings, petticoats, and garters all displayed the remarkable ability to untie themselves, come out from under her clothes of their own power, crawl around the ground, and return to her body, tying themselves neatly in place. She also told people who were brought before her how much money they had in their purses.[53]

When Anne began to exhibit the symptoms, her father arranged for a number of doctors from nearby Oxford and Newbury to examine her. Their inability to find any natural cause of her ailment strengthened the suspicion that witchcraft had been responsible.[54] Not everyone, however, was convinced that Anne was the victim of a supernatural illness. As in many cases of possession, the suspicion of deception naturally arose. The strength of that suspicion became apparent after Anne was moved first to Staunton, Oxfordshire, where she spent some time first at the house of her brother Harvey, and then to the University of Oxford, where she stayed with Dr Thomas Holland, the Regius Professor of Divinity and the rector of Exeter College, who was the husband of Anne's sister Susan.[55] Anne apparently already knew many of the members of the college, some of whom later accompanied her to Abingdon.[56]

While staying at Holland's residence, Anne continued to exhibit her symptoms of possession, and it is quite possible that they became more pronounced as she became the main theatrical attraction in Oxford, sometimes commanding an audience of 40 people at one time. The similarities between possession and theatre have been noted before: both possession and attempts to end it by means of exorcism involved the recitation of a script and the staging of an action.[57] The main question was whether God or the human actors wrote the script. This is the question that the large number of fellows, students, and dons who visited Holland's home to view Anne's behaviour were asking. Many of these visitors noted inconsistencies in the demoniac's actions or discovered that she could not pass various tests they devised to prove the authenticity of her fits. Dr John Harding, the Hebrew reader for the university and the president of Magdalen College, observed that while claiming to be able to read while blind, she could not continue her reading once the lights went out.[58] A student at the college, the second son of the Scottish earl of Murray, discovered the different means she used to untie her shoes and garters and move them along the floor.[59]

Like many demoniacs, Anne claimed that witches were responsible for her afflictions. In fact she named three women, Elizabeth Gregory, Mary Pepwell, and Agnes Pepwell, and she also claimed that she had had visions of these women's familiar spirits. It is not entirely clear why the Gunters preferred charges of witchcraft against these three women. We do know, however, that witchcraft accusations served the function not only of explaining misfortune but also of eliminating socially undesirable people or one's personal rivals. There is evidence from later depositions in Star Chamber that the Gunter family had long been at odds with the three accused women and their families. Testimony from various sources revealed that Brian Gunter had been involved in a fight with members of Elizabeth Gregory's family at a football match and that his neighbours held him to be responsible for the death of her two brothers-in-law.[60] Indeed, Elizabeth Gregory, upon coming to the Gunter residence, accused Brian of being a 'murdering bloodsucker' and promised revenge.[61] Further tension might have arisen from the fact that the three women, being from the lower levels of society, threatened to drain the resources of the more well-to-do members of society, like the Gunters, or simply that they, being aggressive and contentious women, did not conform to the ideal of feminine conduct that was being proclaimed at the time. Agnes Pepwell had in fact been suspected of witchcraft for many years, while Elizabeth Gregory, whose mother-in-law, Katherine Gregory, was reputed to be a witch, was a 'notorious scold'.[62] When Brian Gunter had himself been gravely ill in the summer of 1604, he had suspected Elizabeth Gregory as the cause of his misfortune, and indeed, after scratching her head, he had quickly recovered, thereby confirming his suspicion.[63]

The trial of Elizabeth Gregory and Agnes Pepwell (Mary Pepwell had fled) took place at the Lent assizes held at Abingdon on 1 March 1605.[64] Although Gunter marshalled some 15 witnesses, and the presentation of the evidence involved some 'very long discourses', the jury decided on a verdict of not guilty. Two developments during the trial appear to have been decisive in producing this verdict. The first was the determination of Thomas Hinton of Chilton Park, a cousin of one of the judges, to expose Anne's fits as counterfeit. Not only did he succeed in making a declaration of his incredulity before the court, but he also spoke with others who attended the proceedings, including Sir Francis Knowles and Alexander Chokke, a justice of the peace.[65] The second development was the selection of Chokke and two other justices of the peace as members of the jury. Chokke, who was appointed foreman of the jury, became increasingly sceptical regarding the authenticity of Anne's fits when he observed Anne's behaviour during the trial. The same was true of the other two JPs, who interviewed Anne just before the trial began.

The acquittal of Gregory and Pepwell by no means settled the issue. In the following months Anne Gunter came under the care or observation of many different persons, all of whom became more sceptical of the authenticity of her alleged demonic affliction. The first were the members of the Royal College of Physicians. Just before the trial, the recently appointed bishop of London, Richard Vaughan, asked the fellows of the college to examine the young demoniac. Three of the fellows visited Anne and concluded on 4 March that she was feigning possession.[66] A few weeks later Dr Richard Haddock, a physician in Salisbury, reached a similar conclusion regarding the authenticity of Anne's malady. Acting at the request of Henry Cotton, the bishop of the diocese, Haddock examined Anne and concluded that the pins she vomited up were the same ones that he had secretly marked beforehand.[67]

Anne's fits continued through the summer of 1605, and at the end of August they attracted the attention of King James himself when he visited Oxford.[68] It is not surprising that the king, who prided himself on the detection of fraudulent accusations of witchcraft (as in the Margaret Aitken case), would express interest in a case of possession of this sort. Between August and October 1605 the king interviewed Anne Gunter on at least four separate occasions, at Oxford in August, twice at Windsor in October, and one more time at Whitehall.[69] At some point between the first and second interviews the king referred the case to Richard Bancroft, the archbishop of Canterbury. Bancroft in turn placed Anne in the custody of his chaplain and main assistant, Samuel Harsnett.

Harsnett, like Bancroft, had a special interest in cases of possession. During the previous ten years he had spearheaded a clerical campaign to discredit a rash of exorcisms that were being performed both by Jesuit seminary priests like William Weston and by puritan ministers like John Darrell. The purpose of the Roman Catholic exorcisms had been to prove to a heretical English nation that the Catholic Church was the one true church, one of the marks of which was the power to perform miracles. The greatest of these so-called miracles was the casting out of devils. The puritans, on the other hand, using only the scripturally warranted methods of prayer and fasting, were conducting their exorcisms to counter the claims of the papists. The motive of the Anglican clerical establishment was to discredit both groups of exorcists by revealing the fraudulence of their efforts.[70]

With Anne committed directly to his charge at Lambeth Palace, Harsnett was eventually able to extract from her an admission of the fraud she and her father had perpetrated. She admitted that her father had made her fake many of her alleged symptoms and accuse Gregory and the Pepwells of witchcraft. It has been suggested that Harsnett may have coerced her into making this confession.[71] That is unlikely, however, since Anne made confessions on numerous occasions, not only at Lambeth Palace, but also before the king at Finchingbrooke and later in the Court of Star Chamber. At the end of October Harsnett reported to James that the girl had confessed on oath to what she had already admitted voluntarily.[72] Anne had also admitted her trickery to one Ashley, a servant of the archbishop, with whom she had fallen in love while in detention at Lambeth Palace. Harsnett had apparently encouraged this romance in order to obtain Anne's unsuspecting admission to her deceptive behaviour.[73]

At some point during Anne's stay at Lambeth Place, Harsnett called in a London physician, Dr Edward Jorden, to examine her.[74] Jorden also had previous experience with demoniacs, having only three years before testified in court that the fits of another possessed girl, Mary Glover, were the result of hysteria, or what was then referred to as the suffocation of the mother. In that same year Jorden had published a treatise on the subject.[75] Somewhat surprisingly, he did not reach the same conclusion regarding Anne's affliction, possibly because the girl had ceased having fits when he examined her, so he had no direct evidence of her malady. All he had to go on was the information that pins and pieces of glass had been discovered in Anne's stools, leading him to conclude that she had swallowed the objects, perhaps in her fits. There was clearly nothing supernatural about her behaviour, but the evidence seemed to point more to fraud than to disease as the cause of Anne's affliction. Indeed, in his testimony Jorden referred to Anne's 'sundry feigned fits' while in the custody of Harsnett.[76]

Having interviewed Anne directly, and having received reports from Harsnett and others, the king concluded in a letter to the earl of Salisbury on 10 October that the star demoniac of Oxford and Berkshire was 'never possessed with any devil, nor bewitched'. He based his diagnosis on the fact that she appeared to have been cured by a non-medicinal potion given her by a physician, either Haddock or Jorden, together with a tablet to be hung around her neck. He also claimed that her vomiting of pins was the result of various pinpranks and that the swelling of her belly was attributable to the disease called suffocation of the mother.[77] Finally, he reported that Anne, who had sought Ashley's 'love most importunately and immodestly', was now asking permission to marry him. James's report therefore, while admitting the possibility of illness, emphasized the girl's deceit. It is even possible that Anne was the 'little counterfeit wench' whom James later referred to in an undated letter to his son.[78]

When the king wrote this letter to Salisbury, he already suspected that Anne's counterfeit possession was part of a plot 'against one Gregory for some former hatred … borne unto her'. In a draft of his letter to the earl of Salisbury he indicated that he was planning to have Agnes Pepwell examined by the archbishop of Canterbury and certain legal officials in order to press her to confess the truth, claiming that she had previously lied when she had been given the benefit of royal protection. In particular, the king wanted to know what had been admitted to her in a conversation with William Gunter,

Anne's brother. The king also had in his possession an incriminating letter from Anne Gunter to her father.[79] As early as October 1605, therefore, the government was contemplating legal action against the Gunters.

The prosecution of the Gunters finally commenced in February 1606, when Coke exhibited an information against Brian and Anne Gunter in the Court of Star Chamber. The charge was that the two had conspired 'by false and wicked devices to bring [Gregory and the two Pepwells] into infamy and cause them to be reputed and taken for witches and thereupon also to cause them to be indicted and arraigned for witchcraft.'[80] It was claimed that Master Gunter, who by now was imprisoned in Lambeth Palace, had put his daughter's head in the smoke of burning brimstone, administered intoxicating drinks to her, forced her to swallow salad oil to make her vomit, beat her, thrust pins into her while she was asleep, and then, as in modern cases of child abuse, sworn her to secrecy.[81]

The king did not intervene in the court's proceedings, as he had in the trial of Barbara Napier and her assizers in 1591. There is considerable irony, however, in the fact that the legal machinery used in this case to support a claim of conspiracy to indict for witchcraft represented royal power in its most untrammelled English form. The Court of Star Chamber was a conciliar court; it was in fact the council sitting as a judicial rather than as an administrative body. It owed its origin to the king's prerogative – the power he exercised by himself rather than in conjunction with parliament – and for that reason was also known as a prerogative court. Star Chamber represented direct royal power, and in this case James's power was being used not to prosecute witches but their false accusers.

Unfortunately we do not have a formal record of the court's decision, since most decrees of the court have been lost. It is likely, however, that Brian Gunter was convicted and fined, while Anne, having confessed to the king and the court, apparently received a royal pardon and a dowry.[82] Much more important than any sentence, however, was the discrediting of a counterfeit possession and the demonstrable proof, so often lacking even in mere acquittals for witchcraft, that an alleged practice of witchcraft had never taken place. The trial of the Gunters in Star Chamber had a lasting impact on witch-hunting in England, beginning a long decline that was interrupted only by the campaign conducted by Matthew Hopkins and John Stearne during the civil war.

Whether the investigation changed the witch *beliefs* of James is difficult to determine. Recognition that a person had been falsely accused of witchcraft often encouraged the growth of judicial scepticism but rarely did it foster a philosophical scepticism regarding the reality of the crime. This explains why the decline of witchcraft prosecutions throughout Europe in the late seventeenth and early eighteenth centuries long preceded the emergence of the belief that witches did not exist. It is entirely plausible, however, that the exposure of Anne Gunter as a fraud made the king question the reality of the crime. Thomas Fuller suggested as much when he declared that the frequency of forged possessions in England led the king 'flatly to deny the workings of witches and devils as but falsehoods and delusions'.[83]

Samuel Harsnett, the cleric who took the lead in exposing Anne Gunter, shows how the deduction could be made. In *A Declaration of Egregious Popish Impostures* (1603) Harsnett claimed that the power of the devil is greatly limited in this world and that he generally works through natural causes. Appealing in good Protestant fashion to the sovereignty of God, Harsnett asserted that the age of miracles is past. Christ and the apostles had performed exorcisms, but there was no longer any need for such signs of divine power.[84] Harsnett did not unequivocally deny the possibility of witchcraft, but he ridiculed those who believed in it and challenged its existence in numerable instances.[85]

Even if James did continue to believe in the possibility of witchcraft, he became even less committed to prosecuting those accused of that crime. This became evident in the summer of 1616 when he interviewed another demoniac who had accused nine women of causing his afflictions by witchcraft. John Smith, a 13-year-old boy from Leicester, had experienced such severe fits that two men could not restrain him; he made sounds like horses, dogs, or cats whenever a demon in that animal shape would assault him; and he beat his breast violently hundreds of times without causing himself physical damage. By chance James visited Leicester on one of his progresses four weeks after the nine witches named by the boy had been tried and executed. The king examined the boy and immediately suspected fraud, which was confirmed by clerics in the service of the archbishop of Canterbury.[86] The exposure of the boy came in time to acquit five more witches he had named, but the assize judges who had presided at the first trial, Sir Humphrey Winch and Serjeant Crew, were reprimanded for allowing the executions.[87]

The progression of James's views on witchcraft can be plotted by comparing his reactions to four people who had accused others of witchcraft: the Scottish witches Agnes Sampson and Margaret Aitken and the English demoniacs Anne Gunter and John Smith. The king's interest in these four people (three of whom he interviewed personally) was driven by intellectual curiosity, a wish to display royal Solomonic wisdom, and a desire to test empirically the claims of people to have had contact with the supernatural realm. In the case of Agnes Sampson James eventually became convinced of the woman's guilt. The exposure of Margaret Aitken as a fraud in1597 apparently raised doubts in James, but the fear of yet another treasonous attack led him to continue the witch-hunt even after the privy council had withdrawn some of the commissions of justiciary. The turning point came in England in 1605 during his interviews with Anne Gunter, which led him to support the government's countersuit against the young demoniac and her father. The king's reprimand of Winch and Crew in 1616 represented an even more direct royal repudiation of witch-hunting and the final transformation of the king from royal witch-hunter to royal sceptic.

The transformation of King James's views on witchcraft in England had little impact in Scotland, where he no longer resided, and where a different witchcraft statute, a different conception of the crime, and a different set of procedures in trying witches were in effect. In Scotland witch-hunting continued in James's absence, inspired to some extent by the king's witchcraft treatise, which had affirmed the reality of the crime and endorsed the routine practice of pricking the witch for the devil's mark. In England, where ideas of the pact with the devil found scant confirmation in witchcraft trials, James's treatise did not have a comparable effect. During the 1640s, however, witch-hunting in England as well as Scotland reached new levels of intensity, and some of the king's ideas and recommendations found a receptive audience in England at that time. To that period of witch-hunting in both kingdoms we now turn.

4 Witch-hunting in revolutionary Britain

In 1643, during the civil war that involved the armies of England as well as those of Scotland, Scottish authorities engaged in a frenzy of witch-hunting every bit as intense as in the 1590s. Scottish witch-hunting had entered a period of restraint after the large panic of 1597 had come to an end in the wake of the exposure of Margaret Aitken as a fraud. There had been occasional prosecutions, such as that of Margaret Barclay and Isobel Crawford in 1618, discussed in Chapter 2, and there was a spate of trials in 1628–30 after the privy council supported the kirk in one its periodic campaigns for moral reform. But the country had not engaged in a witchcraft panic for more than 45 years. The hunt that began in 1643 lasted almost two years and was characterized by many of the features of the earlier panics: the trying of several witches at one time, charges of devil worship and nocturnal assemblies, and a high conviction rate. This witch-hunt died out after it had claimed the lives of more than 100 victims, but another, much larger hunt began in 1649, the year that King Charles I was executed. That hunt, which continued into 1650, involved the judicial prosecution of at least 230 persons, of whom 150 are known to have been executed. When English military forces occupied the country in 1651 and English judges assumed jurisdiction over the prosecution of crime, there was a sharp decrease in the intensity of witch-hunting. The Scottish urge to prosecute witches persisted, however, and in the last two years of the English occupation the trials resumed in earnest. Only when the protectorate – the form of government in England, Scotland and Ireland established in December 1653 – came to an end in May 1659 did the witch-trials cease. After the restoration, however, Scotland returned to the business of witch-hunting with a vengeance, prosecuting more than 600 people for the crime in 1661–2.

Scotland's period of intense witch-hunting during the civil war had its parallel in England, where the single largest witch-hunt in English history took place in 1645–7 in the southeastern counties of the kingdom. Like the Scottish hunt of 1643–4, this English campaign against the devil's confederates followed a period of relative leniency in dealing with respect to this crime. During the 1630s in particular, prosecutions in England had almost come grinding to a halt. That trend was dramatically reversed in 1645. The hunt was directed and coordinated by the self-styled witch-hunters Matthew Hopkins and John Stearne, who travelled around the region identifying witches who were reportedly infesting local communities. Like the Scottish witch-hunt of the early 1640s, this hunt also involved the trial of large clusters of witches and the expression of unprecedented charges of commerce with demons. Two years after the hunt finally came to an end, another witch-hunt took place in the northern English county of Northumberland. In its inspiration and dynamics this hunt resembled the Scottish witch-hunt that took place at the same time, and it even employed Scottish personnel in the detection of the culprits. Like the Scottish witch-hunt of 1649, it also continued into the following year before coming to an end.

The Northumberland witch-hunt of 1649–1650, which may have claimed more than 20 victims, was not as large as the massive Scottish hunt of the same years. Even more important, it marked an end to intense witch-hunting in the southern kingdom. The only significant cluster of witch-trials in England in the 1650s occurred at Maidstone in Kent in 1652, where six witches were executed. After that date there were only occasional prosecutions, a pattern that set England on a different demonological path from that of Scotland.

It was no coincidence that both England and Scotland experienced intense periods of witch-hunting during the 1640s. The mid-century was a period of civil war and revolution in both British kingdoms. The turmoil began in Scotland in 1637 with resistance to attempts by Charles I (r. 1625–49) to impose a new service book, modelled on the English Book of Common Prayer, on the more Reformed or Calvinistic Scottish church. Resistance by the Scots led to the signing of the National Covenant in 1638, the abolition of episcopacy, the establishment of an exclusively presbyterian system of church government, and two wars with the king's English army, known as the Bishops' Wars, in 1639 and 1640. The second Bishops' War resulted in the defeat of the English army and the Scottish occupation of northern England. The difficulty Charles had in paying for the war and the costs of the Scottish occupation forced him to summon two English parliaments in 1640, and his failure to come to terms with the second of those parliaments, the Long Parliament (1640–53), led to civil war between English armies loyal to parliament and those that supported the king. In 1643 the English parliament signed a military alliance with the Scots, the Solemn League and Covenant, which pledged the English to establish a presbyterian system of church government, similar to that which was already in place in Scotland.

The English–Scottish alliance endured until the defeat of royalist forces and the capture of the king by the Scottish army in 1646. After the Scots turned Charles over to the English in exchange for the payment of their troops, the English alliance with Scotland disintegrated. The king's negotiations with the Presbyterian party in England, which wished to reach a settlement with him, led to a second civil war in 1648, in which Scots known as Engagers supported the king and his newfound English Presbyterian allies against the more radical Independent party. This party, which included Oliver

Cromwell and Henry Ireton, took a hard line in negotiating with the king and supported the introduction of a form of church government in which each congregation would be independent of each other. A church of this sort was anathema to presbyterians, who wished to maintain a structure of church government in which the clergy exercised a significant degree of influence in both state and society.

The Independents, who had the support of the effective and religiously inspired New Model Army that had been organized in 1645, prevailed in the second civil war of 1648 and then proceeded to try King Charles for making war on his people and therefore committing treason against his 'political body', identified in contemporary political theory as the kingdom or the state.[1] The king's execution in January 1649, followed by the abolition of the monarchy and the establishment of a republic, marked the high-point of the revolution.

Political events after that date followed very different courses in England and Scotland. In the southern kingdom efforts to push the revolution forward and establish a genuinely godly commonwealth resulted in the army's dismissal of the Long Parliament (known as the Rump Parliament after December 1648) and the appointment of the so-called Parliament of the Saints in 1653. Only with the dissolution of this assembly and the establishment of the protectorate did a conservative reaction to the revolution begin to gather strength. Between 1653 and 1658 Oliver Cromwell, who was named protector of the republic, presided over a regime more committed to the maintenance of order than the establishment of a godly state. This counter-revolutionary trend resulted ultimately in the restoration of the monarchy, the church, and the House of Lords in 1660.

In Scotland the turning point in the revolution came earlier, after the English invaded the country in 1649, defeated royalist forces at the battle of Dunbar in September 1650 and then governed Scotland as an occupied country for the next eight years. During this period the government at Westminster brought England and Scotland, as well as Ireland, into a full incorporating union, anticipating the union of the kingdoms of 1707.[2] This Cromwellian union, as it is usually referred to, came to an end with the collapse of the protectorate in May 1659. It was replaced by the revival of the personal union with the restoration of Charles II in 1660.

The entire period from 1638 until 1660 was a revolutionary one in Britain. Historians may quibble over the point at which the revolution came to an end. A case can certainly be made for 1651 in Scotland and 1653 in England. The important consideration for our purposes, however, is that the 1640s and to a lesser extent the 1650s formed a politically tumultuous period in which the traditional political and religious order in both countries was changed in fundamental ways. What is more, the wars fought to implement these political and religious changes resulted, ether directly or indirectly, in the death of about 190,000 English and 60,000 Scots. These figures represented roughly 3.7 and 6 per cent of the respective populations of the two kingdoms.[3] The designation of this entire period as revolutionary is based on a recognition of the depth and extent of the changes in the political landscape and the violence that attended those changes.

This chapter argues that the increase in witch-hunting in Scotland as well as England during these years was the product not only of the political changes that took place during these years but also the commitment of radical Protestants in both countries to bring about a program of moral reform. This argument can hold water only if we recognize that the revolutions in both Scotland and England were inspired in large part by religion. There has never been much doubt about the primacy of religious concerns in the Scottish revolution. The National Covenant of 1638, as its title indicated, defined the relationship between the Scottish nation and God, while the Solemn League and Covenant of 1643 created a military alliance with England in order to advance the cause of the reformed religion in both kingdoms. Later divisions within Scottish politics were based on the claim that those who had sided with the king had breached the covenant.

In contrast to Scotland, the religious inspiration of the English revolution is often minimized or discounted. There were, to be sure, other important causes of this fundamental transformation of political institutions, just as there were in Scotland. The growth of royal absolutism, the perceived violation of legal rights, and economic decay all played a role in fomenting political discontent. But the major lines of conflict, as in Scotland, were drawn between those Protestants who wished to achieve further reform and those who opposed them. The revolution in England is, after all, widely known as the Puritan Revolution, and its direction came from men who wished to purge the English church of its Roman Catholic trappings and bring it into conformity with the example of the 'best reformed churches' on the continent. English soldiers went into battle singing hymns and carrying banners that read 'Antichrist must down' and 'Sacra Scriptura'. The bogeyman of the King Charles's regime, William Laud, the archbishop of Canterbury, had been committed to a restoration of many of the ceremonies and liturgies that puritans considered to be popish. Described and even depicted in woodcuts as the Antichrist, he was impeached for treason in 1641 and executed in 1645, the year before parliament dismantled the episcopal structure of the English church. The execution of the king, who had supported Laud's ecclesiastical program, was carried out by puritans who cited biblical as well as legal justifications for their action. No wonder that the civil wars of the 1640s have been labelled England's wars of religion.[4]

Witch-hunting in revolutionary Scotland

There were three periods of intense witch-hunting in Scotland during the mid-century decades. The first occurred in 1643–4 and was centred mainly in Fife. A much larger upsurge of prosecutions in Scotland took place in 1649, the year the king was executed, and it continued into 1650. These trials were spread out throughout the country and were particularly strong in East Lothian and Ayrshire. The third period of witch-hunting spanned the years 1657–9, the final years of the protectorate. All in all, more than 1,000 people were formally accused of witchcraft during the revolutionary period.[5] The only decade in Scottish history in which more witches were tried than in either the 1640s or the 1650s was the 1660s, and the heavy toll in that decade was due almost entirely to the massive witch-hunt that occurred in 1661–2, shortly after the revolution had ended.

How do we connect this intense period of witch-hunting in Scotland with the revolutionary developments that occurred at the same time? The answer lies in major changes in the administration of justice, the campaign by both church and state to realize a godly society, and changes in the witch beliefs of the educated elite.

Judicial changes

During the period from 1641 to 1650 local Scottish communities arrested and conducted preliminary investigations of more than 500 witches. Most of these prosecutions occurred during either the witch-hunt of 1643–4 or the larger panic of 1649–50. Although we do not know the outcome of most of these prosecutions, a large number apparently resulted in executions. This outcome had much to do with the ability of local governments to prosecute witches with an unprecedented degree of freedom from central governmental control.

The shift away from central jurisdiction was most evident in the decline in the number of cases heard in the court of justiciary, the central criminal court in Edinburgh. During the period from 1641 to 1650, only 47 cases reached the justiciary court. Most of these cases originated in the counties near Edinburgh. Although the justiciary court had jurisdiction over the entire kingdom, the cost of bringing witnesses and the accused to Edinburgh usually meant that a disproportionate number of cases originated in Midlothian, the county in which Edinburgh was located, the neighbouring county of East Lothian, or Fife, the county lying north of Midlothian, across the Firth of Forth.

The low number of cases that reached the justiciary court during the revolutionary period meant that there was little chance that the central government would be able to mitigate the severity of the hunt. As we have seen, the percentage of acquittals of witches in the justiciary court was higher than in the other tribunals where witches were prosecuted. We do not know the fates of most of these 47 witches; only eight were definitely executed.

During the same period of time there was an even more dramatic reduction in the percentage of trials initiated by the privy council. During the 1620s and 1630s the privy council had authorized more than 85 per cent of all witchcraft prosecutions by granting commissions to local authorities to conduct the trials by themselves. During the 1640s this percentage dropped to a mere 21 per cent, accounting for the prosecution of 112 witches in all. The reason for this drastic reduction in the percentage (but not the number) of privy council cases was the revolutionary legislation of 1641, which deprived the king and privy council of much of its power and transferred it to the Scottish parliament.[6] This move had the potential to completely eliminate the council's traditional role in witch-hunting, but concern over prosecuting witches during the panic of 1643–4 led parliament to extend the council's traditional jurisdiction.[7] The council continued to grant commissions of justiciary to try witches until its abolition in 1650, more than one year after the execution of Charles I.

The commissions that the enfeebled privy council did manage to grant during these years, especially during the panics of 1643–4 and 1649–50, were not sufficient to meet the demand from local communities to try the witches in their midst. An undated memorandum of 1649 accompanying a request for a new commission to try some 29 witches in East Lothian highlighted the problem. The memorandum, which prominent burgesses and lairds from the county sent to Thomas Crombie, one of the privy councillors, expressed anger that a previous commission to try an unspecified number of witches (apparently in 1644) had not given the appointed judges power to summon jurors 'under a penalty'.[8] The new commission was to remedy this defect. The memorandum also expressed the hope that, since many other witches besides those listed in the petition had been delated, Crombie would 'get out the commission not only against these already apprehended and confessing but also that such as are or shall be delated thereafter'.[9] This was therefore a request for a standing commission, similar to those issued during the witchcraft panic of 1597. The council denied this request and did not even grant a particular commission for the witches named in the petition, for in 1661 13 of these beleaguered suspects were once again included in another commission, this time granted by parliament.[10]

In response to this demand for the government to authorize witchcraft trials, the committee of estates began granting commissions in 1649. The committee, which was established in 1640 and lasted until 1651, was set up to exercise a variety of judicial and executive functions between sessions of parliament.[11] It functioned more as a commission than a committee in that its activities were not subject to parliamentary approval. Its responsibilities included the maintenance of law and order when the system of criminal justice had been suspended or was not working properly. It did not become involved in witch-hunting until 1649 and 1650, when it issued 58 commissions to local authorities throughout the country to try a total of 180 witches.[12] It also authorized the justice deputes Alexander Colville and James Robertson to try Jean Craig for witchcraft at Tranent on 4 April 1649.[13]

Shortly after the committee began granting commissions, parliament itself issued a limited number of commissions, granting a total of 17 commissions to try 20 persons between May 1649 and December 1650.[14] The slow pace with which it granted these commissions over a period of 19 months suggests that the parliament had little enthusiasm for witch-hunting, and its instructions to the committee of war in the shires to inquire whether any torture had been used against any person suspected or declared guilty of witchcraft offers an explanation for its procedural caution.[15] Parliament also resisted persistent pressure from the general assembly to grant standing commissions to local authorities.[16] Like the privy council, parliament was aware of the procedural dangers of allowing local authorities to try witches without the supervision of men trained in the law.

With parliament dragging its feet, the task of granting local commissions to try witches fell mainly to the committee of estates, but this body also failed to meet the demands of witch-hunters in the presbyteries. The committee's decision to follow the practice of the privy council and parliament by issuing particular commissions was too slow and cumbersome to satisfy the urgent desire of local communities to rid themselves of all the witches in their midst. This difficulty in obtaining the speedy authorization of witchcraft trials explains the urgency of a request from the presbytery of Dunfermline to parliament in 1649. Noting that the gaols, especially in Inverkeithing and Dalgety, were filled with witches who had no money to sustain themselves in times of dearth, the presbytery asked parliament either to send a justice depute to try these 'servants of that prince who revels in the children of disobedience' or to grant a standing commission of local gentlemen to do the same, as the general assembly had urged in 1643.[17] The general assembly made another request for a standing commission to try witches in 1649, emphasizing 'the great charges, besides the loss of time, that people from all corners of the country have in attending here upon particular commissions'.[18] There is no record that either a justice depute was assigned to the area or that a standing commission was appointed.

Faced with pressures like these, the committee of estates delegated a subcommittee to consider the flood of petitions for commissions, noting that the meetings of the privy council were infrequent and the committee of estates was in recess. This subcommittee was to last only until the privy council or parliament should 'take some other course'.[s] On 18 May parliament did establish a committee along these general lines, but neither this new committee, the plenary committee of estates, nor parliament itself granted very many witchcraft commissions after that date.[20] The apparent reluctance of any institutional body in Edinburgh to meet the local demand for witch-trials suggests that the central Scottish authorities were concerned that witch-hunting was once again in danger of getting out of control. This concern found expression in parliament's insistence that commissioners deal only with 'confessing witches and such against whom they shall find malefices clearly proven'.[21]

The difficulty local communities had obtaining permission to try witches explains why in some cases they apparently brought them to trial by their own authority. One of the most remarkable features of witch-hunting during this decade is the number of witches who were executed by tribunals that had no official jurisdiction over the crime. We know about these prosecutions mainly from contemporary letters and local histories and the records of church courts where these witches were examined. A total of 180 witches who were not mentioned in the records of the other courts or councils appear in these sources for the period 1641–50. As might be expected, these trials, which were conducted entirely by local authorities, often resulted in executions. Of the 73 witches tried in this manner whose fates are known, only 11 escaped with their lives. Thirty of the executions took place near Mordington and are known only from references in a contemporary correspondence.[22] The church courts were responsible for at least one such execution. In 1648, when neither privy council, the committee of estates, nor the justiciary court was apparently functioning properly, the presbytery of Dunfermline took justice into its own hands and executed William Crichtoun for witchcraft. The execution took place a few days after he confessed, apparently with the support of the local magistracy.[23]

The experience of the presbytery of Irvine reveals how difficult it was to get the committee of estates to provide the permission to hold a local trial. The process began when the presbytery requested a commission to try Elizabeth Graham of Hilwinning, after the local pricker, Alexander Bogs, had located the devil's marks on her body.[24] The commission, which also authorized the trial of three other witches from the presbytery, was granted, although 'with difficulty', on 9 November. Graham was convicted and executed, although she refused to confess, and one can safely assume that the others were executed as well.[25]

The commission to try Graham and her associates was the only warrant that secular authorities within the presbytery of Irvine received during the witch-hunt. This created a serious problem, since the number of suspects increased dramatically during the next six months. In April 1650 the bailies of the burgh of Cunningham asked the presbytery to send ministers to a trial of 12 witches that was to be held later that month, so that they might secure a 'farther acknowledgement of their guilt'.[26] This request suggests that it was the secular authorities, rather than the presbytery that had taken the initiative in this phase of the witch-hunt. There are no references to these 12 witches in the records of the privy council, the court of justiciary, or the committee of estates, but a report that 12 witches had been executed at Irvine at this time almost certainly refers to this group of witches.[27] It is quite possible that the burgh proceeded against them by their own authority.

On 22 April the presbytery reported that the sin of witchcraft was growing daily and that in several parishes 'many of the hidden works of darkness' were being 'brought to light in the mercy of God'.[28] One witch, Margaret Cooper, had been apprehended by the bailies of Cunningham and had confessed to renouncing her baptism, copulating with the devil, and taking a new name from him.[29] Another 12 witches had confessed to similar apostasy. The presbytery had also received reports that several persons in Dalry, situated about three miles north of Kilwinning, had been apprehended.[30] On 30

April the presbytery examined some of these witches and decided to seek a commission to try them. There is no record of such a commission having been granted by the privy council or the committee of estates, but one week later it was reported that four witches were to be executed at Irvine on the following Saturday.

These executions did not stop the witch-hunt. Confessions by Geillis Buchanan and Janet Hill of Ardrossan gave it new life, and the presbytery once again became actively involved in it. On 7 May the presbytery decided to petition the committee of estates for a commission to try the two witches. A similar strategy was adopted three weeks later after the examination of two more confessing witches from the area. [ae] At this point the bailie depute of Cunningham rebuked the presbytery for having apprehended witches without a warrant from the burgh. This rebuke, however, did not stop the presbytery from petitioning the committee of estates once again to grant a commission to try several more witches so that 'the land may be purged of this abominable sin'.[32]

The land was not purged. The committee of estates did not grant most of the commissions that the presbytery and presumably the burgh had requested, and shortly thereafter the second largest witch-hunt in Scottish history came to an end. As large as it was, the toll it took in human life would have been much higher if the committee had responded to all the requests that it had received and if more local authorities had taken justice into their own hands.

In any event, the history of Scottish witch-hunting entered a radically different phase in 1651, when the English began a military occupation of the country that would last until 1660. The sharp reduction in the number of witchcraft trials and convictions between 1651 and 1656 can be attributed almost entirely to the judicial changes that accompanied the Cromwellian occupation of the country. The conduct of criminal trials by English commissioners for the administration of justice who had no ties with the communities where the witches lived, the operation of a system of circuit courts such as the Scots themselves had been unable to implement up to that point, and the English insistence that cases could not proceed without a private complainant or accuser conspired to keep the number of prosecutions and the number of convictions at a minimum.[33] Only six witches were tried by the justiciary court between 1652 and 1656, and only one of them, John McWilliam of Dunbarton, was executed.[34] The English insistence that convictions had to be based on evidence of maleficent magic (as opposed to the pact with the devil) also contributed to the sharp reduction in the number of successful prosecutions.[35]

Although the English were lenient in their treatment of witches, they did not eliminate all prosecutions for moral crimes. As men who could still be identified as puritans, the English commissioners were committed at least in principle to the establishment of a godly society in Scotland as well as in England. The English judges who released witches 'to go home again upon caution' at Stirling in September 1652 were not as lenient in their treatment of 'adulterers, buggerers, incestuous persons, and such as had lain with beasts'.[36] In 1656 John Nicoll reported that 'an hermaphrodite clad in woman's apparel' was executed in Edinburgh for lying with a ewe, while three months later a circuit court at Dumfries convicted and burned William McShaffie for bestiality.[37]

The most surprising judicial development with respect to witchcraft during the 1650s was the revival of witch-hunting in 1657 and its intensification in the following two years. This can be explained in large part by the policy of the Cromwellian government to establish commissions of the peace on the English model and thus allow local gentry to resume their traditional role in punishing crime.[38] This policy formed part of a broader plan to involve more Scots in the administration of the country.[39] The JPs actively encouraged witch-hunting. In February 1659 the justices of East Lothian held a month-long quarter session at Stenton to try witches. Whether JPs used torture in examining witches cannot be determined,[40] but they clearly took steps to identify the witches in their shires. In Ayrshire, for example, the JPs asked ministers to identify witches in their parishes and bring them to their attention 'for taking present course with them'.[41] In East Lothian the justices also employed the services of John Kincaid, the pricker from Tranent, to confirm their suspicions of the witches' guilt.[42] The increase in the number of witchcraft trials and executions in the late 1650s can also be attributed, at least in part, to Kincaid's activities.

The revival of Scottish witch-hunting in the late 1650s could not match the intensity of the prosecutions of 1643–4 or 1649–50, probably because all the later cases were tried before judges from the central courts, either in Edinburgh or on circuit. There was no return to the system of conciliar or parliamentary commissions, for the obvious reason that the Scottish privy council and parliament did not function during these years. The number of witches prosecuted in 1657–9 was also dwarfed by the numbers tried in the massive witch-hunt of 1661–2, when the privy council and parliament resumed the practice of granting commission to local authorities to try witches by themselves. Nevertheless, the surge in prosecutions reflects the persistent desire on the part of local communities to fulfill the wishes of the general assembly to create a godly society.

One indication of the religious inspiration to witch-hunting during these years was the demonic content of the charges brought against witches. In marked contrast to the dittays produced in the period from 1652 to 1656, which emphasized acts of maleficent magic, the trials of 1658 and 1659 almost always included the charges of making pacts with the devil, copulating with him, and meeting with him and other witches. Janet Man of Stenton, for example, confessed in 1659 that Allison Fermers, who had since been burnt as a witch, brought her to meet the devil, who was dressed in grey clothes and a hat, 'like a gentleman', in the west chamber of her house. She confessed that the devil desired to lie with her and that she had no power to resist his advances. On another occasion she named 11 other witches who accompanied her to a nearby location, where they all danced.[43]

Witch-hunting and moral discipline

The intense witchcraft prosecutions of 1643–4 and 1649–50 were facilitated by the triumph of the covenanters in the Scottish revolution. In these years clerical and lay elites were able to proceed against witches with much greater freedom than they had at any time since the 1590s. The witch-hunt of 1643–4 took place after the signing of the Solemn League and Covenant with England, while the prosecutions of 1649 came after the more extreme covenanters had passed the act of classes, excluding from office all the Engagers who had sided with Charles I in 1648.

Radical covenanters, both clerical and lay, were responsible for the intense prosecutions of the 1640s. They were also responsible for the revival of witch-hunting in 1658 and 1659, once the English allowed them to resume their traditional duties in local government. The reason for their incessant pursuit of witches was their determination to bring about the moral reform of society. The frequent reference to witchcraft as a sin rather than a crime, the citation of scripture to justify the execution of witches, and the reference to God's will that witches be punished all point to this inspiration. The clearest expression of this religious mission comes from the acts of the general assembly. In 1643 the assembly recommended that parliament grant standing commissions lest 'this work which the Lord has so miraculously begun perish in our hands'.[44] In 1649 it ordered a fast mainly because of 'the continuance and increase of sin, especially of the abominable sin of witchcraft, which abounds in the land and which appears from the many and frequent discoveries thereof in all the corners of this country'.[45] This order served as the inspiration for the witch-hunt in the presbytery of Irvine, discussed above, and also the prosecutions at Inverkeithing, where a witch-hunt involving 19 women was directed by Mr Walter Bruce, who among other things was reported to have prayed publicly and exhorted at the execution of a witch.[46]

The religious rationale for witch-hunting also was apparent in the commissions issued by the committee of estates in 1649. Take, for example, the commission granted to try the warlock Robert Maxwell, of Little Fordell, in May of that year. The warrant for the commission began by reporting that Maxwell had confessed to 'sundry points of the crime of witchcraft', as attested by the minister and several of the elders of the parish, and that the presbytery of Dunfermline had found the depositions sufficient for granting a commission. It then inserted a rationale for its own action, stating that the committee desired 'to purge the land of sin and wickedness'.[47] In similar manner John Crooks, minister at Glenluce petitioned parliament in June 1649 for a new commission to try five witches for the 'advancement of the Gospel and the punishment of vice'.[48]

When intense witch-hunting resumed in the late 1650s the religious motive for prosecuting witches once again gained prominence. In June 1658 a group of witches in the parish of Alloa in Clackmannanshire made confessions before the justices of the peace and the presbytery of Stirling. At the request of these men, Major James Holborn, commander of the military forces in the region, and Matthias Symson, the minister at Stirling, wrote to the commissioners for the administration of justice seeking their determination what could be done 'for the discovery and punishment of that devilish crime that the accursed may be destroyed from amongst us, lest wrath be upon us from before the Lord'.[49] The commissioners responded to this plea, which echoed a concern expressed by the general assembly in 1583, by authorizing the trials that led to the execution of at least six witches in 1659.[50]

Scottish witch beliefs during the revolution

The religious inspiration and rationale for witch-hunting was also evident in the content of the charges brought against witches during the revolutionary decades. As discussed in Chapter 1, witchcraft in the northern kingdom had always been viewed as a religious as well as a secular crime, an offence against divine law as well as the law of Scotland. In keeping with this view of the crime, Scottish witches, unlike their English counterparts, were burned at the stake in the manner of heretics, not hanged like murderers and other felons. The pact with the devil had been accepted as part of Scottish demonology since the 1560s, and charges that witches gathered collectively to worship the devil had worked their way into many witchcraft trials since 1590. The devil's mark had become a standard feature of Scottish witch-hunting long before the revolution.

The Scottish witchcraft prosecutions of the revolutionary period, therefore, were not responsible for introducing continental witch beliefs into Scotland, as these were already present. The trials of the 1640s and 1650s were distinctive, however, in the emphasis they placed on the sexual relations of witches with the devil, which in some cases were described in great detail. This became apparent in the trial of Janet Barker and Margaret Lauder before the justiciary court in December 1643. The incident that triggered this prosecution was Barker's curing of a young man, John Scott, of a grievous sickness. Barker confessed to having used charms to heal Scott, but the remainder of her confession dealt only with her alleged relationship with the devil. This included several sexual encounters, in which the devil was described as being 'heavy above her like an ox and not like any man'. The devil also lay with Margaret Lauder several times, the last being a few weeks before her confession, when he lay with her 'after a beastly manner'.[51]

Witchcraft trials that featured commerce with demons, sometimes without any reference to *maleficia*, were made routinely when confessing witches named a number of accomplices, and especially in those prosecutions where ministers took a leading role in identifying the accused. The confessions of the Inverkeithing witches in 1649 referred to the meetings they had with the devil, the imprint of his mark upon their bodies, and his carnal copulation with them. The witches examined by the presbytery of Irvine in 1650 confessed to their 'renunciation of their baptism, carnal copulation with the devil and the taking of a new name from him'.[52]

The pronounced emphasis on the witch's copulation with the devil was a product of the obsessive concern of the kirk with sexual offences during the revolutionary period. The overwhelming majority of the discipline cases adjudicated in the presbytery of Kircaldy between 1645 and 1649, for example, were sexual offences, especially fornication and adultery.[53] The sexual crimes of adultery, incest, homosexuality, and bestiality were all prosecuted with greater intensity than ever before during the 1640s.[54] The prosecution of witchcraft, which like these sexual offences was considered a sin as well as a crime, was also a major target of the moral reformers. Emphasizing the sexual nature of the witch's crime might very well have been a way of illustrating their connection. Even if they were not linked, witchcraft and sexual sins were the issues that had top priority within the kirk during these revolutionary years. On a Sunday in March 1650 the minister in Burntisland, after giving his sermon but before the blessing, first read publicly the act of the general assembly against the 'promiscuous dancing of men and women' and then read the names of three women in the parish suspected of witchcraft as well as the names of three women and one man who had fled, asking anyone who had dittays against these people to appear before the court.[55] Even during the period of the English occupation in the 1650s, a circuit court cited witches together with those accused of adultery, incest, sodomy and bestiality.[56]

The link between sexual crimes and witchcraft in the heightened moral climate of the revolutionary period became most apparent in the prosecution of James Wilson for incest, adultery and bestiality in December 1649. Wilson first came to the attention of judicial authorities in February of that year, two weeks after the execution of the king, when he was cited before the kirk session for adultery with Elspeth Edie, a confessing witch. Wilson confessed not only to adultery with Edie when they were both married but also fornication with her after both of their spouses had died, about 18 years previously. This confession opened up a thorough investigation of Wilson's sexual history. In August he confessed 'with many tears' before the session that he had committed adultery with Janet Walker, another confessing witch, and one week later he confessed to having committed incest with his wife's sister about 34 years before, resulting in the conception of a child that had been baptized at Leith. Wilson's reputation for having sex with witches was reinforced when Margaret Halberstoun, who was arrested on suspicion of witchcraft in the summer of the same year, confessed to having committed adultery with him. On the basis of these confessions, the session recommended to the sheriff of Linlithgow that he seek a commission to try Wilson for incest and adultery. He was convicted by the justiciary court and executed on 20 December 1649.[57] Whether the pattern of having sexual intercourse with witches reflected his own sexual preferences or the fact that female sexual offenders were often charged with witchcraft is unclear. The important consideration, however, is the way in which the two offences were linked in the minds of authorities, especially at this time.[58]

This prosecution of sexual offences and witchcraft, as well as other crimes that were also considered sins, such as blasphemy, formed part of a broader campaign to create a godly society, a goal that both clerics and laymen had pursued with varying degrees of intensity since the Reformation. During the revolution this program of moral reform became the most ostensible way to prove that Scotland was a covenanted state. The prosecution of witches assumed top billing in this national war on sin, probably because it was viewed as the most abominable of all sins. Throughout the 1640s the general assembly pursued a twofold policy of encouraging ministers to be more vigilant in the detection of witchcraft in their parishes on the one hand and of putting pressure on parliament to facilitate its prosecution on the other.[59] Under the influence of the kirk, therefore, witch-hunting became part of a crusade for moral reform, and in particular for the regulation of sex outside the prescribed boundaries of matrimony.

The covenanters' program for moral reform also involved the elimination of magical practices. This had been the major concern of the ministers who had drafted the witchcraft act of 1563, and the acquisition of political power in the 1640s gave them the opportunity to enact that agenda. Part of this program to eliminate magical practices involved the prosecution of white magicians or charmers for witchcraft. Prior to 1640 most charmers had been prosecuted by the church courts, which meted out mild punishments to those whom they had disciplined. In some cases, however, accusations of charming had led to prosecution for witchcraft. The initial charges against Agnes Sampson in 1590, for example, focused almost entirely on her practice as a healer. Accusations of charming also occupied the main portion of Sampson's dittay when she was tried for witchcraft in the following year.[60]

During the 1640s the secular courts began prosecuting significant numbers of charmers for witchcraft. In November 1643, for example, the justiciary court tried and executed John Burgh of Fossoway for witchcraft on the basis of charges that he had 'practised, used and exercised devilish charms of witchcraft and sorcery upon diverse persons, as well men as women'.[61] Many of the witches rounded up in the early stages of the large witch-hunt of 1643–4, including Janet Barker of Edinburgh, were first suspected of witchcraft for having used charms.[62] Charming was defined as witchcraft on the basis of an interpretation of scripture, not Scots law. The indictment of John Burgh, for example, claimed that the practices of 'witchcraft, sorcery, charming, and soothsaying' were ordained by scripture to be punished by death.[63] In 1646 the general assembly proposed that the witchcraft act of 1563 'be enlarged and extended to charmers', but the parliament did not follow through with the appropriate legislation.[64] After 1660, therefore, most charmers were once again prosecuted in the church courts. Even so, the church continued to view their magical practices as witchcraft. As late as 1728 the synod of Merse and Teviotdale condemned a particular type of charming known as scoring the brow, a magical practice used to protect those who had been harmed by others, as 'a sort and degree of witchcraft, not to be tolerated in a reformed land'.[65]

The immediate effect of the emphasis on diabolism in the witchcraft prosecutions of the 1640s was the rapid expansion of the number of suspects. The main reason for the large number of witches in 1643–4 and 1649–50 is that the witches prosecuted during those years named a number of accomplices who allegedly had been with them at the sabbath. Throughout Europe large witch-hunts developed only when the crime was defined in diabolical terms and witches named their alleged confederates. This was no less true in England than in Scotland during the 1640s.

Witch-hunting in revolutionary England

The revolutionary decade of the 1640s witnessed an intense upsurge in witch-hunting in England as well as Scotland. The total number of people investigated and tried did not match the corresponding figures for Scotland, but the numbers were high enough to reverse the gradual decline that had set in after the prosecution of Brian and Anne Gunter in the Star Chamber in 1606–7. Although we have reliable statistics only for the English home circuit, they suggest that there were more prosecutions and executions in the 1640s than in any other decade of English history, even in the 1590s, when witch-trials appeared to have reached their peak.[66] Most of the English prosecutions took place between 1645 and 1647 when the self-styled witch-finders Matthew Hopkins and John Stearne directed a large witch-hunt in the southeastern counties of the country. All in all, the towns that Hopkins and Stearne visited prosecuted about 240 witches, at least half of whom were executed. This was a major witch-hunt not only by English standards but by continental European standards as well.[67]

The collapse of the East Anglian witch-hunt in 1647 did not spell the end of witchcraft prosecutions in England. In 1649, the year of the king's execution and the abolition of the monarchy, a cluster of trials took place in the northern towns of Newcastle upon Tyne and Berwick upon Tweed as well as in the surrounding villages of Northumberland, resulting in about 20 executions in all.[68] This hunt was much smaller than that of Hopkins and Stearne, but it had some similarities with that campaign. There was also a close Scottish connection. These trials, which were held near the Scottish border, coincided with the massive Scottish witch-hunt that took place during the same two-year period. Some of the procedures followed were the same as those used by Scottish witch-hunters, and a Scottish pricker was called in to help town authorities identify the alleged confederates of the devil. The witch-hunt in Newcastle, moreover, was inspired by the same type of campaign for comprehensive moral reform that set in motion the large Scottish witch-hunts of 1643–4 and 1649–50.

The third and final hunt in revolutionary England took place at Maidstone, Kent, in 1652. This was a much more limited operation than the previous two campaigns. Sixteen people were tried at the assizes, and all but two of them were convicted. The judge, Peter Warburton, reprieved or reduced the sentences of eight witches, leaving only six to be hanged.[69] The charges of diabolism brought against the accused, including copulation with the devil and the unusual confession that the devil had impregnated one of the witches, suggests comparisons with, and perhaps even the influence of, the trials in East Anglia and Northumberland.[70] Like the other two witch-hunts, the Maidstone prosecutions also raised concerns regarding the legal grounds upon which the witches had been executed.[71] This growing concern with the excesses of witch-hunting explains why England did not, like Scotland, continue to prosecute witches in significant numbers after these hunts had ended.[72] After 1652 witch-hunting in England resumed the decline that had begun in the early seventeenth century. By 1685 the last English witch had been led to the scaffold.

Intense witch-hunting in England during the 1640s can be attributed to many of the same considerations that explain the greater intensity of Scottish witch-hunting: the conduct of witch-trials without supervision by judges from the central courts; the ability of local magistrates to use torture or other forms of physical mistreatment to secure confessions; the determination of zealous Protestant clergy and magistrates to discover and prosecute witches as part of a program of moral reform; and the definition of witchcraft as a religious crime involving commerce with demons.

Prior to the outbreak of the civil war, witch-hunting in England was not characterized by any of these features; by 1645 witchcraft prosecutions bore all these characteristics. It was almost as if Scottish witch-hunting, including the Scottish pricker hired by Newcastle, came to England for a brief period of time and then retreated. It is no coincidence that this transformation of English witch-hunting into something that resembled the prosecutions north of the border began at the time when English puritans and Scottish covenanters were engaged in a common military enterprise that had a religious goal of bringing the churches of both countries into conformity. Nor is it a coincidence that the clergy in both countries intensified their demands for witchcraft prosecutions as part of a more general program of moral reform.

The military operations of the civil war had no direct bearing on witch-hunting. Witch-hunting and military fighting rarely mixed well in early modern Europe.[73] The fear that armies might move into one's county or neighbourhood, which was present in Suffolk in 1645, did, however, lead elites and villagers alike to identify sources of internal and moral subversion within the community. War also created economic insecurity, dearth, inflation, and disruptions of family life that contributed to the personal tensions that found expression in witch-hunting. Most important, the civil war and the revolutionary changes that it triggered created disruptions in the judicial machinery that allowed witch-hunters to win convictions, often by employing illegal or at least unprecedented judicial techniques.

The judicial machinery

The English civil war caused widespread disruption in the operation of the judicial machinery, especially the functioning of the semi-annual county assizes. Many of the witchcraft prosecutions of the revolutionary period resulted in convictions and executions because the men who conducted the investigations were not subject to the close supervision of assize justices travelling on circuit. This absence of central judicial control was evident in the witch-trials at Chelmsford, Essex, in the summer of 1645. These were the first trials in which Hopkins and Stearne, as well as Sir Harbottle Grimstone, had a hand. One of the reasons that these men succeeded in securing 19 convictions is that the earl of Warwick, a nobleman from the region who was serving as a commander of the Parliamentarian forces, stood in for the assize judge when the war had made his presence impossible. The effect of this substitution on the toll taken by witch-hunting in the summer of 1645 cannot be exaggerated. With no professional knowledge of the law, Warwick could not prevent unqualified witnesses from testifying, deny the validity of confessions that were coerced or adduced under torture, or use his influence to direct a verdict in summing up the evidence. In particular, Warwick was unable or unwilling to exclude the evidence that the Chelmsford witches had confessed after being kept awake for 72 hours on the pretext that the authorities were waiting for the witches' hungry imps to appear and receive nourishment from their mistresses.

Most of the prosecutions during the East Anglia witch-hunt were tried before the assizes in whatever makeshift manner they may have been assembled. In a few cases, however, the quarter sessions, which were the regular meetings conducted by justices of the peace in various county towns, held the trials themselves. Quarter sessions often took cognizance of minor crimes classified as misdemeanours, and they frequently conducted the initial examinations of witches, but they were expected to reserve those cases for the assizes, which took cognizance of felonies like murder, grand larceny, and witchcraft. In the tumultuous and disruptive years of the civil war, they did not observe these traditions but proceeded to trial and execution by their own authority. Like the men whom the Scottish privy council appointed to serve as commissioners of justiciary, the justices of the peace who staffed the meetings of the quarter sessions in England for the most part did not have legal training.[74] The procedural irregularities and the high rate of conviction in the witchcraft trials conducted by the quarter sessions in 1645 and 1646 can be attributed in large part to the determination of the justices of the peace who conducted these trials to secure the conviction of the witches infesting their communities.

A number of municipal courts also managed to try and execute witches by their own authority, without the supervision of assize judges travelling on circuit. In Aldeburgh, Suffolk, the trial and execution of seven witches in 1646 was conducted entirely by burgh authorities, since Aldeburgh had its own power of gaol delivery, which exempted it from the jurisdiction of the assize judges.[75] At Faversham, Kent, the mayor Robert Greenstreet and the other godly magistrates of this strongly puritan town were able to examine, try, and execute three witches in 1645 by their own authority because the town, as one of the Cinque Ports, also had its own courts, which exercised jurisdiction over all crimes, including felonies like witchcraft.[76] In similar fashion, the town of Newcastle was able to proceed against witches by its own authority, since it too had its own power of gaol delivery. This meant that the godly magistrates who took office shortly after the execution of the king could try the witches by their own authority rather than referring the matters to the assizes in the county of Northumberland.[77] Witches tried by local municipal authorities, without the presence of a judge from the central common law courts at Westminster, stood little chance of being acquitted, just like the Scottish witches tried by the magistrates of Scottish burghs. The absence of judges explains why a number of procedural irregularities took place during the trials, included the swimming of the suspected witches in Suffolk.

The most unusual judicial experiment during the revolutionary period was parliament's appointment of a special court of oyer et terminer to try a cluster of witches held prisoner in Bury St Edmunds, Suffolk, in 1645. Commissions of this sort, which replaced the standard commissions of assize, were usually named to deal with an emergency situation. In this case it was the concern with the high number of imprisoned suspects, which had sparked a fear that 'some busy men had made use of some ill arts to extort such confession from them'.[78] The commission therefore reflected a spirit of judicial caution. It was, however, an exception to normal judicial practice, having been issued by parliament at a time when the office of the lord chancellor, the official who usually issued such commissions, had been vacant since 1642.[79] It was also unusual in that this puritan parliament appointed two clerics, Samuel Fairclough and Edward Calamy, to sit with the lawyers and local gentry on the bench.

The special commission of oyer et terminer for Suffolk bore a number of similarities to the witchcraft commissions granted by the Scottish committee of estates in 1649 as well as to the special court of oyer et terminer to try the witches who would crowd the gaols in Salem, Massachusetts, in 1692. Like these other examples of specially delegated judicial power, the Suffolk special commission found 17 witches guilty and ordered their execution, but the appointment of a qualified judge to head the commission, Serjeant John Godbold, and the commitment of Fairclough to obtaining sufficient evidence of the diabolical pact kept the number of executions fairly low.[80] Fairclough's role was crucial to this moderate outcome. In two assize sermons he insisted that, although a confession was essential for conviction on the basis of the demonic pact, confessions must be 'purely voluntary and unconstrained and the truth evidenced by collateral circumstances and other concurring and convincing evidence'. In making these warnings Fairclough anticipated the position that Increase Mather would take in 1692 when he warned the members of the Salem commission that they must exercise 'exquisite caution' in dealing with witchcraft cases.[81] If the clerics involved in Scottish witchcraft cases had urged similar caution, the death toll in the northern kingdom might have been substantially reduced.

Torture, swimming, and pricking

The absence of central judicial supervision in the trials of 1645–6 explains why evidence obtained by torture was admitted as evidence in English witchcraft trials. Whether the techniques used to extract these confessions qualified as torture has long been a matter of controversy. The reason for the controversy is that neither Hopkins nor the investigating officers ever employed the more brutal methods of interrogation used in witchcraft trials on the continent or in the interrogation of suspected traitors in England. Hopkins never used or attempted to use the *strappado*, the rack, the boot, or even the thumbscrews used in Scotland. The main method was keeping witches awake for as many as 72 hours, sometimes walking them, as he did the 80-year-old cleric, John Lowes. Hopkins's justification for this tactic was that he and his assistants were waiting for the witches' hungry familiars to appear and seek nourishment.[82] This rationale, however, cannot disguise the fact that the torture of forced sleeplessness, the dreaded *tormentum insomniae*, was one of the most effective means of extracting a confession and was recognized as torture by European jurists.[83] This technique of watching the witch was almost certainly borrowed from Scotland where, as we have seen in Chapter 2, it was used frequently during the seventeenth century. New England witch-hunters who watched the witches during the Salem episode in turn borrowed the technique from Hopkins, revealing once again that witch-hunting in Britain was a transatlantic phenomenon.[84]

The use of torture in the witch-hunt of 1645–7 stood in violation of English law. So too did the extra-judicial procedure known as the water ordeal, which Hopkins and local magistrates utilized on numerous occasions, including the investigation of John Lowes, who was swum in the ditch surrounding Framlingham Castle in 1645. As we have seen, this procedure was a popular version of the ordeal by water used in the Middle Ages. James VI had recommended its use in pre-trial proceedings, but it had no standing in either English or Scots law. It was also subject to the theological objection that the evidence it offered must come from the devil, since God could not be expected to produce such a 'marvel' on demand.[85] Hopkins's encouragement of it as a means to confirm a witch's guilt eventually prompted a rebuke from Serjeant Godbold, who ordered that no more witches in Suffolk were to be subject to the procedure.[86]

Witch-finders in the prosecutions at Newcastle in 1649 and Maidstone in 1652 introduced another investigatory technique that also derived from Scotland but had no precedent in English law. This was the practice of pricking the witch to find the devil's mark. As discussed in Chapter 3, James VI had endorsed this procedure in his witchcraft treatise, and it had become common in Scotland during the seventeenth century. Pricking, however, had been unknown in England, both because English magistrates and judges did not accept the demonological theory that underlay it and because it put the accused at a judicial disadvantage. As we have seen, pricking in Scotland often had the same effect as torture. Even if it did not elicit a confession, it provided evidence of the witch's guilt and thus prejudiced the case against her.

Without a cadre of experienced prickers to call upon, the Newcastle magistrates had to seek assistance from across the border, where pricking had begun to emerge as a semi-profession.[87] Shortly after receiving a petition from individuals demanding the discovery and prosecution of witches, the corporation sent two sergeants to Scotland to hire an unnamed pricker to help them identify the devil's confederates in their midst.[88] The corporation agreed to pay him 20s a piece for his services. After townspeople had made known the names of 30 suspects, the pricker stripped them and thrust long pins into their bodies. His probings confirmed that 27 of the suspects had made pacts with the devil, and this evidence was used to convict 14 women and one man of witchcraft. These witches were executed, together with another witch from the county of Northumberland, in August 1650.[89] The pricker did not confine himself to Newcastle. The members of a guild in the border town of Berwick upon Tweed had sent for the same man on 30 July 1649,[90] and after providing his services there and at Newcastle he went into the villages and towns of Northumberland, where he received upwards of £3 for each witch he discovered. Only after Peter Ogle, a justice of the peace, seized him and forced him to post bond for an appearance at the quarter sessions did the pricker flee back to Scotland, where it was reported that he was apprehended, convicted, and executed, bragging in his gallows speech that he had been responsible for the death of more than 200 women in England and Scotland.[91] The man who thrust pins deep into the arms of three witches at Maidstone three years later apparently was recruited locally.[92] In any case, the practice had no warrant in English law. Like the antics of the Newcastle magistrate who drove the accused witch Anne Bidelstone through the streets holding a rope that was attached to the witches' bridle (an iron muzzle that fit over the witch's head), pricking was not authorized by Newcastle's municipal charter and was 'repugnant to the known laws of England'.[93]

Puritanism and witch-hunting

The driving force of the witch-hunts in East Anglia and Newcastle was puritanism, the movement to bring the Church of England into greater conformity with the 'best reformed', that is, Calvinist churches on the European continent and in Scotland. There was nothing in Calvinist theology that led directly to witch-hunting, but theology was not the defining feature of English puritanism, especially in the early seventeenth century, when all religious factions shared the essentials of Calvinism. Rather it was the religious zeal that characterized their determination to turn England into a godly community by imposing a strict moral discipline on the community. Puritan zeal gave them the reputation of being 'the hotter sort of Protestants', and this commitment to the cause of reform provides the key to their interest in witch-hunting.

Witch-hunting in England may not have required the stimulus of religious zeal, as Keith Thomas has argued, but it is difficult to deny that it played a major role in the prosecutions of the 1640s.[94] The determination with which Hopkins, Stearne, and others went about their self-appointed mission of discovering witches and bringing them to the gallows cannot easily be explained without reference to their commitment to the creation of a godly society. All the principal parties in the East Anglian witch-hunt counted themselves among the elect. Hopkins, the son of a godly minister, spoke frequently of his religious mission, while his reference to the devil's marrying witches according to the service prescribed in the Book of Common Prayer displayed the typical puritan distaste for the ceremonies of the established church.[95] Stearne was almost a caricature of the godly layman, while Sir Harbottle Grimstone, the JP who managed the initial prosecutions in Essex, once referred to William Laud, the archbishop of Canterbury, as 'the sty of all the pestilential filth that hath infested the state and government of this commonwealth'.[96]

Puritan clergy played a central role in turning the witch-hunt of 1645–7 into a war against Satan, similar to the one that had been raging in Scotland for more than half a century. As a result of the religious changes that took place when the civil war broke out in 1642, many puritan ministers had received appointments to benefices in the very region where Matthew Hopkins's witch-hunt took place. Essex, where Hopkins lived and where the hunt began, was the most solidly puritan county in the country. The new puritan clergy had replaced the 'scandalous ministers' that parliament had ejected in the early years of the war.[97] English ministers could not participate in witchcraft trials, but they could influence how the population viewed the crime, mainly from the pulpit. The clergy also preached the sermons at the semi-annual meetings of the county assizes. In these sermons, such as those delivered by Samuel Fairclough during the witch-hunt in Suffolk, they always emphasized the spiritual nature of the crime; *maleficia* played little or no part in their evangelical concern.

One of the themes of puritan preaching during the entire revolutionary period was millenarianism, the belief that the last judgment was imminent and that Christ would come again to rule for a thousand years. Inspired mainly by Revelation, the last book of the New Testament, millenarians believed that the Antichrist had appeared and that the devil was very active in the world. Much of the strength of the parliamentary cause can be attributed to this conviction. It helped to justify the attack upon the old regime in 1641, and it gave purpose to the military campaigns of the parliamentarian army. It also helped to justify witch-hunting.[98] The millenarian, convinced that the reign of King Jesus was about to begin, felt compelled to prepare the way of the Lord by cleansing the world of its diabolical contaminants. In this way millenarianism channelled godly zeal into the hunting of witches. One of the pamphlets written against witchcraft in 1645 referred to 'these times wherein the devil reigns and prevails' and then urged men to prosecute witches as a means of remedying the situation.[99] In his commentary on the witch-hunt in East Anglia John Stearne quotes Revelation frequently and looks forward to Christ's conquest, when there will not be any more witches.[100] Two years later, the London puritan minister Nathaniel Homes spoke of the activities of the devil on earth as 'a presage of the last days'.[101] Alan Macfarlane has observed that in many of the Essex villages where witches were prosecuted in 1645 popular millenarian sentiment was especially strong.[102] This sentiment inspired witch-hunting in these puritan communities and it confirmed the widespread belief that witchcraft was a religious crime.

The puritan desire to establish and enforce a godly discipline by prosecuting witches was evident in the witch-hunt at Newcastle in 1649–50. This hunt, which was conducted by the newly installed leadership of the corporation, formed part of a broader program of enforcing a strict code of morality in the town; the puritan magistrates also convicted numerous townspeople for drunkenness, blasphemy, and idle living.[103] The Newcastle campaign against immorality, however, was unique in its primary focus on witchcraft. In this respect it resembled campaigns for moral reform in neighbouring Scotland. There is little doubt that the Newcastle magistrates, like all godly laymen in the mold of John Stearne in Essex, considered witchcraft a sin and the pact with the devil as its essence. Otherwise the Newcastle magistrates would not have employed a pricker to find the devil's marks on the accused.

The religious definition of the crime

A further indication of the influence of puritanism on English witch-hunting during the revolutionary period was the emphasis placed on the spiritual nature of the crime. For Protestant demonologists the essence of the crime of witchcraft had always been the pact with the devil, not the performance of harmful magic. For that reason Protestant theologians like William Perkins made no distinction between white and black witchcraft; in some ways the so-called good witch was more dangerous than the perpetrator of maleficent magic.[104] In this respect Protestant demonologists were following the reasoning of St Augustine in the fifth century when he argued that all magic, white or black, was the work of the devil. The English divines at the Westminster Assembly, which was convened in 1643 under Scottish pressure and attended by Scottish observers, explicitly defined the crime in these terms in 1645. In their semi-official commentary on the scriptures, these ministers interpreted Exodus 22:18 to support the claim that even if no injury (i.e. *maleficium*) was perpetrated, 'the witch deserves present and certain death for the contract itself'.[105] John Stearne subscribed to this definition of the crime in the preface to his treatise on the East Anglian witch-hunt. By their diabolical practices, wrote Stearne, witches are guilty of 'the greatest apostasy from the faith, for they renounce God and Christ and give themselves by a covenant to the devil, the utter enemy to God and all mankind'.[106] This religious definition of witchcraft also found expression in the witchcraft statute passed by the legislature of the puritan colony of Massachusetts in 1648. This act decreed that 'If any man or woman be a witch, that is, hath or consulteth with a familiar spirit, they shall be put to death. Exod. 22. 18. Levit. 20. 27. Deut. 18. 10. 11.'[107]

One indication of the climate of puritan opinion regarding the crime of witchcraft was the apparent effort by some 'overly rigid Presbyterians and Independents' to make witchcraft and sorcery a crime punishable in the church courts. This proposal evoked a firm response from the puritan lawyer William Prynne, who cited the Bible to support his claim that not only witchcraft but also sodomy and buggery, like murder, were all by God's precepts civil crimes, punishable by the civil magistrate.[108]

This Protestant initiative did not succeed, and witchcraft remained a civil crime, but the number of cases involving charges of diabolism in one form or another increased dramatically in the 1640s. In 1645 we find the first English confession of a face-to-face pact with the devil, the first English report of the devil appearing as a man, the first English accounts of sexual intercourse with the devil, and the first English confessions to attendance at regularly scheduled, weekly witchcraft assemblies. The possession of demonic imps or familiars, the staple of English diabolism, figured in three-quarters of the narratives written during these years.[109] The imps in these accounts, moreover, became more bizarre, described variously as a mouse, a polecat, a black horse, a long-legged greyhound with a head like an ox, a fat spaniel without any legs, and a black rabbit.[110]

Jim Sharpe has shown how difficult it is to identify all these beliefs in diabolical witchcraft in the 1640s as having been 'continental' in origin, imposed by Hopkins and others familiar with European witchcraft treatises.[111] The prominence of demonic imps or familiars in the confessions by itself suggests that at least some of these ideas were homegrown and of popular origin. Evidence of an interaction between continental and English as well as learned and popular ideas can be seen in the confessions of the devil appearing in the form of an imp (rather than as a man or a goat) and of a familiar providing sexual gratification to the witch, as when Ann Usher described the sensation of having 'two things like butterflies' in her secret parts.[112]

Whether there was an element of Scottish demonology in this mix of continental and native English witch beliefs is difficult to determine. The frequent reference to English witches' having made a 'covenant' or 'solemn league' with the devil in the 1640s suggests this possibility. Diane Purkiss has speculated that Scottish witch beliefs may have entered Essex through the port of Manningtree,[113] while the Westminster Assembly of Divines, which was convened in 1643 with the intention of establishing a presbyterian form of church government in the southern kingdom, could easily have served as another conduit.[114]

It is not necessary, however, to establish direct Scottish influence on English witch beliefs to appreciate their close kinship during these years. Many of the ideas that found expression in the confessions of witches during the revolutionary period owe their similarity to the common efforts of English puritans and Scottish covenanters to wage war against Satan and his malignant confederates. The similarities are most apparent in the frequency of charges of sexual intercourse with the devil. Like the Scottish confessions elicited during the 1640s, the confessions of the English witches examined by Hopkins and Stearne were filled with references to illicit sexual relations between the witch and the devil. This was evident in the very first confession of Elizabeth Clarke at Manningtree in 1645, who reported that she had had carnal copulation with the devil three or four times in a week and that he would 'lie with her half a night together in the shape of a proper gentleman'.[115] To some extent this confession was the product of this widow's erotic imagination, but like all such confessions it was coaxed or extracted by puritan zealots who were determined to establish a godly society. The general assembly of the Church of Scotland would have been proud of their efforts.

The end of intense witch-hunting in England

In England the reaction to the tactics of Hopkins and Stearne arose during the trials, and it found its most eloquent expression in John Gaule's treatise, *Cases of Conscience Touching Witches and Witchcrafts* (1646). Gaule, the vicar of Great Staughton, Huntingtonshire, was no friend of witches. Like most demonologists, he professed a firm belief in their reality, claiming that to deny their existence was to send the sceptic down the slippery slope to atheism. But Gaule objected strenuously to self-styled witch-finders on the grounds that they often used 'unlawful and indirect means of discovery' and allowed the conviction of 'ten that are innocent before he discovers one that is guilty'.[116] In a direct rebuke to Hopkins he deplored the practice of tying up a witch with cords and keeping her 'without meat or sleep for the space of 24 hours'.[117] While admitting the sufficiency of a witch's confession for conviction, he warned that 'it would be well considered whether she was forced to it, terrified, allured or otherwise deluded'.[118] Knowing that juries in England could convict on the basis of circumstantial evidence, Gaule recommended that juries in witchcraft cases be empanelled not of 'ordinary country people, but of the most eminent physicians, lawyers and divines that a country could afford'.[119] In a further rebuke to Hopkins, Gaule said that those juries should not convict simply on the basis of the pact with the devil; evidence of 'some kind of fact' was also necessary.[120]

Gaule's concern with the legal procedures employed by Hopkins and Stearme was reinforced by the objections presented by unknown persons, probably justices of the peace, to the judges of the Norfolk assizes held at Norwich in 1647. One of the queries was whether accused witches would not swear that they suckled evil spirits 'till they have used unlawful courses of torture to make them say anything for ease and quiet, as who would not do?'[121] Hopkins responded to these queries in a brief defensive pamphlet, *The Discovery of Witches* (1647), but the work did not swing public opinion in his favour. English pride in the safeguards afforded by the common law had taken precedence over the desire to reform English morals. By the time of his death in 1647 he had been completely discredited.

The reaction against Hopkins and Stearme was based more on their violation of due process than disbelief in the content of the witches' confessions. It was in other words a reaction based on judicial rather than philosophical or religious scepticism. This criticism of the East Anglian witch-hunt did not bring witch-hunting in revolutionary England to a complete halt. As we have seen, a relatively severe witch-hunt took place in Newcastle only two years after Hopkins's death. In 1652 there were a couple of trials in London,[122] and in the same year a much larger witch-hunt in Kent resulted in 14 convictions.

Criticism of the Maidstone trials dealt a final blow to large-scale witch-hunting in England. The initial criticism came, as we have seen, from the assize judge, Sir Peter Warburton, who reprieved or commuted the sentences of eight of the witches and tried desperately to stop the execution of three of the remaining six. A more systematic critique of the legality of the witch-hunt came the following year from the pen of Sir Robert Filmer, the royalist political theorist whose work will be discussed more fully in Chapter 6.[123] Filmer recommended the establishment of clearly defined criteria, similar to those used in jurisdictions following inquisitorial procedure, for the conviction of a witch in an English jury trial. As we have seen, those standards could not be enforced when the decisions of juries were inscrutable and their verdicts irrevocable. Nevertheless, Filmer's pamphlet exposed the weakness of the verdicts that juries had already returned and offered advice to future juries on how to deal with this crime.

The confessions adduced during the 1640s also raised doubts about the some of the witch beliefs that flourished in the 1640s, especially those that dealt with the pact with the devil. These beliefs were not banished from the mental universe of literate Englishmen; they surfaced again after 1660, when witchcraft theory experienced a robust and somewhat surprising revival.[124] But charges of diabolism appeared only occasionally in English trials in the late seventeenth century. In marked contrast to the situation in Scotland, where hundreds of Scottish witches were charged with making pacts with the devil and attending meetings with him during those years, large-scale witch-hunting based on charges of devil worship had come to an end in England.

Conclusion

Regardless of what happened in the 1660s, the fact remains that during the revolutionary period magistrates and judges in Scotland and England subjected more individuals to witchcraft prosecutions than at any comparable period of time in British history. The series of accusations, trials, convictions, and executions serves as a grim reminder of what happens when the normal machinery of justice is rendered inoperative, when powerful men become paranoid of rebellion in all its forms, when millenarian and reforming zeal blends with paranoia, and when religious reformers, in an effort to reform popular culture, combine prosecution with theological instruction. All this took place during, and in large part because of, the Scottish and English revolutions.

5   The great Scottish witch-hunt of 1661–2

During 1661 and 1662 Scotland experienced the largest witch-hunt in its history. Within the space of 16 months no fewer than 660 persons were publicly accused of various acts of sorcery and diabolism.[1] The hunt began to the east of Edinburgh in the villages and small burghs of Midlothian and East Lothian, where 206 individuals were named as witches between April and December 1661. The hunt did not remain restricted to that area, however, as the privy council busily issued commissions to local authorities throughout the country to try suspected witches. We do not know how many people were executed during the hunt, but the report of John Ray, the English naturalist, that 120 were burned during his visit to Scotland suggests that the total number was substantial.[2] It is true that some of the witches tried in the justiciary court were acquitted, and a number of those who were named as accomplices never actually came to trial. This should in no way detract from the size and importance of the hunt. At no other comparable period of time in Scottish history were so many people accused of witchcraft within such a brief period of time. Indeed, the hunt, which involved four times the number of persons accused of witchcraft at Salem, Massachusetts, in 1692, was comparable to the large witch-hunts that occurred on the European continent during the sixteenth and seventeenth centuries.[3]

The prosecutions of 1661–2 constituted a distinct operation, separate from the prosecutions of 1658 and 1659.[4] As we have seen, intense witch-hunting resumed in Scotland in 1658 after the English commissioners for the administration of justice had discouraged prosecutions for six years. The number of witchcraft trials grew steadily until May 1659, when the government of England and Scotland collapsed. The trials did not resume until April 1661, nearly a year after the restoration of Charles II. This two-year hiatus in witch-hunting requires that we consider the prosecutions of 1661–2 as a separate, self-contained witch-hunt with its own dynamic, even if some of the witches prosecuted in 1661 and 1662 had been brought to the attention of authorities during the 1650s.

There are two further reasons for considering this witch-hunt as a distinct operation rather than an extension of the prosecutions of 1658 and 1659. The first is the sheer size of this witch-hunt, which dwarfed the prosecutions of the late 1650s. The second is the exceptionally large number of individuals who were named by witches who had already confessed. In the prosecutions of 1658 and 1659 relatively few of the witches named their alleged confederates. In 1661 and 1662, however, witches routinely confessed that they had met the devil and other witches in various locations. This process of naming the witches' confederates accounts for a majority of the names of the witches that appear in the judicial records.

The great Scottish witch-hunt of 1661–2 has attracted a fair amount of historical attention, but historians do not agree on the reasons why it took place at this particular time. Most of them have linked it one way or another to the political and administrative changes that took place at the time of the restoration. 'Whatever satisfaction the return of King Charles the Second might afford to the younger females in his dominions,' wrote one nineteenth-century commentator, 'it certainly brought nothing, save torture and destruction, to the unfortunate old women, or witches of Scotland.'[5] In particular, historians have attributed this hunt to the end of English rule in Scotland. During the protectorate, Scotland had been joined to England in an incorporating union, and Englishmen had assumed jurisdiction over criminal prosecutions as commissioners for the administration of justice. These English judges had been reluctant to prosecute and especially to execute suspected witches, and consequently the number of witches believed to be at liberty had steadily increased. As soon as Scots, who customarily exercised much less restraint in the prosecution of this crime, regained exclusive control of their judicial system, they set out to rid the country of the large 'backlog' of witches that had accumulated.[6]

This venerable political interpretation does not offer a complete explanation of this massive witch-hunt, but it does provide us with a good starting point, for the English judges who adjudicated criminal causes were more lenient than their Scottish predecessors and successors in the treatment of accused witches. Such a policy was to be expected from a group of justices trained in English law, which did not allow the use of torture in the interrogation of witches, the means by which many witchcraft confessions were obtained both on the European continent and in Scotland. For this reason, and also because the belief that witches made explicit pacts with the devil and worshipped him in large nocturnal gatherings did not gain wide acceptance in England except during the revolutionary period, there were relatively few executions for witchcraft in that country. Even more unusual in England was a rapid increase in the number of suspects as confessing witches implicated their alleged cohorts, often under the pressure of judicial torture. No wonder, therefore, that the English judges in Scotland, whom Cromwell intended to use as agents in a reform of Scots law, should have imposed English standards in the prosecution of this crime.

There is in fact a good deal of evidence to support the contention that the English judges did actually inaugurate a reformed 'English' policy towards suspected witches. As we have seen, a Scottish official reported in 1671 that during the English occupation the judges 'would put no person to death without proven malefice against them and when nobody was insisting'.[7] When the commissioners heard charges against 60 persons accused of witchcraft in 1662, they found 'so much malice and so little proof against them' that the justices refused to condemn any of them.[8] At about the same time a circuit court at Stirling cited a number of witches but gave them liberty to return home upon caution.[9] And when the commissioners received the confession of John Bayne, a warlock from Kincardineshire in 1654, they ordered a commission to be sent to the governor of Inverness for a re-examination.[10] Overall, between 1653 and 1657, the commissioners succeeded in keeping the number of prosecutions and executions to a minimum, the latter totalling only 12 known cases.[11] As we have seen, in 1658 and 1659 there was a notable increase in judicial activity against witches, resulting in 38 executions in the latter year alone,[12] but even then the judges came under sharp criticism for being too lenient. 'There is much witchery up and down our land,' complained Robert Baillie in 1659, 'though the English be but too sparing to try it, yet some they execute.'[13] Even at Tranent, where the commissioners sentenced 11 witches to death in 1659, the elders of the kirk recalled one year later that some who had been accused and imprisoned had subsequently been released, while others who had been accused had not even been imprisoned.[14]

The leniency of the English judges, their refusal to allow the application of judicial torture, and their scepticism regarding the veracity of confessions obtained by local authorities all contribute to an explanation of why witch-hunting assumed such moderate proportions during the Cromwellian period. Of equal or greater importance was the disbandment of the Scottish privy council and parliament in 1650. As we have seen, both of these bodies had issued large numbers of commissions of justiciary to try witches in the 1640s. These structural changes in the administration of justice meant that witchcraft trials now had to take place in the circuit courts or the central court of justiciary, rather than in ad hoc tribunals consisting of local bailies and lairds. The end result was a dramatic reduction in the chances that a suspected witch would even be brought to trial, let alone be convicted.

These chances of successful prosecution became even smaller during the two-year period that preceded the hunt, for on 6 May 1659, the date marking the end of the protectorate, the judicial machinery of Scotland ground to almost a complete halt.[15] This created a serious legal crisis that only compounded the economic crisis that had been developing for a number of years. 'Scotland's condition for the time is not good,' wrote Baillie, 'exhaust[ed] in money; dead in trade; the taxes near doubled; since the sixth of May without all law, nor appearance of any in haste.'[16] Other Scots also complained bitterly about the interruption of justice, cataloguing the adverse effects of the situation.[17] For those who expressed concern about the prevalence of witchcraft, the cessation of criminal justice was particularly regrettable. 'Because the laws are now silent,' complained the earl of Haddington after nearly two years of judicial paralysis, 'this sin [witchcraft] becomes daily more frequent'.[18]

The question remains, however, whether the leniency of the English commissioners, the absence of the Scottish privy council and parliament during the period of the commonwealth and union, the English regulation of local jurisdictions, and the interruption of legal proceedings in 1659–61 actually led to an accumulation of suspected witches, thus creating a demand for legal action that only a hunt as great as that of 1661–2 could satisfy. This is a reasonable hypothesis, but a difficult one to substantiate, since there is only fragmentary evidence concerning witches who had managed to avoid formal accusation, trial, or conviction during the Cromwellian period, only to be caught in the wide net of the panic of 1661–2. We do know, for example, that Margaret Cant of Aberdour, who had been arrested for witchcraft in 1654 but subsequently released, was apprehended again by the restored Scottish authorities in 1661.[19] In similar fashion, Christian Wilson of Dalkeith, who had been released from prison on bond when the English entered Scotland in 1650, was eventually burned for witchcraft in 1661.[20] Another four witches from Newbattle who had been named by a confessing witch in 1656 were not imprisoned until 1661,[21] while Janet Millar, delated by six confessing witches in 1650 and eventually arrested and induced to confess in 1659, was not actually prosecuted until 1661.[22] More surprisingly, at least 18 of the witches tried and executed in 1661 had been named in the witch-hunts of 1644 or 1649, but their prosecutions had failed.[23] In these instances it was the Scots themselves, rather than the English, who had frustrated the prosecutions sought by local authorities.

But even if all the witches of 1661 had in fact been suspected of diabolical activity during the 1650s, and early attempts to prosecute them had been frustrated in one way or another, the restoration of the traditional authorities cannot by itself explain this witch-hunt. It cannot, for example, explain why the hunt was restricted to a relatively small area during the greater part of 1661. Nor can it account for the long duration of the hunt. Even more important, it cannot explain why the accusations were made in the first place. The most that can be said is that the end of Cromwellian rule and the restoration of the regular judicial machinery and personnel in 1661 provided a necessary precondition of the hunt. If the English commissioners had not been succeeded by a Scottish justice general, if the privy council and parliament of Scotland had not been restored, and if the regular judicial institutions had not been returned to smooth working order, the great Scottish witch-hunt of 1661–2 probably would never have occurred.

But what was the real driving force behind the hunt? Who set the machinery of justice in operation and then maintained it? The tendency of most historical scholarship has been to blame the clergy not only for this particular hunt but for all witch-hunting in Scotland.[24] Whether the clergy of 1661 were trying to prove that they were as zealous against the 'powers of darkness' as their predecessors in the 1640s or reacting against the Cromwellian policy of laicization in the interests of 'religion and justice',[25] they certainly appear to have played an active part in the prosecutions of 1661–2.

There are solid grounds for identifying the clergy as the source of much of witch-hunting zealotry in early modern Scotland. They waged an unremitting war against the forces of Satan throughout this period, especially during the 1640s, when the covenanters were in power. Ministers were also primarily responsible for continuing this struggle in the late seventeenth and early eighteenth centuries, when secular officials had become much more reluctant to prosecute those who had aroused suspicion. But the clergy's role in this largest of all Scottish witch-hunts, which occurred after the covenanters had lost power, reveals the limitations of clerical influence in witch-hunting and points to laymen as the main inspiration for the prosecutions.

Scottish ministers were not inactive during the witch-hunt of 1661–2. Working with the lay elders of their parishes in the kirk sessions, they conducted some of the initial examinations of persons arrested for witchcraft, allowed the suspects to be searched for the devil's marks, and took depositions from witnesses before referring the cases to the appropriate secular authority.[26] In this capacity the clergy occasionally acted without proper restraint. They extracted a number of confessions from accused witches, and when the justiciary court acquitted one witch in 1661, the kirk session of Dalkeith prepared a second set of charges to prevent her release.

During this witch-hunt, however, the examinations conducted by the kirk sessions did not always lead to witchcraft trials. Quite to the contrary, their jurisdiction over slander had the opposite effect. Thus, at Dalkeith on 30 July 1661, at the height of the witch-trials, the kirk session heard the complaint of John Hume against John Dobie for saying he would wager 500 marks that Hume's wife would be convicted of witchcraft if tried.[27] Hume's wife was never named as a witch. At Newton, Midlothian, where no fewer than 28 witches were named in 1661, the kirk session warned John Nielson three times for calling Margaret Allen a bitch and a witch.[28] The Newton session also ordained during the summer of 1661 that anyone who slandered the child of a person who had either been convicted or delated for witchcraft should suffer publicly before the congregation, and the kirk session of Inveresk issued a similar warning that applied to friends as well as children of witches.[29] Action of this sort, while incapable of preventing all villagers from making further accusations of witchcraft, nonetheless did keep the hunt from becoming larger than it actually was and might have even helped to bring it to an end.

If the kirk sessions did not always promote witch-hunting in 1661–2, the presbyteries, which consisted of the clergy from a number of parishes, were even less responsible for fuelling the flames of this witch-hunt. As we have seen, presbyteries played a crucial role in witch-hunting during the 1640s, but they were far more reluctant to intervene in the prosecutions of 1661.[30] Perhaps the presbytery of Dalkeith, in which jurisdiction a majority of the accusations were made in 1661, still remembered the reprimand it had received in 1609 when it had proceeded against the suspected witch Geillis Johnstoune. At that time the privy council had protested against the 'preposterous' form of proceeding undertaken by the presbytery, noting that the case should have been referred to the lord of regality or the justice general and his deputes.[31]

In any event, the Dalkeith presbytery in 1661 remained inactive in the face of the crisis developing around it.[32] As long as witchcraft remained a statutory crime triable in the secular courts, the clergy could only play a limited role in its prosecution.[33] The main burden of prosecution fell on the shoulders of lay judicial authorities, both in the localities and in Edinburgh. Local gentry and bailies were, after all, the men who were authorized by the privy council or parliament to try the witches on the basis of the commissions of justiciary they granted. They were also the men most responsible for the judicial abuses that sullied the reputation of local Scottish justice during the great witch-hunt of 1661–2. Almost all of the charges of illegal pricking and torturing witches during these years were directed against laymen, not clerics.[34]

The clergy could of course use the power of the pulpit to make their parishioners more attentive to the dangers of witchcraft, and there is some evidence that the clergy acted in this way before and during the prosecutions of 1661–2.[35] The minister of Inveresk, for example, notified his congregation that a woman who had been imprisoned on suspicion of witchcraft would have to be released unless someone brought charges against her, and he also warned them not to harbour two witches who had fled from Chrichton after being imprisoned for witchcraft.[36] But if the clergy railed against witches and alerted the population to the activities of the devil's confederates, they were not alone. The cleric Robert Baillie may have bemoaned the prevalence of witchcraft in 1659, but he was joined by the laymen Alexander Brodie, Andrew Hay, John Nicoll, and John Lamont. And it was the petition of a layman, the earl of Haddington, that moved parliament to delegate a commission to try the witches who were allegedly infesting his lands in Samuelston and thus to begin the hunt in April 1661.[37]

Haddington's petition and parliament's quick response suggest that this witch-hunt, like any other, required not only adequate judicial machinery to bring witches to trial but a fear of witchcraft among influential members of society and a commitment by the ruling elite, especially those who exercised secular power, to activate that machinery. Three months after Haddington's petition, heritors in the parishes of Musselburgh, Dalkeith, Newbattle, Newton, and Duddingston, all within Midlothian, complained to the privy council about the number of witches in their locality. In response to this complaint, the council ordered three justice deputes to travel to Musselburgh and Dalkeith to try accused witches.[38] These towns, where the same judges had been sent a month before by order of parliament, became two of the most important centres of witchcraft prosecution during the hunt.[39]

The privy council's decision to send justice deputes to the parishes where witch-hunting was most intense reflected the gravity of the situation as well as the fear that this witch-hunt might spiral out of control. With the circle of accusations widening and the gaols filled beyond capacity, the usual method of granting commissions of justiciary to try individually named witches could not keep up with the demand. This had become evident in the witch-hunt of 1649–50, when neither parliament, the committee of estates nor the privy council could satisfy the requests from the presbytery of Irvine for permission to try the steadily growing number of witches in their parishes. The only other option was to issue a general or standing commission to local authorities, such as the presbyteries of Dunfermline and Irvine had requested at the time. As we have seen, the privy council and parliament had consistently refused to grant such standing commissions, despite frequent entreaties from the general assembly. The assignment of a justice depute, which the Dunfermline presbytery had considered an acceptable option in 1649, was therefore the course of action that the council adopted in 1661. Recognizing the gravity of the situation, the lords of the council assigned not one but all three justice deputes to hold witchcraft trials in the towns and parishes of Midlothian southeast of Edinburgh.[40] Their number included Sir George Mackenzie, who had secured his appointment as justice depute only three months before.[41] As we shall see, Mackenzie's experience as a judge in these trials had a lasting effect on the history of witch-hunting in Scotland.

How did the situation reach such a state of desperation that Mackenzie and his colleagues had to be sent to the afflicted area to try those witches? What had triggered this witch-hunt and why were so many people being accused? The petition of the earl of Haddington to parliament provides a number of clues:

> That upon several malefices committed of late within and about my lands of Samuelston there being several persons suspect of the abominable sin of witchcraft apprehended and searched, the marks of witches were found on them in the ordinary way. Several of them have made confession and have delated sundry others within the said bounds and have acknowledged paction with the devil.[42]

It is clear from this statement that malefices, that is, harmful deeds attributed to the witches' superhuman, mysterious, or extraordinary power, provided the original grounds for suspecting at least some of the Samuelston witches. Such *maleficia*, or acts of harmful magic, were often incorporated into the dittays of the accused, and since witnesses could often be induced to testify to their reality, they helped to bring about convictions. But *maleficia* do not appear to have been the only reason for Haddington's concern. Nor do the charges of *maleficia* brought against those witches who were examined by the kirk sessions and tried by the court of justiciary in 1661 reveal much that was by itself capable of causing a large-scale panic. The witches were accused of a wide variety of harmful deeds, such as injuring or causing the death of their neighbours, making them tremble or sweat, preventing them from arriving at their destinations, riding horses to death, turning over stones to prevent corn from growing, and burning barns.[43] These were, of course, serious charges, and they were probably the reason why Haddington's tenants threatened to leave his lands if the witches were not prosecuted.[44] But it is clear that Haddington was concerned with more than the alleged practice of sorcery and his tenants' fear of it. What bothered him most was the fact that the people accused of committing *maleficia* had confessed to making pacts with the devil and had implicated a large number of confederates. It was the belief that sorcerers made explicit pacts with the devil, copulated with him, renounced their baptism, and worshipped him that distinguished European witchcraft of the fifteenth, sixteenth, and seventeenth centuries from the simple black magic found in all parts of the world at all periods of time. And it was the belief that witches worshipped the devil collectively in large numbers and thus constituted an enormous conspiracy to subvert the Kingdom of God that aroused the fears of European authorities, lay as well as clerical, and led to the large witch-hunts of the sixteenth and seventeenth centuries. Haddington's petition to parliament in 1661 simply expressed the same fears that had dominated European elites for nearly 200 years. He might have been able to cope with a few isolated individuals tampering with the normal processes of nature, but large-scale apostasy and recruitment by the devil was something of an entirely different order.

Another phrase in Haddington's petition, the indication that the 'marks of witches were found on them in the ordinary way', suggests why he and other Scots were especially concerned with the 'abominable sin of witchcraft' at this particular time. As we have seen, searching a suspected witch's body for marks that were insensitive to pain and did not bleed had by this time become one of the most distinctive features of Scottish witch-hunting. It had gained a royal endorsement in James VI's *Daemonologie* and had become a routine procedure shortly after the witch's arrest. Technically, finding the devil's mark did not by itself secure the conviction of the accused; it only served as a preliminary indication of guilt that would lead either to further interrogation or to trial. In practice, however, it was crucial in confirming the suspicions of authorities, prejudicing the case against the accused, and in some cases actually forcing the accused to confess. It also served the purpose of transforming accusations of *maleficia* into cases of diabolism. The devil allegedly gave his mark to the witch when she made her pact with him. Locating the marks, which were found on witches' shoulders, necks, arms, legs, and in one case 'between her thigh and her body',[45] could therefore transform a charge of *maleficium* into one of apostasy.

The validity of the devil's mark was not universally recognized. European demonologists were divided on its legal value. Sir George Mackenzie claimed that it possessed relevancy only if the witches themselves confessed that they had received it by their own consent, it being 'equivalent' to a pact.[46] As might be expected, accused witches challenged its probative value. On the same day that the ministers and elders of the Newbattle kirk examined Margaret Litle for withcraft, Janet Litle was interrogated for having said that 'every man and woman had so many marks like witches'.[47] Her remark shows that scepticism of witchcraft, especially its diabolical dimension, could just as easily arise among villagers as with a learned judge such as Mackenzie.

During the witch-hunt of 1649–50 a number of professional witch-finders who specialized in pricking suspects in order to find the marks became active in Scotland. These 'prickers', whose number included John Kincaid and his protégé David Cowan, operated for profit and may have even used their craft as a pretext for extortion.[48] But irrespective of their motives, they satisfied the demands of local magistrates and even some witches themselves, who naively sought out the prickers in order to establish their innocence.[49] The prickers appear to have been most active during the early months of 1659, just before the interruption of justice, and again in 1661, when witches were pricked almost as a matter of course.[50] This suggests that the prickers were at least partially responsible both for the substantial increase in the number of prosecutions and executions in 1659 and the hunt that began in 1661.

There is also a strong geographical connection between the activities of the most famous pricker, John Kincaid, and the prosecutions of both 1659 and 1661. Kincaid lived in Tranent, East Lothian, and although he travelled about the country, he was most active in his home county and in neighbouring Midlothian. In 1659, 18 of the 38 individuals executed for witchcraft resided in East Lothian, and almost all of them submitted to searches by the pricker, who in a number of cases was specifically identified as Kincaid.[51] When the machinery of justice was once again set in operation in April 1661, the first witches brought to trial came from Samuelston, East Lothian, which is only six miles from Tranent. Since these witches confessed after marks were found on their bodies, they were probably searched by Kincaid, who was active during the entire hunt. It might also be suggested that one of the reasons why the hunt was at first confined to East Lothian and Midlothian was that Kincaid and his associates operated mainly in that area.[52] A further reason for the heavy concentration of prosecutions in that region was the thorough administration of justice there by the justiciary court.

Who were the witches?

The witch-hunt of 1661–2 received its direction mainly from the judges, magistrates, clergy, and local gentry who controlled the judicial machinery and used it to obtain confessions, depositions, implications, and convictions. Consequently, the reasons the hunt took place reside primarily in the beliefs, fears, policies, and activities of that ruling elite. But popular fears, suspicions, and accusations also played an essential role in the process, mainly by determining which people would be prosecuted and providing evidence of the alleged witches' maleficent deeds. Why then did certain individuals incur the suspicions of their neighbours?

The most obvious social characteristic of those accused of witchcraft in 1661–2 is that 84 per cent were adult females. In this respect the Scottish witches of the early restoration period conformed closely to the stereotype of the witch that had developed in Scotland and in most of western Europe during the prosecutions of the sixteenth and seventeenth centuries. But this fact by itself cannot provide an adequate explanation of the pattern of accusations. The important question is why certain women were singled out by their neighbours for prosecution while others were not. The reasons for suspecting a person of witchcraft could be many and varied, but four considerations seem to have been dominant in this witch-hunt: magical practices, moral deviance, personal temperament, and economic circumstances.

A large number of the women accused of witchcraft in 1661 and 1662 were healers who used charms to cure their patients.[53] The practice of charming was frowned upon by the kirk, which periodically conducted campaigns to eliminate it, on the grounds that it was considered superstitious and diabolical in its origin. Villagers and townspeople who brought charmers to the attention of the authorities and then testified against them in court were usually concerned when the charmer's power was used to bring misfortune or harm to them, their families, or their neighbours. The diabolical source of charming, like the pact with the devil and the witch's gatherings, were of relatively little importance to them.

The case of Agnes Johnston, a midwife in Edmiston, shows how charming could easily lead to charges of witchcraft. Johnston was delated before the Newton kirk session in August 1661 for putting salt in the mouth of Agnes Alexander when she was in labour and saying the following words: 'Our Lady said, and sooth she said, that afterbirth shall never bade, and that a little after she was brought to bed.' Johnston claimed that she had learned this charm from women in the parish of North Leith but could not remember their names. When asked how she cured a young boy, Thomas Thomson, who had a sore eye, she replied that she had a young child blow three times through a stone held on the lad's eye.[54]

When the two beneficiaries of this charming were called to testify on 18 August, however, they only increased the suspicion of the charmer. Agnes Alexander claimed that Johnston had caused her grief, and Thomas Thomson testified that he would have nothing to do with her.[55] One week later the session at Newton received a report from the elders at Edmiston that Johnston was under very ill repute and that they hoped very soon that the civil magistrate would charge her with witchcraft.[56] By that time these communities had probably learned that in late July two witches at Musselburgh had confessed that Johnston and others had met the devil at Wolmet Bank.[57] It was not until December however, that Johnston was finally imprisoned for witchcraft in Newton, and on 5 January 1662 the kirk session reported that she had escaped.[58] There is no record of where she went or whether she was ever tried for her alleged crime.

The charges against Janet Cock of Dalkeith, who was executed for witchcraft in November 1661, reveal that she also used charms to cure people. Her methods, which often involved laying the parts of newly killed animals on her patients' bodies, added credibility to the charge that she practised harmful magic and kept company with the devil.[59] In the formal charges against accused witches charms and malefices were usually kept separate, as they were in the dittay against Isobel Ramsay, who was also executed in August 1661.[60]

Many of the women accused of witchcraft had previously been suspected of, or even prosecuted for, various forms of moral deviance. Helen Cass, for example, who was executed at Dalkeith in August, was widely known to be sexually promiscuous, especially with English soldiers, as early as 1655,[61] while Christian Wilson had been delated for cursing on the Sabbath in 1658,[62] and Helen Concker had committed fornication with John Wysurd before being committed to the tollbooth for witchcraft in 1661.[63] In Scotland the charge of moral deviance usually arose when the witch was examined before the kirk session or the presbytery. The charge was brought by the session, but it was based upon the witch's reputation in the community. In that sense the charge of witchcraft came from below rather than above. As with charming, the charge of sexual immorality supported a diabolical interpretation of the crime. Just as charming implied a pact with the devil, so charges of sexual immorality made the charge of copulation with Satan plausible.[64]

Even more widespread than specific charges of deviance was the irascibility attributed to many of the witches accused in 1661. Of course the charge that the accused had been angry with her husband or a relative or neighbour was often made simply to provide a plausible emotional backdrop to the alleged pact with the devil. But the testimony of witnesses against the accused, which remains the most reliable evidence regarding the personality and behaviour of the witch, reveals an exceptionally high incidence of angry, vengeful activity on the part of the witches of 1661. The incidents that triggered these outbreaks of anger often had economic origins. Christian Wilson, for example, sought revenge against William Richardson for felling one of her hens,[65] while Janet Cock had an argument with James Douglas over the raking of dung,[66] and Margaret Allen 'conceived malice and hatred' towards Thomas Hoye because he had taken some of her husband's land.[67]

The alleged anger of witches was often directed against male members of the community who occupied positions of social or economic superiority over them. Many of the witches accused in 1661 and 1662, especially widows like Janet Lyle, Beatrix Leslie, Christian Patersone, and Margaret Porteous, appear to have lived in straitened economic circumstances. Sir George Mackenzie was speaking from his experience as a justice depute in Midlothian in 1661 when he observed that the 'persons who are ordinarily accused of this crime are poor, ignorant creatures'.[68] One such witch had confided to him at her examination that she was 'a poor creature who wrought for her meat'. The woman, who might very well have been the 60-year-old widow Janet Lyle from Edmiston, said she had confessed to Mackenzie not because she was guilty but because as a defamed witch no would ever give her meat or lodging. Faced with that prospect she said she 'desired to be out of the world'.[69]

In some cases the witch's antagonist actually denied her an act of charity she had requested, such as when Walter Lithgob, a cook, refused Janet Cock the broth she had asked for and he gratuitously threatened to scald her with it instead.[70] Janet Millar allegedly enchanted the milk of Helen Black when the latter refused to give her some butter, while Margaret Hutchinson became angry at Harry Balfour because he refused to do some work for her.[71] But it is not possible to conclude from this and other similar incidents that most of the witches prosecuted during this witch-hunt were making their wealthier and more individualistic or 'capitalistic' neighbours feel guilty by demanding that they adhere to communal standards of social justice. Alan Macfarlane has argued that such a situation prevailed in Essex in the sixteenth and seventeenth centuries, while Paul Boyer and Stephen Nissenbaum have shown that a somewhat different type of conflict between medieval corporate ideals and a nascent spirit of capitalism explains the pattern of accusations at Salem.[72] It is difficult, however, to establish any such broad trends on the basis of a few isolated witchcraft accusations from the towns of Midlothian and East Lothian in 1661. Not only did Scottish society lag far behind that of Essex in the development of early capitalism, but those Scottish accusations that had an economic foundation often reflected little more than a jealousy and hostility common to many pre-capitalistic societies.

What is most striking about the witches accused in this witch-hunt is that so many of them conformed to the traditional stereotype of the poor woman who aroused suspicion, fear, and discomfort among her neighbours. As far as can be determined, this stereotype persisted throughout the hunt and did not break down as the first suspects began to implicate others. Such a change did occur at Salem and in many of the German witch-hunts studied by Erik Midelfort.[73] In the later stages of these hunts a large number of men, including some of the wealthier and more influential members of the community, incurred accusations of witchcraft, thereby creating a sense of alarm within the ruling elite and stimulating a crisis of confidence in the legal institutions used to prosecute witches. Scotland did eventually experience a crisis of confidence, but it did not derive from a change in the status of the victims of the hunt. The witches remained the most vulnerable as well as the most easily suspected members of the community.

The crisis of confidence

The crisis of confidence in Scotland began when the judges of the justiciary court, which had assumed primary responsibility for trying witches in Midlothian and East Lothian, came to the realization that a number of accused witches, especially those named in the later stages of the hunt, were in fact innocent. The judges appear to have become most sceptical regarding accusations made by dying and confessing witches, who often gave no evidence concerning the activities of their alleged confederates except that they had seen them at one of their nocturnal gatherings (which were actually rather tame affairs by continental standards) at such places as Wolmet Bank, Libberton Kirk, or Newton Dean.[74] Very few of the witches thus named ever came to trial, at least in the justiciary court. Some of them may have avoided prosecution because local communities, burdened with the cost of maintaining large numbers of witches in jail, and unable to locate individuals who were willing to testify against them, decided to set them free. A few witches imprisoned in 1661 were released for precisely these reasons,[75] but it is much more likely that the judges simply refused to hear such cases. There is no doubt that the judges had begun to question seriously the validity of accusations made by confessing witches. In one case, the court not only accepted the retraction of a witch's confession but also sentenced him to be whipped and placed in a house of correction for implicating so many honest people.[76]

Even when suspects had been accused by individuals who were not themselves witches, and the trials actually did take place, the judges of the justiciary court proceeded in a cautious, sceptical manner. In a number of cases they declared certain articles against accused witches to be irrelevant, a procedure that laid the foundation for no fewer than 14 acquittals. In two cases, those of Janet Cock and Margaret Hutchinson, acquittals were followed either by re-apprehension of the accused or formulation of a new dittays against them.[77] Both Cock and Hutchinson were eventually convicted and executed, but in another similar case, that of Janet Millar, the judges denied the request for a second trial, despite the submission of a new dittay, on the grounds that the witch had already been declared not guilty by the assize.

The case of Janet Millar reveals the complexity of the judicial process during the revolutionary and post-revolutionary years, the dangers that witches faced from prosecution by more than one jurisdiction, and the commitment of trained judges to due process. Millar had been delated by six confessing witches in 1650, but she did not appear before a court until 1659, when the kirk session of Kirkliston examined her on 14 August.[78] She confessed ten days later, but the session, requiring more verification, requested the presence of the lairds of Dundas and Carlowrie and two JPs from the sheriffdom of Linlithgow. In their presence Millar admitted that she had made a confession, denying that she had been tortured but claiming that the constable, Robert Wilson, had promised her that if she were to confess she might return home afterwards.[79] In 1661 Millar was confined to the tollbooth in Edinburgh, but since no witnesses would come forward, the justice deputes sent her back to Kirkliston on 5 July to be tried by such commissioners as the parliament or the council should nominate.[80] This trial was to have taken place on 10 September, but on 20 August Millar was tried with a number of witches from Duddingston and was declared not guilty by a plurality.[81] At an unknown date, new dittays were drafted. The justice deputes, however, would not allow her to be tried at Kirkliston, as previously planned, since she had already been acquitted. In this way the judges adhered to the tradition in Scots law that witches should not be tried twice for the same crime.[82]

Acquittals for this or any other reason, if numerous enough, could have a profound effect upon the momentum of a witch-hunt by short-circuiting the chain of accusations, reducing the willingness of local authorities to initiate new cases, and calling into question the means by which the witches had been apprehended and examined. Even more important, the process leading to acquittal often allowed the judges themselves to clarify the reasons for their caution. There is little doubt that Sir George Mackenzie's involvement in this witch-hunt as a justice depute influenced the development of his relatively moderate, cautious attitude towards the prosecution of witches, which he later formulated in *The Laws and Customes of Scotland in Matters Criminal*.[83] It is also possible, though impossible to prove, that the growing scepticism of Mackenzie and his colleagues explains why the justiciary court almost completely stopped adjudicating cases of witchcraft in 1662.[84]

The cessation of judicial activity by the justiciary court did not, however, put an end to the prosecution of witches at this time. Quite to the contrary, the news of the burnings in Edinburgh, the sense of alarm that had arisen within the ruling elite, and the accumulation of routine suspicions throughout Scotland led the privy council to issue an unprecedented number of commissions to try suspected witches during the first six months of 1662.[85] The records of these trials are no longer extant, nor are the fates of most of the accused known, though it is likely that many were executed. As long as the council continued to issue these commissions, the hunt could have been sustained, even without the assistance of the justiciary court. But by the spring of 1662 the council had begun to manifest the same scepticism that had affected the justiciary court. In a proclamation issued on 10 April, the council noted that great numbers of suspected witches had been apprehended, hurried into prisons, pricked, tortured, and abused, with the unfortunate result that many innocent people had suffered. It therefore ordered that a suspected witch could not be arrested without a special warrant from the council, the justice general, or his deputes, or from the sheriff, justices of the peace, stewart, bailie of regality, or magistrates of the burgh where the suspected witch resided. It also prohibited pricking or torture except by order of the council and forbade the use of any other unlawful means to extract confessions.[86] As a further indication of its new policy, the council imprisoned Kincaid and John Dick for their activities as prickers.[87]

By this decisive action the council dealt three strong blows to the witch-hunt of 1661–2 and to the entire process of witch-hunting in Scotland. First, the requirement that a special warrant be obtained before arrest made it difficult for local communities to proceed peremptorily against suspected witches. Second, the prohibition of torture, while not absolute, discouraged the use of a judicial tool that was responsible for many of the confessions and implications made during this and other witch-hunts. In this respect the council was simply adopting the policy that the English commissioners had implemented when they controlled criminal justice during the 1650s.[88] Finally, and most important, the imprisonment of Kincaid and Dick put almost a complete end to the activities of the prickers, who had been partially responsible for starting the witch-hunt of 1661–2 and had helped to define its early geographical boundaries.[89]

A few months after issuing this order, the privy council granted its last commission of 1662, and during the next two years it granted only three more. Since parliament had already issued its last commission on 12 July 1661, the day of its adjournment, and since the justiciary court had already stopped hearing all but a few isolated cases, the witch-hunt of 1661–2 came to a halt. The end of the hunt in many ways constituted a turning point in the history of Scottish witchcraft, for after 1662 one can detect a general, although not strictly progressive, decline in witchcraft prosecutions until the last execution in 1727.[90] Seen in this light, this witch-hunt assumes an importance comparable to that of the auto-de-fé that occurred at Logroño in northern Castile, on the border of the Basque country, in 1610. In the wake of the Logroño trials, which resulted in 11 executions for witchcraft and the publication of an edict of grace that induced a further 1,802 individuals to confess to that crime, the Spanish Inquisition adopted policies that led to a dramatic reduction in the number of witchcraft prosecutions in all of Spain throughout the remainder of the seventeenth century.[91]

The person most responsible for the change in the official Spanish attitude towards witchcraft was the inquisitor Alonso de Salazar Frías. Salazar had taken part in the Logroño trials but had disapproved of some of the procedures employed by his colleagues. He had also become sceptical regarding the confessions prompted by the promulgation of the edict of grace, and after an extensive investigation of the evidence he concluded that none of the 'witches' had actually performed the deeds to which they had confessed.[92] In 1614 he drafted a new set of procedural rules for the supreme council of the Inquisition in Madrid, *la Suprema*, which was adopted for use in all subsequent witchcraft trials. These rules in effect brought witchcraft executions to an end in the Inquisition, although they continued in the secular courts.

Salazar's counterpart in Scotland was Sir George Mackenzie, who played an active role in the trials of 1661. Mackenzie's cautious and moderate stance towards witchcraft, like that of Salazar, did not derive from a philosophical scepticism. Although he did not think that witches were very numerous, he believed in the reality of witchcraft and took issue with the sceptical arguments of the German humanist physician Johann Weyer.[93] Like Salazar, Mackenzie exhibited a judicial scepticism that had emerged from his involvement in the prosecution of witches and his scholarly investigations of witchcraft prosecutions in the past. The numerous miscarriages of justice that he had either witnessed or studied convinced him that of all crimes witchcraft required 'the clearest relevancy and most convincing probation'.[94] He condemned judges who burned people by the thousands for their alleged witchcraft, and he defended the 'poor, ignorant creatures' who were so often accused.[95] Most important, he gave expression to all those doubts and reconsiderations that had begun to prevail in 1661 and 1662. He insisted that the justiciary court exercise exclusive cognition of the crime and he discouraged the council's practice of issuing commissions to 'country men' and inferior courts.[96] He condemned the art of pricking as a 'horrid cheat', and he argued that the devil's mark, which 'useth to be a great article with us', was not relevant unless the witch confessed that she got the mark by her own consent.[97] Finally, he insisted that the implication of the accused by other confessing witches was not by itself sufficient for conviction.[98] These observations read like a commentary on the experiences of 1661–2. It appears as if Mackenzie, one of the most intelligent participants in the great Scottish witch-hunt of these years, was writing its final footnote.'[99]

Let me add one more. This hunt took place at a time when royalist and counter-revolutionary sentiment was strong. The restoration had been popular in Scotland,[100] and it had led to a repudiation of the revolutionary changes that had occurred during the previous three decades.[101] It is possible that royalist professions of hatred for revolution and rebellion created a public mood, at least in some communities, that was especially conducive to witch-hunting.

One sign of that mood was an anti-covenanter 'pageant' staged by royalists in the town of Linlithgow on 29 May 1661, the first anniversary of the restoration of Charles II, shortly after the witch-hunt had begun.[102] The 'chief author' of this pageant was Robert Mill, one of the bailies of the borough, who had the support of the minister, James Ramsay, the future bishop of Dunblane.[103] In an expression of their support for the restored royalist regime these men framed a large ark, representing the ark of the covenant, to which the men attached a number of pictures.[104] These included an old hag, representing a witch, holding the National Covenant of 1638 in her hand; a Whig (a radical covenanter) holding the Remonstrance of 1650, which had condemned the acceptance of Charles II as king without his having promised to uphold the Covenant; and the parliamentary committee of estates bearing the inscription 'An Act for Delivering up the King.' Atop the ark stood the devil, with the inscription: 'Stand to the Cause!' The architects of this pageant also included a picture of a figure representing Rebellion in a religious habit, holding *Lex Rex*, the radical statement of covenanter political theory by Samuel Rutherford, in one hand and an inscription reading 'The Causes of God's Wrath' in the other. Another inscription read: 'Rebellion is the Mother of Witchcraft.' After some kirk stools and logs of wood had been thrown into this mix, the men who staged this spectacle, who were intoxicated, set the frame with all its fixtures and appendages ablaze, toasting the king's health.[105]

This incident may have been isolated, but the reference to witchcraft shows that some local Scottish authorities, who were understandably eager to give evidence of their royalism and consolidate their power, had little difficulty linking the rebellious sin of witchcraft, described as such in 1 Samuel 15:23, and the rebellious political activities of the covenanters. Perhaps the royalist association of these two apparent threats to the established order helps to explain why many members of the ruling elite were especially eager to proceed against witches at this time.

If the great Scottish witch-hunt did in fact gain strength from the anti-revolutionary fervour of local royalist authorities, it did not occur mainly because of such sentiment. This hunt had a number of more important causes. It took place, first of all, because the prosecution of so many suspected witches had been frustrated in one way or another between 1649 and 1660, because the traditional machinery of justice had been set into operation once again in 1661, and because Scottish courts no longer were obliged to employ English procedures in the prosecution of this crime. More specifically, it took place because John Kincaid and other professional prickers had confirmed that numerous suspected sorcerers in the Lothians had made pacts with the devil, and because a frightened earl of Haddington succeeded in bringing judicial relief to his locality. Once the hunt had begun, it increased in size and scope because confessing witches implicated large numbers of confederates and because magistrates in other areas, plagued by fears such as those of Haddington, secured commissions from the privy council to conduct witchcraft trials. At every stage, of course, the hunt required the support of the king's government. As soon as judges like Mackenzie and members of the privy council began to suspect that some of the individuals convicted of witchcraft were in fact innocent, the hunt could not be sustained. The members of Charles II's Scottish government must accept some responsibility for allowing the witch-hunt to take place, but they were almost solely responsible for bringing it to an end.

6 Absolutism, state-building, and witchcraft

The effort by royalists at Linlithgow to depict rebellious covenanters as witches in 1661 presented in visual form the close connection between witch-hunting and politics, especially ecclesiastical politics, that had long existed in Scotland. By proclaiming that rebellion was the mother of witchcraft, the royalist revellers were arguing that it was the spirit of political and religious rebellion during the past 20 years that had led to the recent increase in the number of witches.

There was of course no evidence of any such link between the covenanters and witchcraft. Quite to the contrary, it was the covenanters who had been in the vanguard of witch-hunting in Scotland during the revolutionary period, just as puritans had taken the lead in hunting witches in England. Blaming the covenanters for the rise in the number of witches was therefore a piece of political and religious propaganda. As such, however, it was remarkably effective, for it used the traditional association between rebellion and witchcraft to indict a political faction that in their defeat could now be clearly labelled as rebels.

Witchcraft and rebellion

The link between witchcraft and rebellion had a biblical foundation in 1 Samuel 15:23, 'Witchcraft is as the sin of rebellion.' During the early modern period demonologists developed this connection. Like the devil himself, who began his malevolent career with an act of rebellion against God, demonologists viewed the witch as the quintessential rebel. As a heretic and apostate the witch was considered guilty of *lèse majesté* or treason against God;[1] as a devil-worshipper she was part of an enormous political conspiracy; as a lower-class peasant she was striving to turn the world upside-down, inverting the divinely established hierarchical order of society and rejecting all its moral norms.[2] William Perkins, the English theologian who wrote *A Discourse of the Damned Art of Witchcraft* in the early years of the seventeenth century, had the image of the rebel-witch in his mind. 'The most notorious traitor and rebel that can be', wrote Perkins, 'is the witch. For she renounceth God himself, the king of kings, she leaves the society of his Church and people, she bindeth herself in league with the devil.'[3]

In Scotland James VI had given substance to the identification of witches as rebels in 1591 when he accused the witches of North Berwick of both witchcraft and treason. He made the same identification in 1597 when he learned that witches were trying to drown him, as discussed in Chapter 3. During the revolutionary period royalists often exploited this association between rebellion and witchcraft, laying the foundation for its specific use against covenanters at Linlithgow in 1661. A royalist pamphlet published during the second civil war, *A Wonder, A Mercury without a Lye* (1648), claimed that God disliked rebels as much as he did witches.[4] In 1646 royalists accused Thomas Larkham, a radical puritan clergyman who had recently returned from Massachusetts, of 'faction, heresy, witchcraft, rebellion and treason'.[5]

During the interregnum no less a royalist than Thomas Hobbes made a similar association in discussing the danger of popular men in *Leviathan* (1651). Referring to the possibility that such men will undermine obedience to the law, Hobbes wrote: 'And this proceeding of popular and ambitious men is plain rebellion, and may be resembled to the effects of witchcraft.'[6] Hobbes, a materialist, was the ultimate sceptic regarding the reality of witchcraft, and he had no tolerance for the religious zealotry that inspired witch-hunts, but he did give the powerful state he envisaged the right to punish witches for the threat they posed to the order of society.[7]

Parliamentarians were unable to respond to these arguments in kind, since the accusation that royalists were rebels was not plausible. Parliamentarians were therefore left with two alternatives. The first was to belittle the royalist claims, as when *The Parliaments Post* began its bi-weekly report of military developments in August 1645 with the statement that Cavaliers, 'unable to prevail with our men, hath met with some of our women, and it hath turned them into witches'.[8] The other option was to claim that witches were in league with the royalists, such as when they asserted that a witch captured by the army of the earl of Essex as she was sailing down the Newbury River was a royalist spy.[9] This claim, even if it could be substantiated, had little traction, since it could not exploit the traditional link between witchcraft and rebellion.

The royalist condemnation of witchcraft as a form of rebellion raises the issue of the connection between witch-hunting on the one hand and both absolutism and the process of state-building on the other. Before evaluating these theories, a brief discussion of terms is in order. Absolutism was both a theory and a practice. As a theory it exalted the power of the king, giving him all the attributes of sovereignty, including the right to make law. It also freed the king from most of the restrictions of the law, at least when he was acting in the interest of the state. Absolutism cannot be equated with the doctrine of the divine right of kings. That theory, endorsed and in many ways refined by King James VI, declared that God, not men, placed kings on the throne. The doctrine of divine right was often used to support the theory of absolutism, but subjects who insisted on limiting the power of the king could, and often did, subscribe to the doctrine. In any event, the theory of divine right, taken by itself, is not central to the question whether absolutism and witch-hunting were connected.

The practice of absolutism consisted of the implementation of policies designed to give the king the tangible power that political theorists claimed he had; it was by definition a program and a process. The program involved the reduction of the rival power of the nobility, the elimination or dramatic restriction of the power of representative assemblies (parliaments, estates, or diets), and the use of both the judicial system and armed force to suppress rebellion and maintain order throughout the king's domain. Absolutists also sought to secure judicial decisions affirming that when they pursued policies to benefit the entire realm, their power was not subject to the law.

A policy of royal absolutism inevitably involved a program of state-building. A state is a formal, public, and autonomous political organization, staffed by officials who have the legally sanctioned authority to require obedience from the inhabitants of a specific territory over an extended period of time.[10] The state is a coercive institution, and its status depends to a great extent on its ability to enforce its edicts and writs throughout the territory over which it claims sovereignty. State formation or state-building involved territorial expansion and consolidation, the development a centralized administration, the suppression of dissent, the inculcation of habits of obedience among the entire population, control of the church, and the creation of a standing army. These policies all strengthened royal power and suppressed local autonomy. It is understandable, therefore, why rulers who had an image of themselves as absolute rulers would pursue these centralizing policies. State-building and absolutism are so closely linked that some historians refer simply to the formation of 'absolutist states'.[11]

During the past 30 years scholars in the area of witchcraft studies have argued that there is a close correlation between absolutism and state-building on the one hand and witch-hunting on the other. These scholars have focused on the role of the state in the judicial process, the disciplining of the population to promote obedience to an absolute ruler, and the link between demonological and absolutist ideas.[12]

The kingdom of Scotland provides an ideal test case for this thesis. In the foundational text for the scholarly study of witch-hunting in Scotland, Christina Larner argued that witch-hunting in Scotland, as in many other places in Europe, was integrally connected to the process of state-building and the effort to establish absolutism.[13] Subsequent scholarship has endorsed the core of Larner's argument while modifying and embellishing it in a number of respects.[14] Other scholars have attempted the much more difficult task of applying it to England, where the processes of state-building and witch-hunting followed very different paths.[15]

The main elements of Larner's thesis are as follows. Beginning in the late sixteenth century, the Scottish state took deliberate steps to secure a monopoly of witch-hunting, demanding that only the central court of justiciary or individual commissioners authorized by the central government could try witches. These efforts formed part of a broader effort to make the state 'absolutist'. It was appropriate, therefore, that King James VI, who claimed absolute power by divine right, should have taken a lead in witch-hunting, which he encouraged in his witchcraft treatise, *Daemonologie*. The large witch-hunts of 1590–1, 1597, 1628–30, 1649–50, and 1661–2, which when taken together account for about 60 per cent of all Scottish prosecutions, were either initiated by the state or were encouraged by officials in the central government.

The key to state control of prosecutions was central management – the careful review of petitions submitted to the privy council requesting authorization to try witches in the localities. This process of central management allowed the ruling elite to control and manipulate 'the demand for and the supply of witchcraft suspects'.[16] Central management also explains how national hunts could develop, since the privy council could coordinate witch-hunts in different parts of the country. The efforts of the privy council to encourage and promote witch-hunting formed part of a broader concern to create a godly state – an enterprise in which local communities were also involved. Thus Scottish witch-hunts can be compared to continental European hunts whose purpose was to discipline the population in the interest of reformed religion and the social order, a process of 'acculturation' that the French historian Robert Muchembled has claimed was a major objective of officials involved in witch-hunting.[17]

Linking state-building with absolutism, Larner states in the conclusion of her study that the Scottish witch-hunt 'spanned a period that began with the divine right of kings and ended with the decline of the doctrine of the godly state'. Her interpretation of Scottish witch-hunting is therefore essentially political, one that 'rests essentially on the themes of political sociology: power, dominance, ideology, and legitimation'.[18]

There is much of value in this interpretation of Scottish witch-hunting, especially in its emphasis on political and legal developments. By focusing on absolutism and state-building it removes witch-hunting from the periphery of European history and places it at the very centre of political development. The problem with the thesis, however, is that it exaggerates the role of the Scottish state as an agent of witch-hunting, and it fails to recognize that throughout the period of witch-hunting – and not merely towards its end – the state had as much to do with placing limits on witch-hunting as with promoting it. The intensity of Scottish witch-hunting, moreover, can be attributed as much to the weakness of the Scottish state, and in particular its failure to develop a powerful central judicial establishment, as to its strength.

The Scottish state and witch-hunting

During the period of witch-hunting Scottish monarchs and their ministers made sustained efforts to build a strong, powerful state with an absolute monarch at its head, but they achieved only limited success. In the late sixteenth century, when the process of witch-hunting had begun in earnest, Scotland possessed the formal structure of a unitary state, in which all local powers were subordinated to the king, privy council, and parliament, but in reality the Scottish state was a fragile creation, and the process of state-building confronted a series of obstacles. First, the state exercised effective power only in the Lowlands; in the Highlands leaders of the clans performed many of the functions of the state, and the king's writ often did not run in those locales. Even in the Lowlands the effective exercise of central state power was problematic. The church, while technically subordinate to the state in jurisdictional matters, often commanded greater and more fervent allegiance than the state and sometimes found itself in disagreement or open conflict with the officers of the state. The bureaucracy of the Scottish state was pitifully small, even smaller than that of its southern English neighbour, whose central administration was in turn a pale reflection of that of France. The revenue that the king relied upon to run this feeble structure was far smaller than any state of comparable size in Europe. The power of the monarch who controlled this fractured state was limited by law, custom, and the practical necessity of negotiating with the nobility, who exercised nearly autonomous power in certain localities and who constantly threatened the monarch with rebellion.

The weakness of the Scottish state was particularly evident in the administration of criminal justice. The central criminal court, the court of justiciary in Edinburgh, was staffed by the justice general, whose role after 1628 was largely honorific, and justice deputes who acted as his surrogates. Unwilling or unable to burden the justiciary court with a large volume of cases, and unsuccessful in its efforts to create a properly functioning circuit court system, the privy council occasionally appointed one or more of the justice deputes to conduct trials in the localities or, more commonly, granted commissions of justiciary to local elites to try the prisoners themselves. The officers of the state also had to rely on the church courts in the parishes, known as kirk sessions, and the presbyteries, which consisted of representatives from several parishes, to conduct the initial interrogation of persons suspected of certain crimes, including witchcraft, and refer them to central authorities for trial. The legislative assembly of the kingdom, the Scottish parliament, had a relatively minor place in the administration of justice. Summoned only occasionally, it assumed the function of the privy council of granting commissions of justiciary when it was in session.

Scottish local courts could be considered only tangential components of the state apparatus. The jurisdictional map of Scotland was a maze of courts possessing different and sometimes overlapping jurisdictions. The courts of burghs functioned with minimal regulation by the central government, and the heritable sheriffships (royal courts in the localities) and regalities (grants of jurisdiction on a nobleman's land), which continued in Scotland until the parliament of Great Britain abolished them in 1747, represented the very antithesis of state power, which by definition is public. Officials of the Scottish state often tried to restrict the powers of local courts, and in the prosecution of witches they succeeded to some extent. The problem was that the government in Edinburgh still needed to rely on local authorities to maintain order and prosecute crime; hence the practice of granting commissions of justiciary. These commissions derived their power from the state, but since they were temporary bodies appointed for a specific task, they were not part of the state apparatus. At best they can be considered intermediary authorities, providing a tenuous connection between central and local government.

A further weakness of the Scottish state derived from its relationship to the English state during the period of intense witch-hunting. Subject to English overlordship during the Middle Ages, the Scottish state had by the sixteenth century established its autonomy, but English victories against the Scots in 1513 and 1542 and English assistance in achieving a Protestant reformation in Scotland during the 1560s had guaranteed the continuation of a measure of English influence in Scottish affairs. The nexus between the two kingdoms became even stronger in 1603, when James VI of Scotland became James I of England, thus bringing about a regal or personal union of the two kingdoms. This union kept the two states separate but linked them in ways that have never been reversed. In some respects the regal union of 1603 turned Scotland into a satellite state of England and made it questionable to what extent the Scottish state was still sovereign. That sovereignty was completely destroyed during the Cromwellian period, when the country was absorbed temporarily into a single commonwealth of England, Scotland, and Ireland, and permanently when England and Scotland were united in the United Kingdom of Great Britain by the treaty of union of 1707.

However weak or fragile the Scottish state was in the early modern period, there were repeated attempts to strengthen it between the accession of James VI in 1567 and the Act of Union in 1707. Many of these efforts were linked to the absolutist policies of the Stuart kings. The question at hand is to what extent these policies had an impact on the intensity of witch-hunting.

Criminal justice and state power

As we have seen, Scottish witches were tried only in the secular courts. The church courts played an important role in pre-trial examinations of witches, but they were not permitted to try Scots for this crime or any other felony. The Scottish government jealously protected its jurisdiction against efforts by the church to exceed the boundaries of its jurisdiction, thus reinforcing efforts it had made during the reign of James VI to assert royal control over the church.[19] The exclusive trial of witchcraft in the secular courts did not mean, however, that the state, as defined above, took an active role in the prosecution of witch-hunting. The state's involvement in witch-hunting can best be assessed on the basis of the extent of its role in the prosecutions and the degree to which officers of the state, in particular the members of the privy council and the royal judges, superintended criminal prosecutions.

As we saw in Chapter 2, James VI's judicial reforms of 1587 authorized the lord advocate to start a prosecution by his own authority, even if the injured party did not file a complaint. This innovation, which represented one feature of inquisitorial procedure, allowed the main legal officer of the Crown to bring a witch to trial without first submitting the charges to a grand jury, as in England. The question, however, is how often the lord advocate exercised this arbitrary power of indicting witches and thus began a witch-hunt. Did he act in the manner of public prosecutors on the European continent, especially in the German territories, who started witch-hunts by arresting and interrogating suspected witches solely on the basis of rumour?

The answer is: not very frequently. The number of Scottish witches who were originally identified and charged by the king or central judicial authorities was negligible. Even the witches whom James VI personally interrogated in 1590, when he suspected that they were involved in a plot to kill him, had been accused of witchcraft before he took interest in them.[20] James did, however, pursue them with determination, and the government was responsible for drafting the indictments against them. He was also personally responsible for initiating the prosecution of the jurors in the trial of Barbara Napier for wilful error when they acquitted her of some of the charges enumerated in her dittay. The king played a much smaller role in the large witch-hunt of 1597. As we have seen, he became personally involved in these prosecutions only after he suspected that witches had once again tried to harm him.[21] The other indictments drafted by the lord advocate during the period of the witch-trials arose in response to charges brought by the witch's neighbours that witches had harmed them by maleficent means.

The initiative for Scottish witchcraft trials, therefore, came almost entirely from local communities. In this respect Scotland was little different from England, where virtually all prosecutions originated in charges of *maleficia* that arose among villagers and townspeople. Scotland was also not that different from numerous German territories, where most prosecutions came 'from below', not from state authorities who assumed the responsibility of bringing witches to justice. Even in territories like the electorate of Trier, the site of a massive witch-hunt between 1589 and 1591, the original accusations came from the common people, not from the bishop and his legal representatives, as was once believed.[22]

A stronger argument for the involvement of the Scottish state in witch-hunting focuses on the steps that central state authorities took once the initial accusations had been lodged. One of the most distinctive features of Scottish witch-hunting was the way in which the central government authorized all witchcraft trials, either by arranging for prosecution in the central court of justiciary in Edinburgh or by granting commissions to local authorities to try witches in the localities. It denied the church courts, the sheriff courts, and the burgh courts the right to try witches by themselves, insisting that any local authorities who wished to have witches prosecuted submit the request to the privy council, which would then decide the manner of prosecution. In this way the officers of the Scottish state guaranteed they would have a hand in each and every witchcraft prosecution.

This acquisition of a power to determine whether and how all Scottish witchcraft cases should be tried must be counted among the achievements of the Scottish state during this period. Indeed, one of the connections between witch-hunting and state-building in Scotland lies precisely in the privy council's success in forcing local authorities to recognize the state's authority in this jurisdictional area. The crucial questions, however, especially in evaluating Larner's thesis, concern the purposes such control served and the effects it had. In particular, did the privy council use its powers to promote witch-hunting by regulating the demand for and supply of witchcraft suspects and by actually coordinating prosecutions in different parts of the country?

In this respect three points need to be made. First, the refinement of this system in 1597 was intended much more to control and place limits on the process of witch-hunting than to promote it. In 1597 the government had issued general or standing commissions that allowed local authorities to prosecute any witches who might be found in their communities.[23] It had also issued some of these commissions to one or two individuals. These commissions were in fact warrants for open-ended witch-hunts in which the number of victims could increase quickly. It soon became clear to the government that these commissions had allowed the process of witch-hunting to get out of control, leading to terrible miscarriages of justice. In a series of steps discussed in Chapter 2, the government assumed much tighter control over the granting of these commissions, giving them to large groups of commissioners (often numbering more than eight) and authorizing them to try only those individuals whose names were listed on the document.

This new policy meant that, if local elites wished to prosecute witches, they needed to send a petition, supported by documentation, to Edinburgh in order to obtain permission to try witches who were already in their custody. The government would then respond either by directing the trial to be held in the court of justiciary, or by issuing a commission of justiciary allowing the petitioners to hold the trial themselves. This procedure for determining how witches would be prosecuted, which remained in operation until the end of the seventeenth century, was thus intended to restrain witch-hunting rather than to encourage it. The restraining influence was most obvious during the period from 1597 to 1628, when relatively few witchcraft prosecutions took place, and after 1662, when prosecutions entered a period of decline, which shall be discussed in Chapter 8.

The second point is that there is no evidence that the privy council ever used its power to control the flow of prosecutions, to coordinate prosecutions, or to inspire a national witch-hunt. The use of the word 'national' in this context must be qualified, since the five large Scottish witch-hunts hunts during the early modern period did not take place throughout the entire country. These hunts were national only in the sense that they involved more than one region; the witch-hunt of 1597, for example, affected only five counties. But even if we use the word national in that restricted sense, there is no evidence that the privy council did anything to give witch-hunting a national character. It certainly had a mechanism for doing so, especially if it had been willing to grant standing commissions to authorities in different counties, but it rarely did so. Even more indefensible is the claim that the Scottish government used its powers over witchcraft to create 'national unity'.[24] The connections between the prosecutions in different parts of the country can be explained by the ability of local elites (clerical and lay alike) to share their fears and anxieties with others in their proximity, not by provocation, instigation, or coordination by the privy council in Edinburgh.

The third point is that the central government's management of prosecutions does not in any way indicate that the officers of the state experienced or participated in 'witch panics' during the years of crisis. The word panic has been appropriately used to describe large witch-hunts that got out of control, especially those fuelled by the naming of accomplices. It is, for example, proper to label the large-scale prosecutions in German states like Bamberg and Würzburg during the 1620s, as well as those in Sweden in 1668–76, as panics. Some of the smaller, more limited hunts in the Jura region studied by William Monter may also be referred to in this way.[25] In those continental European witch-hunts, moreover, an argument can be made that state authorities contributed to the panic by assuming control of the investigations, torturing accused witches, and demanding the names of the witches' accomplices. The Scottish privy council made no such contribution to the development of large Scottish witch-hunts. As we have seen, they did not assume the responsibility for initiating prosecutions, and they did not engage in a process of torturing witches to secure the names of alleged accomplices, except in 1590–1. Even during the 1640s, a time when witch-hunting became more intense than it had ever been before, the privy council resisted demands from local presbyteries that it grant general commissions.[26] An account of the Scottish 'witchcraft panic' of 1597 reveals that members of local elites in Aberdeenshire and elsewhere became terribly frightened about the existence of a diabolical conspiracy, but nothing about the conduct the lords of the privy council during that crisis suggests that they too experienced overpowering fear or terror. If anything, the council took action in 1597 to stop the panic, not to encourage it.[27]

One reason for the inapplicability of the word panic to the attitude of the privy council is that the councillors who considered petitions from the localities were not themselves members of the local community. They may have feared witchcraft in a general sense, as a threat to religion and the social order, but they did not participate in the local dynamics of witch-hunts. In this respect they can be compared to the English justices of the assize, the judges of the English central courts who went on circuit twice every year, who were not allowed to preside over trials in their native counties. Those justices rarely became involved in witch panics, and they generally demonstrated a high degree of impartiality in presiding over witch-trials. Unlike the judges in many small German states who exercised jurisdiction over tiny geographical areas, they did not share the fears of the witches' neighbours.

If officers of the Scottish state did not initiate or deliberately promote witch-hunting, they did nonetheless bear some responsibility for the high number of executions. Their complicity in these prosecutions was most evident during times of intense witch-hunting, when the number of petitions coming to the privy council or parliament was overwhelming. In those situations the privy council or parliament, incapable of actually weighing the evidence in a judicial manner, and unable to direct too many trials into the court of justiciary, routinely issued commissions of justiciary to local elites. Even though the privy councillors did not actually try these cases, they became complicit in their outcome, which almost always meant the execution of the witch.

The first source of their complicity was their requirement that, in order to receive a commission to hold a trial, local elites had to present evidence of the witch's guilt, preferably in the form of a confession. This requirement encouraged local elites, in their determination to secure the trial and conviction of the witch in their custody, to use various forms of judicial coercion, all of which were illegal, in order to obtain the confession. The irony is that the original pretext for treating the prisoners in this way was the privy council's demand for a confession, a requirement that was intended as much to prevent miscarriages of justices as to secure the conviction of witches.

The second way in which the privy council was complicit in the conviction and execution of witches was in its delegation of most trials to legally untrained commissioners in villages and towns.[28] The council made these assignments simply because it did not have the judicial personnel to funnel all requested prosecutions into the justiciary court in Edinburgh or to send trained justices on circuit. This practice of authorizing witchcraft trials by local commissioners had devastating consequences for accused witches. Unlike the trials held in the court of justiciary, where the trial was conducted by a trained judge and the evidence was debated at length,[29] trials in the localities, were usually conducted in summary fashion. As in the court of justiciary, juries determined guilt or innocence, but the possibility of an acquittal by the neighbours of the accused, some of whom had brought charges against the witches, was slim. As Sir George Mackenzie wrote in 1678, 'scarce ever any who were accused before a country assize of neighbours did escape that trial'.[30]

The lairds and bailies who served as commissioners of justiciary in these witch-trials were not acting in a private capacity. They conducted the trials on the basis of properly delegated authority, and the fact that they went to great lengths to obtain commissions, sending agents to Edinburgh with the required documentation, suggests that the rule of law was perhaps more firmly established throughout the kingdom than is usually conceded. The process, however, involved the local elite's use of the judicial authority of the state for its own ends rather than the central government's imposition of its will on subordinate authorities in the localities. The lairds and magistrates who conducted these local trials were acting in the interest of their communities and their churches, not as executors of a central governmental policy.

The role that the state played in the process was minimal. The privy council was not 'in effect conducting the trial itself' when it decided whether or not a trial should be held.[31] The council's deliberations, however lengthy, dealt with presumptions rather than proof of the witches' guilt. Their consideration of the evidence submitted to them (usually in the form of the witches' confessions) could not possibly have met the requirements of a proper trial. If the lords of the council knew that they were in effect conducting the trial themselves, they would have been complicit in the fate that awaited almost all of the witches who were tried in this way. The ultimate reason for that complicity, however, was the difficulty devising an alternative system of administering criminal justice in the localities. The problem was the weakness of the Scottish state, not its strength.

Moral discipline and the state

One of the main sources of witch-hunting zeal throughout Europe was the determination of lay and clerical elites to create a godly state, a political community characterized by the practice of a strict Christian morality. The kingdom of Scotland provides the best example of a polity in which this religious inspiration of witch-hunting was evident. In Scotland, where witchcraft was referred to in court records as a sin as well as a crime, committed against the laws of God as well as the law of Scotland, the prosecution of witches formed a major part of a Protestant campaign to achieve the moral reform of society.

The campaign to create a godly state was undertaken mainly by the reformed Protestant church, which considered witchcraft one of an entire litany of sins that needed to be punished, if not eradicated, to achieve an ideal Christian community. In this pantheon of vice, witchcraft took its place alongside fornication, adultery, incest, blasphemy, cursing, and Sabbath-breaking.[32] The main agents of efforts to prosecute these forms of moral deviance were the courts of the reformed kirk – parish sessions, presbyteries, and synods – that were erected with the primary purpose of imposing a moral discipline on the population. A campaign against witchcraft, however, could not be achieved through these courts alone. Since witchcraft was a felony that could be tried only in the secular courts, the kirk could only participate in the preliminary examination of the accused before turning the testimony over to the civil magistrate. Faced with this restriction, ministers found themselves either exerting informal pressure on lay magistrates to take action against witches, urging parliament to pass legislation against witchcraft, or pressuring the privy council to intensify its prosecution of the crime. As we have seen, much of this pressure on the secular government came from the general assembly, especially during the period of its greatest influence during the revolutionary period.

The question remains whether this Protestant campaign to create a godly state by prosecuting witches had anything to do with broader process of state-building that we have been discussing. One way of addressing this question is to ask whether the government supported or initiated any such moral campaigns for political purposes. Conducting campaigns for moral reform has often proved a successful tactic for winning popular support and even legitimizing regimes in European history. A strong case can be made that the local authorities who came to power in England and Scotland in the 1640s, most notably at Newcastle in 1649, started witch-hunts in order to legitimize their recent acquisition of power. The question however is whether central authorities in Scotland took the initiative in hunting witches to strengthen the state.

In 1628 the Scottish privy council did take the initiative in inaugurating a campaign to prosecute various forms of moral deviance, including witchcraft.[33] The witch-hunt of 1628–30, which was one of the largest in Scottish history (although not on the scale of the hunts of 1649–50 or 1661–2), originated in such a godly enterprise. It is difficult to comprehend, however, how either this campaign or the like-minded witch-hunt of 1649–50 served the purposes of state-building. The witch-hunt of 1628–30 is best understood as the product of religious zeal among laymen determined to serve the purposes of reformed Protestantism, not the consolidation of secular power.

Nor is it plausible that witch-hunts fostered habits of obedience to political as well as religious authority. Robert Muchembled has argued that witchcraft prosecutions, which formed part of a broader campaign by the forces of reformed Catholicism to destroy superstition and bring about moral reform, produced a more homogeneous population and thus promoted obedience to the 'absolute king and to God'.[34] A case can be made that the moral and social discipline enforced by the kirk sessions and presbyteries in Scotland contributed indirectly to state formation by making the task of governing easier and reducing the need for coercion.[35] It is difficult, however, to see how the kirk's examination of witches could have made the population more docile or politically subservient. To be sure, witchcraft was viewed as a form of rebellion in Scotland, but the witches themselves could rarely be identified as political dissidents, even in 1591. The only tangible effect of the trials on the behaviour of the population was that they encouraged women to adhere to traditional standards of feminine conduct in order to avoid persecution.

Political obedience was inculcated by trying and executing traitors, not witches.

The most untenable argument that witch-hunting served the combined purposes of state-building and absolutism is the claim that the statutory definition of witchcraft as a secular crime was a product of the state's power 'to classify and construct the world, to articulate hierarchies of deviance and conformity'. According to this argument, which was partially inspired by Larner's work but was developed with respect to England (where absolutism never succeeded), witchcraft was a manufactured form of deviance, an abstract or symbolic crime against the state, the ruler, and religion, whose creation and definition was designed to serve the political purposes of judicial elites by enhancing their power. The definition of witchcraft as a political crime thus constituted a formative episode in the development of absolutism, a process arising from a deliberate fusion of institutional centralization with an insistence on confessional uniformity.[36]

The passage and the inspiration of the Scottish witchcraft act of 1563, which defined witchcraft as a secular crime and became the statutory foundation of all Scottish witchcraft prosecutions, provides little support for such a claim.[37] Parliament passed this act mainly in response to pressure from the church to establish a godly discipline in the early years of the Protestant reformation.[38] The committee that drafted the act was dominated by protestant ministers, including John Knox. These men were concerned with a number of moral offences, such as blasphemy, as well as witchcraft. The Scottish government of Mary Queen of Scots had resisted Protestant demands for a program of moral discipline for two years before the meeting of parliament in 1563. Once the act was passed, the Scottish government, which was entrusted with this task of prosecuting witches, showed little interest in witch-hunting. In 1565 the general assembly complained that a number of horrible crimes, including witchcraft, were not being prosecuted.[39] Thus neither the Scottish witchcraft act nor its enforcement had anything to do with efforts of rulers or officials to strengthen the state, much less to achieve royal absolutism. Witchcraft did not become a political crime until James equated it with treason in 1590.

The claim that witchcraft as defined in the act of 1563 was an abstract or symbolic crime also has no foundation. The act condemned the practice of 'witchcrafts, sorcery, and necromancy' on the grounds that those activities had long been considered against the law of God. Just like the English statute passed earlier in the same year condemning *maleficia* (which find no mention in the Scottish act), this piece of legislation was concerned with very specific practices. It did not declare that it was illegal simply to be a witch. Nor did it mention the demonic pact, although that was implicit in the condemnation of necromancy. In any case the explicit or implicit pacts negotiated by ritual magicians were hardly abstract. To argue that the act condemned an abstract crime against the state or ruler is just as misleading as to claim that rulers promoted the prosecution of the crime to enhance their power.

Absolutist theory and witchcraft.

With so few apparent connections between witch-hunting and policies of absolutism and state-building, we return to the question whether there was a link between absolutist theory and the ideology of witchcraft articulated in demonological treatises. The main evidence for such a link comes from the writings of James VI, who wrote a demonological treatise and also espoused a theory of royal absolutism.[40] Stuart Clark has argued that *Daemonolgie* was in fact a political treatise in the sense that it depicted the witch as the inverse of the good ruler. Whereas the good ruler imposed order on his kingdom, the witch was the source of disorder and rebellion.[41] Whether this contrast justifies the claim that *Daemonologie* was a political treatise, in the same category as the *Trew Law of Free Monarchies*, is open to debate; a better case could be based on the explicit connection the treatise makes between witchcraft and treason. But in any event, there is nothing in *Daemonologie* that provides support for royal absolutism, a theory that deals with the relationship between the king and the law.

The same can be said for the work of Jean Bodin, the French political theorist whose *Six Books of the Republic* (1576) not only provided a foundation for the modern theory of sovereignty but also laid the basis for the theory of royal absolutism. Like James, who drew heavily on Bodin's political theory, Bodin also wrote an influential demonological treatise, *De démonomanie des sorciers* (On the Demonomania of Witches, 1580). Like James's treatise, *Démonomanie* affirmed the reality of witchcraft in the face of the sceptical views of Johann Weyer and made specific recommendations for the vigorous prosecution of the crime. Like James, Bodin also claimed that witches were guilty of treason, although more against God, and considered them to be a threat to the good order of the commonwealth.[42] As with James, however, the specific links between a theory of absolutism, as opposed to a set of ideas regarding the maintenance of order and the prevention of rebellion, can only be established implicitly.

If the link between absolutist theory and support for witch-hunting may have been tenuous in the work of James VI and Jean Bodin, it was entirely absent from the works of Sir Robert Filmer and Sir George Mackenzie. Filmer, a squire from the English county of Kent, is known mainly for his extreme absolutist views that found expression in his treatise *Patriarcha*, written on the eve of the civil war but not published until the country was divided again at the time of the exclusion crisis of 1679–80. Filmer's absolutism, which was based on the argument that royal power was essentially that of a father, having descended from Adam and reinvested in the kings of Israel and then the rulers of Europe, was more extreme than that of Bodin or James VI. Filmer argued, for example, that kings had total control over the lives of their subjects, just as fathers had control over the lives of their children, and could tax them without their consent.

More obscure than *Patriarcha* was Filmer's anonymous witchcraft pamphlet, *An Advertisement to the Jury Men of England Touching Witches* (1653), written in the wake of the execution of six witches at Maidstone the previous year. Filmer's ostensible purpose, reflected in the subtitle of the pamphlet, was to reveal the difference between an English witch, defined by the Protestant theologian William Perkins as one who makes a covenant with the devil, and the Hebrew witch of the Bible, who was never reported to have made such a pact. In presenting this comparison Filmer was following the argument of the two great sixteenth-century sceptics, the Dutch humanist and Protestant Johan Weyer and Filmer's fellow Kentishman Reginald Scot. Having thus undermined the relevance of Exodus 20:18, Filmer proceeds to show that the 18 proofs that a witch had made a pact with the devil presented by Perkins were all insufficient to convict a witch. So too were the three means of discovering a witch set forth by King James VI in *Daemonologie* 'in his youth, being in Scotland'. These proofs were finding the devil's mark, swimming the witch, and witnessing her inability to shed tears.[43]

In Filmer's case, therefore, there was no apparent connection between the theory of royal absolutism on the one hand and a belief in witchcraft or a determination to punish it on the other. On the contrary, Filmer's commitment to absolutism might very well have inspired his demand for legal proof in witchcraft cases. The establishment of absolutism depended on the operation of a rational, clearly defined judicial system under central state supervision. Abuses in the system could only undermine the authority of the person or body that exercised sovereignty, which in 1653 was parliament. Parliament had in fact tried to stop the executions at Maidstone but could not save the lives of three of the accused.

Concern for the proper exercise of legal power in an absolutist state was more explicit in the writings of the Scottish jurist and lord advocate Sir George Mackenzie of Rosehaugh. Writing at the end of the seventeenth century, when Charles II and James VII were striving to establish absolutism in Scotland and England, Mackenzie defended royal absolutism in a series of treatises written between 1670 and his death in 1691.[44] In these works Mackenzie defended the institution of absolute monarchy not only on the basis of divine right and inherited patriarchal authority but also on historical grounds, claiming that the people had chosen to be ruled by an absolute monarch in the distant past.[45] Mackenzie's views on this issue conflicted with those of Andrew Fletcher of Saltoun and Gershom Carmichael, who insisted than Scotland had always been a limited monarchy. Mackenzie also argued that it was 'fit for the people that kings should be above the law ... for strict and rigid law is a greater tyrant than absolute monarchy'.[46]

As one of the members of the Scottish government during the restoration period, first as a justice from 1661 to 1677 and then as lord advocate from 1677 to 1686, Mackenzie tried to implement the style of absolutism he defended in print. His suppression of the covenanters for their resistance to Charles II's religious policy was so brutal that he became known as 'Bloody

Mackenzie'. His efforts to strengthen the state focused on making the judicial system more inquisitorial (by giving the lord advocate more discretion and by restricting the powers of juries) and establishing a clearly defined judicial hierarchy in which central judges controlled their subordinates. Mackenzie was proud of his efforts to make the law serve the purposes of royal absolutism. 'No advocate', he declared, 'has ever screwed the prerogative higher than I have.'[47]

With such strong absolutist credentials, one might assume that Mackenzie was a fervent witch-hunter. In one of his earliest assignments as a justice depute he did in fact try a number of witches in Midlothian and East Lothian during the great hunt of 1661–2. But after that experience, and most likely because of what he had witnessed during the trials, Mackenzie became a severe critic of witch-hunting. Like James VI, he never expressed scepticism regarding the reality of witchcraft, but he did insist that the crime of witchcraft was difficult to prove and required judges and juries to proceed with great caution in its prosecution. As an advocate Mackenzie demonstrated remarkable leniency and sympathy in dealing with witches. In one of his pleadings, which were published in 1672, he defended an accused witch, identified simply as Maevia. As lord advocate he was responsible for the acquittal of a number of witches, most notably Bessie Gibb in 1680, on the grounds that there was insufficient evidence against them.[48] Although he defended the legality of torture on the basis of the law of Scotland and the law of nations, he criticized its use in extracting confessions from those accused of witchcraft. In dealing with witches, Mackenzie the absolutist and state-builder, hated and feared by the covenanters for his repressive tactics, became the witches' advocate.

There was no inconsistency between Mackenzie's support for absolutism and his criticism of witch-hunting. Central to Mackenzie's concept of absolutism was royal power exercised by the king's appointed judges who decided cases on the basis of established standards of proof. His objection to witchcraft trials was that local authorities, whom he disparagingly referred to as 'country men', took the initiative in the prosecution, exercised the royal prerogative of torture without proper warrant, and conducted trials without the supervision of professional lawyers and judges. Witch-trials conducted in this manner deprived the sovereign of his obligation to provide justice to his subjects in accordance with due process. The only way to ensure the maintenance of due process was to have centrally appointed judges superintend the entire judicial system. Delegation of judicial powers to legally untrained local magistrates undermined the proper functioning of the state. One would struggle in vain to find in Mackenzie's writings or his policies any evidence of the connection between state-building, much less his style of royal absolutism, and witch-hunting.[49]

Reason of state and witch-hunting

The writings of Filmer and Mackenzie reflect a development in political theory identified by Wolfgang Behringer as Machiavellianism, a political doctrine that venerated the power of the state and tended to devalue religion unless it was instrumental to the ruler. Those who followed this line of thinking, first articulated by Niccolò Machiavelli in *The Prince* (1532) and developed more systematically by Thomas Hobbes in *Leviathan*, entailed a deep suspicion of religious enthusiasm and zealotry on the grounds that it threatened public order. For this reason Machiavellians were generally opposed to the activities of witch-hunters inspired by religious zeal. It was contrary to 'reason of state', the rationale absolutists use to justify their policies.[50]

This suspicion of religious enthusiasm is clearest in the works of Hobbes, who disliked all forms of clericalism, especially that of English presbyterians during the civil war. It is also evident in the activities and writings of Mackenzie, who persecuted covenanters (whom he considered to be traitors and rebels) while treating the witches accused by covenanters much more leniently. Mackenzie appealed to reason of state to justify his policies. 'Necessity of state', wrote Mackenzie in 1691, 'is that super-eminent law to which upon occasion all particular acts must bow.'[51] Filmer's criticism of the puritan magistrates at Maidstone reflected a similar concern with the maintenance of order in the state. All three of these absolutists demanded adherence to strict legal procedure and the subjection of inferior magistrates to the king. Their demand for due process in witch-hunting, like their opposition to religious enthusiasm, reflected a concern for upholding the king's authority.

The concerns of Hobbes, Mackenzie, and Filmer had a precedent in the decision of the Scottish privy council in 1597, when it recalled some of the commissions of justiciary after witch-hunting had spun out of control. At various times in the late sixteenth and seventeenth centuries the privy council succumbed to the entreaties of the kirk and the more zealous members of the council to root out witches and other sinners as part of a campaign to establish a godly state. On each occasion, however, they learned the same lesson as many continental political authorities did after they had authorized witch-hunts: that whatever political benefits might accrue from taking a lead in the war against Satan, the social disruption caused by witch-hunting was far more deleterious to the body politic and ultimately to the ruler. Even James VI, who had personal reasons to hunt witches and equated witchcraft with treason, learned that lesson when he moved to England in 1603. James, whose theoretical absolutism was unmatched by any other English monarch, did much more to limit witch-hunting in his southern kingdom than to promote it. Perhaps even he had come to the realization that his endorsement of witch-hunting in the 1590s in Scotland was counterproductive.

7 Demonic possession and witch-hunting in Scotland

In August 1696 Christian Shaw, the 11-year-old daughter of the laird of Bargarran, in the parish of Erskine, Renfrewshire, began to experience fits and bodily contortions, her body became stiff and motionless, and her tongue protruded at great length. She experienced temporary deafness, blindness, and an inability to speak. She regurgitated hair, straw, coal cinders the size of chestnuts, gravel, pins, feathers of wild fowl and bones of various sorts. At times her head twisted around, as if her neck bone had been dissolved. Her stomach 'swelled like a drum, as like a woman with child'.[1] At times she had difficulty breathing and felt as if she was being choked. During some of her fits she took off all her clothes. Witnesses claimed that on a number of occasions she was carried through her house 'with such a swift and unaccountable motion that it was not in the power of any to prevent her – her feet not touching the ground'.[2] She also conversed with invisible spectres.

After the local physician and apothecary failed to identify a natural cause for Christian's maladies, the members of the family and the local minister reached the conclusion that her afflictions were caused by witchcraft. Christian herself confirmed their suspicions. While experiencing her fits, the young girl accused Katherine Campbell, one of the maids in the house, and Agnes Nasmith, described by her neighbours as 'an old widow woman, ignorant, and of a malicious disposition, addicted to threatenings', of having caused her suffering.[3] Christian later added others to the list of accused culprits.

Since Christian Shaw's afflictions had led to accusations of witchcraft, local authorities brought the matter to the attention of the privy council, which commissioned Lord Blantyre and eight other members of the local elite to interrogate and imprison those suspected of witchcraft and to examine witnesses. In taking this step the council was proceeding more cautiously than in 1662, when they granted commissions to try witches almost routinely in response to petitions from local authorities. Recognizing that justice had not been served in 1662, they demanded more evidence of culpability before authorizing a witchcraft trial. Unfortunately, however, the privy council was not able to conduct the investigation itself. It still needed to rely on local authorities to conduct the investigation.

A judicial inquiry of this sort was likely to find incriminating evidence, and the men assigned this task did not disappoint. During the proceedings three of the accused witches – Elizabeth Anderson (aged 17), James Lindsay (aged 14), and Thomas Lindsay (a minor), all grandchildren of Jean Fulton – confessed and named 21 others who had allegedly gathered with them and the devil. The commissioners arranged for a pricker to search all those who had been named, and he found the devil's marks on most of them. One of the few suspects who passed this humiliating test was Martha Semple, the 18-year-old daughter of Margaret Lang, who was stripped and searched twice in the presence of six men. One observer reported that Semple was the only accused witch who had wept during her interrogation.[4]

The examinations conducted in February led to the drafting of articles against all 24 accused witches. On the basis of these depositions the privy council issued a new commission of justiciary on 9 March to try seven of these individuals. The narrowing of the list of suspects reflected a more discriminating evaluation of the evidence than the council had demonstrated in the past, but this body still decided to delegate responsibility for the trial to an even larger group of commissioners. Before the assize was constituted, the commissioners conducted further pricking of the suspects and made efforts to secure their confessions. During a delay in the proceedings requested by the advocates of the accused, three more witches confessed, although one of them was found strangled in prison. This apparent suicide was attributed to the devil, since the man 'was found sitting in a chair with a cord around his neck, but slack and tied to nothing'.[5] The trial finally commenced on 5 May, and all seven of the accused were convicted and executed at Paisley.[6]

Two years after the Paisley trial, another two young girls who lived near Shaw, Margaret Murdoch and Margaret Laird, accused more than 20 persons of causing them physical harm by means of witchcraft.[7] The two girls experienced many of the same physical symptoms as Christian Shaw. Witnesses claimed that Margaret Murdoch's body stretched back like a bow, while her neck, legs, and arms became so stiff that they could not be moved. Observers reported that when her legs were wrapped around a chair, they could not be separated without breaking. She vomited up pins, straw, hair, wool, rags, and feathers after her mouth had been searched to see if she had been concealing the substances. Her body showed signs of having been pinched and pricked, and one witness said that her flesh was blistered and burnt as if it had been seared by a hot iron. Her mouth was opened 'beyond measure' and her tongue drawn out 'to the tail of her chin'. She sat naked during some of her fits, and sometimes her arms were extended and positioned in such a way that people could not dress her without breaking her bones.[8]

Margaret Laird allegedly experienced many of the same symptoms as Murdoch and Shaw. She fell into a fainting fit and then a deaf fit, and when she recovered she cried out but was unable to speak. Thomas Brown, the minister at Paisley, described her torments as 'preternatural'. She was so badly contorted that three or four people could not hold her using all their power, while her throat swelled so much that attendants had to loosen her clothes. She claimed that the reason for that swelling was that one of her tormentors was pushing a button down her throat. Her hand also became swollen, and her arm became black from the finger ends to the elbow. During some of her fits she declared that the devil was beside her in a chain.[9]

Murdoch and Laird named several tormentors, and when these accused witches were brought into their presence the two girls fell into fits. The charge that they had been harmed by means of witchcraft led to a request to the privy council to authorize the precognition of witnesses, which took place at Paisley and Glasgow in April 1699. These precognitions, which came from a total of 91 witnesses, identified more than 20 suspected witches, many of whom were accused of causing Murdoch's and Laird's fits. Some of those who were accused had been suspected of witchcraft before they were named as the source of the two girls' afflictions. This suggests that the residents of the area were taking this opportunity to implicate individuals long suspected of witchcraft but never prosecuted. Their names might very well have been suggested to Murdoch and Laird while they were in their fits, so that they might identify them as their tormentors.

One of the many connections between the prosecutions of the witches named by Christian Shaw in 1697 and the investigations conducted in 1699 was that Sir John Maxwell of Pollok, one of the commissioners who had investigated and tried the persons accused of causing the possession of Christian Shaw, took the lead in the proceedings at Paisley and Glasgow two years later. Maxwell, the son of a famous victim of witchcraft in 1678, was not as successful in 1699 as he had been with the Paisley witches two years before. In this case the privy council did not find the evidence sufficient for a trial and therefore denied his request for a commission of justiciary.[10] The likely explanation for the council's refusal was mounting scepticism regarding the guilt of accused witches, especially in cases of demonic possession.

The prosecution of the Paisley witches in 1697 and the west country witches in 1699 marked the first times in Scottish history that witches were tried for having caused the demonic possession of their alleged victims. In this respect Scotland had lagged far behind England and the rest of Europe. By 1603 England had experienced no fewer than seven widely publicized cases of possession that had led to witchcraft trials, including that of the Throckmorton children in 1593 and Mary Glover in 1602. In the duchy of Savoy cases of demonic possession had become so common by the beginning of the seventeenth century that the Burgundian demonologist Henri Boguet observed that 'every day [the duchy] sends us a countless number of persons possessed of demons which, on being exorcised, say that they have been sent by witches'.[11] To illustrate the importance of demonic possession in witch-hunting, Boguet began his discourse on witchcraft with a discussion of the charges against Françoise Secretain for having used witchcraft to cause the possession of an 8-year-old girl.[12] In France the possession of Madeleine

Demandols de la Palud and other nuns in an Ursuline convent in Aix-en-Provence in 1611 had led to the execution of Father Louis Gaufridi, a parish priest in Marseilles, for having caused their possession by witchcraft.[13] In an even more notorious case of witchcraft and possession Urbain Grandier, also a parish priest, was executed in 1634 for causing the possession of a group of Ursuline nuns in a convent at Loudun.[14] Between 1627 and 1631 the parish of Mattaincourt in Lorraine was home to no fewer than 85 possessed women and children, and these too had led to witchcraft trials.[15] In the German university town of Paderborn a wave of possessions and exorcisms between 1656 and 1659 led to a witch-hunt that resulted in about 50 executions,[16] while in 1692 a large witch-hunt began in Salem, Massachusetts, when a group of young girls had fits and convulsions that were interpreted as signs of possession.[17]

Theories and interpretations of possession

In Christian demonology possession was the phenomenon in which demons invaded the body of a human being and gained control of the person's movements and behaviour. The victims of this demonic invasion, often referred to as demoniacs, displayed a variety of symptoms, the most common being bodily contortions so severe that their legs could not be uncrossed or their arms straightened without breaking them. Other physical symptoms included uncontrollable fits, skin lesions, turning one's head 180 degrees, demonstration of supernatural strength, vomiting of alien objects, temporary blindness and deafness, and levitation. The changes in personality and behaviour that demoniacs displayed were apparently just as dramatic and unnatural as the changes in their bodies. Demoniacs reportedly spoke in deep, gruff voices, uttered blasphemies and obscenities, spoke in languages they never had learned, cursed and disobeyed their superiors, and revealed remarkable clairvoyance and knowledge of hidden objects. Demoniacs rarely manifested all these symptoms, but when some of them made their appearance, as in the cases of Christian Shaw, Margaret Laird, and Margaret Murdoch, there was little doubt that a demon had entered their bodies.

Possession did not require the agency of a witch. Demonologists held that the devil could, with God's permission, take possession of a human being's body by his own power. The English physician John Cotta, writing in the early seventeenth century, used biblical evidence to illustrate this possibility. Many of the possessions recorded in the gospels, wrote Cotta, were 'works of the devil by himself, solely wrought without the association of man'.[18] The same was true for some of the possessions in Cotta's day. A number of narratives published in Germany during the early modern period detailed assaults of demons on young men and women but did not attribute these attacks to witchcraft.[19] In similar fashion, many of the cases of demonic possession that occurred in seventeenth-century French convents did not lead to accusations of witchcraft, as they had in the cases of Urbain Grandier and Louis Gaufridi.[20] In Russia women known as shriekers howled, screamed, convulsed, and tore off their clothes, leading their neighbours to claim that they were possessed by devils, but neither the shriekers nor the neighbours used this occasion to start a witch-hunt.[21]

Most cases of demonic possession that occurred in seventeenth-century England and Scotland did not fall into this category. Rather they were, in Cotta's words, the 'works done by the devil with respect unto the covenant with man'.[22] The claim that witches were responsible for causing demonic possession became so common in early modern England that the word possession became the equivalent of bewitchment.[23] In these Scottish and English cases the demoniac's afflictions were considered to be *maleficia*, the acts of harmful magic that witches allegedly performed. Dr Thomas Oakes, a physician called in to examine a group of possessed children in Boston, Massachusetts, in 1688, interpreted the distempers of his patients in this way when he concluded that 'nothing but an hellish witchcraft could be the original of these maladies'.[24]

The victims of possession, unlike the witches who allegedly ordered demons to enter their bodies, were usually not considered legally responsible for their afflictions. Since the devil's entrance into their bodies was involuntary, they could not be held legally culpable for actions, which often included unconventional, rebellious, or immoral behaviour. Demoniacs could, however, be considered *morally* responsible for their possession. The reason for this is that possession was often considered to be a punishment for one's sins.[25] In early modern possessions this distinction between demoniac and witch occasionally became blurred.[26] Madeleine Bavent, one of the nuns believed to have been possessed at Louviers, Normandy, in the 1640s, was accused of practising sorcery, attending sabbaths, and copulating with devils. In Lutheran Germany some demoniacs were reported to have made pacts with the devil,[27] while in puritan New England a fear arose that demoniacs, if not dispossessed, would themselves become witches.[28] In Sweden two female demoniacs were accused of blasphemy before the king's council in 1690 and 1708 respectively 'for having let Satan take their body in possession'.[29]

Cases of possession, whether or not they were attributed to witchcraft, have caused major problems of interpretation. When scholars study cases of demonic possession, they often try to discover what was *really* going on. Dismissing the possibility that these afflicted people might have been actually possessed by demons, they usually offer one of two explanations. The first is that the demoniacs were impostors, who faked the symptoms of possession in order to bring attention to themselves, use the excuse that they were under the devil's influence to violate established social and moral norms, or retaliate against enemies by accusing them of witchcraft.[30] The other explanation is that the demoniacs were afflicted by some kind of disease or mental illness, such as hysteria or schizophrenia. Some psychologists choose to interpret the apparent presence of an alien spirit in a person's body and that spirit's control of the person's speech and behaviour as manifestations of a multiple personality disorder.[31]

Scholars studying the case of Christian Shaw have usually followed one of these approaches. The charge that she was the 'Bargarran impostor', who deliberately swallowed the objects she regurgitated, originated in the eighteenth century and is still widely held today.[32] The medical interpretation of what was *really* bothering Christian has been just as durable; Christian has been posthumously diagnosed as having been afflicted by a conversion disorder, a trance disorder, a transient psychotic disorder, or childhood epilepsy.[33]

These interpretations of possession may have some validity, but they cannot provide an adequate historical explanation of demoniacs' behaviour. Christian Shaw may have been faking some of her symptoms, and she also may have been afflicted by some sort of medical disorder, but she was also conforming to widely acknowledged norms of demoniacal behaviour.[34] Demoniacs in all societies act the way in which their religious culture tells them they should act. Either consciously or unconsciously they learn how to act like possessed persons. Just like the French demoniac Marthe Brossier, who in 1599 modelled her behaviour on that of Nicole Obry at Laon in 1566, and just like Anne Gunter, who imitated the convulsions of the possessed Throckmorton children in 1593, Christian Shaw was following a script encoded in seventeenth-century religious life. She learned this script either by reading about other possessions (something many demoniacs did) or through instruction from her parents and ministers. Parts of that script came from the narratives of the Salem cases of possession that were circulating widely in Scotland at the time. Whether ill or not, whether duplicitous or not, Christian was playing her appointed role in a religious drama of the utmost importance to those around her.

In Christian Shaw's case the script was distinctly Calvinist, in that it required that as part of her ordeal she struggle against the temptation, presented by the demons who possessed her, to become a witch herself. This as we have seen was a challenge facing demoniacs in other Protestant and especially Calvinist communities, where the determination whether one was a member of the elect was of the utmost importance. Christian Shaw grew up in a community where piety was defined in terms of election and salvation. Her possession might very well have been the result of a conversion experience that had gone bad.[35] In any case, the narrative of her possession indicates that she withstood these temptations to fall into witchcraft; she refused to renounce her baptism and attend the devil's meetings. According to a letter written by her mother, Christian told the devil on his second appearance to her, 'Thou thinkst to make me a witch, but through God's strength thou shalt never be the better; I charge thee in the name of God to be gone.'[36] This report of the girl's edifying struggle against Satanic temptation, made possible by God's freely granted grace, served as a statement of her own personal, Protestant version of exorcism – a ritualized combat or spiritual warfare that resulted in her dispossession.

Once the narrative of Christian Shaw's possession and dispossession had circulated, it served as a model for the other cases of possession that surfaced in Scotland in the years following the execution of the Paisley witches. The possessions of Margaret Murdoch and Margaret Laird, who lived in the same vicinity as Shaw and therefore probably knew about her possession from oral if not written sources, exhibited many of the same symptoms that Shaw had manifested. Just like Shaw, Murdoch also claimed to have been tempted by the devil to become a witch herself. She testified that the devil came to her with a piece of silver in one side of his mouth and a piece of paper in the other. When Janet Robison, one of the accused witches, asked her to subscribe to the paper, she refused.[37]

Five years after the west county witch-hunt of 1699, the narrative of Christian Shaw's possession provided a script for yet another Scottish possession, which triggered the last Scottish effort to blame witches for sending demons into the body of another human being. The case originated in the fits and convulsions experienced by a 16-year-old blacksmith apprentice, Patrick Morton, in the fishing village and port town of Pittenweem in Fife. Morton's symptoms closely resembled those of Shaw, Murdoch, and Laird. When Morton named a number of witches as the cause of his convulsions, he set off a witch-hunt that led to the imprisonment of seven persons for causing his possession. This witch-hunt, which ended with the release of five of the accused, the death of a sixth (the only man accused) in prison, and the murder of the seventh, will be the subject of Chapter 9. It is important to note here, however, that the reason why Morton's symptoms resembled those of Christian Shaw is that the minister of Pittenweem, Mr Patrick Cowper, had actually read an account of Christian Shaw's possession to Morton when he started falling into his fits.[38] The account of Christian Shaw's possession, therefore, provided a script for demoniacs to follow not only in the west country but also in an eastern Scottish shire that had a history of intense witch-hunting.

The strange history of Scottish possession

Although the devil was certainly a prominent part of Scottish theology and spiritual life during the early modern period, the record of demonic possession in Scotland before Christian Shaw experienced her convulsions and vomiting is threadbare. The narratives of possessions that appear so frequently in France, Germany, and England in the late sixteenth and seventeenth centuries are not found in Scotland until the 1690s. Even more striking, the records of Scottish witchcraft prosecutions offer only one instance of a witch causing the possession of another human being before 1697.[39]

How do we explain the near absence of demonic possession in Scotland during the period from roughly 1590, the beginning of intense witch-hunting, until the mid-1690s, when witchcraft prosecutions were otherwise in a state of decline? Neither Protestantism nor Calvinism can by itself supply the answer. Protestants, no less than Catholics, accepted the possibility and reality of demonic possession. Possession did, after all, have a firm foundation in scripture, the touchstone of Protestant belief. Christ had exorcized a number of demoniacs, and these dispossessions had given rise to charges by his opponents that he drove them out by the power of Beelzebub, the ruler of the demons.[40] All the leaders of the Reformation accepted the reality of possession. At times it was uncertain whether they were considering possession to be spiritual rather than corporal, such as when Melanchthon declared it 'most certain that devils enter into the hearts of some men and cause frenzy and torment in them'.[41] The same ambiguity can be found in Luther's writings, but we do know that Luther once attempted an exorcism himself.[42] Calvin rejected the rite of exorcism as a papal relic, arguing further that the age of miracles had passed, but he did not, as the Jesuit Louis Richeome claimed, deny the reality of possession or the possibility of dispossession.[43]

Protestant demonologists, just like their Catholic counterparts, found a respectable place for possession in their treatises. Certainly King James VI of Scotland – a good Calvinist – had no problem with the reality of possession, which he discussed in his treatise on witchcraft, *Daemonologie*.[44] Even Johann Weyer, the great sixteenth-century sceptic regarding witchcraft, acknowledged the reality of possession. Weyer, whose Protestantism was never in doubt, was far more credulous of reported cases of possession than of allegations of witchcraft. He argued, for instance, that the affliction of nuns in a convent at Wertet in the Spanish Netherlands 1550 should not be attributed to the activity of witches but to direct possession by the devil.[45] One must look ahead more than a century, to the publication of the Dutchman Balthasar Bekker's sceptical *The World Bewitched* in 1691, to see how a Calvinist minister could use biblical scholarship to undermine the belief in demonic possession as well as witchcraft.[46]

Protestant countries, no less than those that were Catholic, witnessed numerous instances of possession in the late sixteenth and early seventeenth centuries. In the northern Lutheran territories of Germany there were actually more reported cases of possessions than in the southern Catholic regions.[47] In the towns of southeastern France and Switzerland, Protestant as well as Catholic communities often attributed demonic possession to witchcraft. In the late sixteenth and early seventeenth centuries the staunchly Calvinist republic of Geneva prosecuted numerous witches for allegedly causing the demonic possession of their victims.[48] And as we shall see, most possession cases in the late seventeenth century came from Calvinist communities in New England, England, the Dutch Republic, and Scotland.

One key to solving this enigma lies in the attitude of James VI towards this phenomenon. As discussed in Chapter 3, James admitted the possibility of possession in his *Daemonologie*, but he denied the possibility that anyone could drive out the invasive spirit unless they followed the traditional Protestant methods of prayer and fasting. In taking this position he not only discredited the public exorcisms that priests had performed in France, most notably at Laon in 1566 and Soissons in 1582, but also implied that the possessions that had been the occasion of those exorcisms were also counterfeit. His comment that the symptoms of possession in those Catholic cases of possession were 'vain' served the same purpose.[49] As we have seen, James said nothing about instances of possession in Scotland, with the exception of a passing reference to a young girl as having been troubled by a spirit.[50] The *Daemonologie*, which became the foundational text of Scottish witchcraft, provided no specific instances of the phenomenon.

At the same time Scots learned that fraudulent possessions were not restricted to Catholic countries. In the years before and after James acceded to the English throne, English churchmen, most notably Richard Bancroft and Samuel Harsnett, uncovered a number of fraudulent possessions that puritan ministers had exploited for purposes of religious propaganda, and in 1605 James himself helped them prove that the Berkshire demoniac, Anne Gunter, also had faked her possessions.[51] Well might James's councillors and churchmen in Scotland have concluded that reports of *no* possessions – Catholic or Protestant, French, English, or even Scottish – could be trusted.[52]

There is fragmentary evidence that Scottish authorities did in fact treat reports of possession in their own country with caution during the 1620s. The evidence comes from John Maitland, the second earl of Lauderdale, during the middle decades of the seventeenth century. Corresponding with the English presbyterian Richard Baxter in 1659 regarding the possessions at Loudun, Lauderdale warned against excessive scepticism regarding witchcraft, demonic possession, and the existence of spirits. Lauderdale attributed this scepticism, which he labelled sadducean and atheistic, to the impostures of Roman Catholic exorcisms, the extreme credulousness of those who attributed everything to witchcraft, and the over-eagerness of judges and juries to convict people of witchcraft.[53]

In order to prove the existence of spirits, Lauderdale recounted the case of a possessed woman who lived in the town of Duns in Berwickshire, when he was a boy, in the late 1620s. Lauderdale's father and the local minister, Mr John Weems, were both convinced that this woman, unlike the nuns at Loudun, was genuinely possessed. To validate this claim, Lauderdale's father and Weems, together with a knight by the name of Forbes[54] and an unnamed minister from the north, went to visit the woman, whom Lauderdale described as a poor, ignorant creature. When Weems spoke to Forbes in Latin, saying, 'Nondum audivimus spiritum loquentem' (Now we will hear the spirit speaking), the demoniac, identified by other sources as Margaret Lumsden, said 'Audis loquentem' (You hear him speaking). The minister, amazed at this response, said 'Miseratur Deus peccatoris' (God have mercy on sinners), to which Lumsden responded, 'Die peccatricis, die peccatricis' (The day of the sinner).[55] Lauderdale was persuaded of the genuineness of this possession because the woman's linguistic facility, such as it was, was not displayed during a public exorcism, as often happened in the large public dispossessions in France.

Lauderdale complained to Baxter that Scottish authorities had given no credence to this woman's possession. When Weems had asked the privy council to declare days of humiliation to relieve her of her suffering, the council brought Lumsden, her mother, and her father-in-law to Edinburgh for examination, and then denied the request.[56] According to Lauderdale, who in 1659 was still a covenanter, the reason for this refusal was that the bishops were then in power and would not allow any fasts to be kept. It is more likely that upon examination the council concluded that Lumsford was faking her possession, just like all those French nuns and English children. Either way, we might conclude that the reason for the low incidence of demonic possession in Scotland during this period was the failure of secular and ecclesiastical authorities to take such reports of possession seriously.[57]

One might suspect that the replacement of those authorities by men who were more committed to doing battle against Satan during the revolutionary decades of the mid-century would have created a climate of opinion more receptive to claims that the devil was taking possession of the bodies of Scottish subjects. As we have seen, the covenanters, who dominated the Scottish church and state from 1638 to 1651, were more credulous of witchcraft and more eager to prosecute those accused of this sin and crime than their predecessors during the 1620s and 1630s. The records of those prosecutions, however, yield no instances of witches having been accused of causing possession. Witches were accused of various *maleficia* during those years, as well as making pacts with the devil and having sex with him, but none of them were charged with commanding him to enter the bodies of other Scots and controlling their bodily movements and behaviour.

One possible explanation for the absence of demonic possession in a world filled with demons comes from the report of a Roman Catholic priest, William Ballentine, to his superiors in Rome about 1660. Ballentine had served on the Roman Catholic mission in Scotland for 12 years and his report, while obviously biased, was well informed. The subject of demonic possession comes up in Ballentine's discussion of the failure of Scottish ministers to give consolation to sinners. The prefect reports that Scottish Protestant ministers, unlike Catholics priests who provide solace through the sacrament of confession, tell such people that their only hope of salvation lay in a public confession of their sins. This, according to Ballentine, led many of these troubled souls to commit suicide rather than to subject themselves to 'public disgrace'.[58]

Ballentine then gives the example of three women troubled in conscience, two of whom 'had been falsely persuaded that they were possessed by the devil'. Having gone to the minister for consolation, they were told that their only hope lay in 'a public manifestation of their whole life story'. All three women were at the point of suicide, when some of their friends brought them to Catholic households regularly visited by Catholic priests. Predictably, this gave them peace of mind and they recovered from their suicidal despair.[59]

These brief comments suggest that the reason for the absence of cases of possession in Scotland during these years was that Scottish ministers viewed possession as a sign of moral failure that prevented the victims from accusing others of causing their afflictions. The problem, according to orthodox Calvinist ministers, lay in the demoniacs themselves. We have seen that there was a tendency in Protestant thought to assign moral responsibility to demoniacs, suggesting not only that their possession was punishment for their sins but also that they stood in danger of becoming witches themselves. As long as this belief in the moral weakness of demoniacs persisted, it was unlikely that demoniacs would risk exposing themselves to disgrace in an attempt to shift blame for their torments to witches. It was not until ministers could construct a different interpretation of possession, in which a pious demoniac like Christian Shaw could successfully resist the temptation to become a witch herself, that cases of possession could be publicized and used to inspire the prosecution of witches.

Possession and the existence of spirits

The turning point in the history of demonic possession in Scotland came in the late seventeenth century, when instances of demonic possession became the persuasive pieces of evidence in a major theological and philosophical effort to prove the existence of spirits. This enterprise, which became the main focus of late seventeenth-century British demonology,[60] made Scottish presbyterian ministers and laymen eager to find evidence of Satan's activities on earth, which they found in the afflictions of Christian Shaw, Margaret Laird, and Margaret Murdoch.

The British discourse on the existence of spirits can be traced back to the late sixteenth century, when Reginald Scot was accused of denying their existence and when King James VI attacked Scot and others on the grounds that they were sadducees, named after the members of a Jewish sect active in Judaea from *c.*200 BCE until 70 CE who denied the existence of spirits and the immortality of the soul.[61] The controversy intensified in the 1680s with the publication of *Saducismus Triumphatus* by the English cleric Joseph Glanvill, who was a member of the Royal Society, and *Satan's Invisible World Discovered* by George Sinclair, the Scottish natural philosopher from the University of Glasgow.[62] Both works, in an effort to provide empirical evidence for the existence of spirits, recounted stories about witchcraft, apparitions, poltergeists, and other preternatural phenomena in order to counter the claims of the seventeenth-century sadducees.[63] Ultimately they were designed to prove the existence of God, for if one did not believe in spirits, the belief in God would likewise vanish. As Henry More, one of Glanvill's allies, put it: 'No spirit, no God'.[64]

The battle between the sadducees and their opponents entered a new phase in 1691 when Richard Baxter, the English minister who had corresponded with Lauderdale regarding demonic possession, published *The Certainty of the Worlds of Spirits*. Baxter's entrance into the debate was significant for the purposes of this discussion because he used many more instances of demonic possession than either Glanvill or Sinclair to prove the existence of spirits. Glanvill and Sinclair had emphasized poltergeists, ghost stories, and especially reports of witchcraft. Baxter, however, turned the reader's attention to possession, including Lauderdale's story and countless similar episodes throughout Europe. These included the story of Mary Hill, an 18-year-old girl from Beckington who vomited up no fewer than 200 pins and whose tongue swelled out of her mouth; a woman believed to be hysterical until she vomited long crooked nails, brass needles, and lumps of hair and meat; a 15-year-old girl from Louvain who in 1571 vomited 24 pounds of liquid a day, followed by the dung of geese and doves, hair, coal and stones; and the demoniac reported by Sebastian Brand who in one year reportedly vomited enough blood to fill 400 chamber pots. Baxter also made mention of Cotton Mather's recently published apocalyptic book, *Memorable Providences Relating to Witchcrafts and Possessions* (1689), which presented an account of the possession of the Goodwin children in Boston. One of the children had been 'visited with strange fits, beyond those that attend an epilepsy'. Their tongues were reported to have 'drawn down their throats' or 'pulled out upon their chins to a prodigious length'. 'Sometimes they would be deaf, sometimes dumb, and sometimes blind, and often all this at once.'[65] Mather interpreted these and other possessions as signs that the rule of Satan was in its final days and the Second Coming was imminent, a theme that Stuart Clark has shown to be central to contemporary accounts of demonic possession.[66]

From a polemical point of view, the attention given by Baxter to possession was a deft move. Demonic possession provided much more certain proof of the existence of spirits than either witchcraft or poltergeists, because in possessions one could actually hear the devil speak and witness the bodily movements he controlled. Baxter's book also had the effect of giving the debate over the existence of spirits a denominational character. During the 1690s, as the controversy over spirits intensified, the anti-sadducees – those who accepted the reality of possessions and witchcraft – tended increasingly to be English dissenters, New England puritans, and Scottish presbyterians.

During the 1690s there were plenty of new narratives that the anti-sadducees could use to bolster their position. First there was the episode of possession at Salem, which had led to the execution of 19 persons for witchcraft in 1692. The first narrative of the case by Deodat Lawson appeared in that year, and it was followed by Cotton Mather's *Wonders of the Invisible World*.[67] Then there was the case of the 'Surey demoniac', Richard Dugdale, a teenage gardener from Lancashire who began to experience fits in 1689 and who testified to the reality of his own possession in 1695. Dugdale's affliction became the subject of a major controversy which peaked in 1697 with the publication of a narrative of his possession, urged by the 'believers of Satan's activating men's bodies by possession, witchcrafts, etc. ... as a very likely expedient for rooting out atheism, debauchery, sadducism, and devilishness'.[68] This pamphlet elicited a sadducean rejoinder from Zachary Taylor, *The Surry Impostor*, taking the position that the whole thing was a hoax.[69]

It is important to appreciate the fact that the possession of Christian Shaw occurred in the midst of this controversy and that it was immediately seen as evidence of the anti-sadducean, presbyterian position. No sooner had the Paisley witches been executed than a number of pamphlets describing the case began to appear, including an anonymous account, *A True Narrative of the Sufferings and Relief of a Young Girle*, published in Edinburgh in 1698. This work has been attributed to Francis Grant, later Lord Cullen, the lawyer who prosecuted the Paisley witches, with the assistance of John MacGilchrist, a Glasgow solicitor who was Christian's uncle.[70] The polemical purpose of *A True Narrative* was clearly indicated in the preface, which used Shaw's possession to affirm the existence of God. Its purpose is also revealed by the title of the London edition of this work, *Saducismus Debellatus* (Sadducism Conquered).[71]

Another anonymous pamphlet, *Witch-Craft Proven*, published at Glasgow in 1697, served the same polemical purpose as *A True Narrative*. This highly credulous work, erroneously attributed to John Bell, makes no specific reference to the Paisley trials, but the place and date of publication and its professed purpose to prove the existence of spirits leave no doubt regarding its inspiration.[72] The author starts by painting a grim picture of a world in which spirits do not exist: 'For if there be no spirits then ... there is no eternal death, life, nor resurrection to be to be expected, nor any local place of punishment for the damned to be tormented in ... nor any heavenly joy and solace to be expected by the truly godly after this life'.[73] He then cites the presence of witches in all ages as evidence for the existence of wicked spirits, and those 'who are in covenant and league with them'.[74]

The publication of *A True Narrative* in 1698 linked Shaw's possessions to others that were reported in the same year, most notably that of Sarah Fowles, an English woman from Hammersmith, who in 1698 claimed to be possessed by the devil and was accused in print of being an impostor.[75] *A True Narrative* also linked Shaw's possession to a case in County Antrim, Ireland, in 1698, described in a pamphlet published in the following year.[76] Antrim, the Irish county closest to Scotland, is located in the Northern Irish province of Ulster. After the flight of the Catholic Irish earls in 1607 James VI superintended the settlement of the plantation of Ulster by Scottish presbyterians and English Anglicans. The county's predominantly Protestant population was therefore divided between the two denominations. This case, as well as the prosecution of a 'Scotch girl' by the kirk in Antrim for charming about the same time, was undertaken by the Irish of Scottish descent, and that community was responsible for the county's reputation for witchcraft. The presbyterians of County Antrim therefore belonged to a British Calvinist network that united presbyterians in Scotland, Protestant dissenters in England, congregationalists in New England, and Scottish presbyterians in Ulster. These 'British' Calvinists shared similar witch beliefs, a similar determination to prosecute witches vigorously when witch-trials were coming to an end, and a widespread belief that during the final days leading up to the Second Coming the devil was assaulting good Christians in various ways, including taking possession of their bodies.

In the Irish possession case reported in the pamphlet, a girl of 19, 'inferior to none in the place for beauty, education and birth', innocently swallowed a leaf of sorrel, which she had received from a beggar after giving the woman bread and beer. Upon swallowing the leaf she began to experience convulsions, and after the doctors had given her remedies to no avail and the minister had laid hands on her, she began to roll about in fits and vomit horse dung, needles, pins, feathers, pieces of glass, nails, eggs, an iron knife and fish shells. Whenever the suspected witch came within a few yards of the girl's house, her symptoms became worse. The witch was arrested, condemned, strangled, and burnt, a mode of punishment reflecting the religious nature of the witch's crime in this Protestant Irish county, just as in Scotland.[77]

In Scotland the narrative of Christian Shaw's possession also provided a script for the possessions of Margaret Laird and Margaret Murdoch in the west country in 1699 and that of Patrick Morton at Pittenweem in 1704. Not surprisingly, the author of one of the published accounts of the Pittenweem witchcraft trials not only compared Morton's affliction to that of Christian Shaw but also put the episode to the same theological use, 'for proving the existence of good and evil spirits'. The same author claimed that there were thousands of witnesses to the influence of evil spirits 'on both hemispheres'.[78]

Seen in this theological and philosophical context, the sudden and belated appearance of cases of possession in Scotland at the end of the 1690s and the first prosecutions of witches for causing demonic possession in Scottish history begin to make sense. In the late 1690s the debate over the existence of spirits, reinforced by a growing belief in Scotland that the Second Coming was near, created a determination among Protestant ministers and pious laymen to look for evidence of Satan's activities on earth. They found it in the demonic possession of Christian Shaw and her imitators. The recent ecclesiastical changes that had occurred in the wake of the Glorious Revolution, which abolished episcopacy once again and established the presbyterian church by law, gave them unprecedented confidence that such possessions would not be ignored or dismissed, as had happened with the possession of Margaret Lumsden in 1629. The decision by the Scottish government to proceed with the prosecution of the student Thomas Aikenhead for blasphemy and atheism in 1696, to the horror of all religious moderates and most English observers, gave them further cause for hope that latter-day sadducees would not succeed in sapping Scottish society of its Christian vitality.[79]

Possession and judicial caution

Cases of demonic possession could have two very different effects on witch-hunting. On the one hand, the accusations, coming from individuals whose suffering was readily apparent, could confirm the reality of demonic power in the world and inspire legal action against the witches who were the alleged cause of the demoniacs' afflictions. This positive impact on witch-hunting usually occurred when cases of demonic possession were something of a novelty in a region. Thus the possessions of the five children of Robert Throckmorton in Huntingdonshire, which was one of the first possessions in England attributed to witchcraft, contributed to the intensification of witch-hunting during the 1590s. In similar fashion, the first case of demonic possession attributed to witchcraft in New England, that of the Goodwin children in Boston in 1688, not only resulted in the execution of an Irish laundress for bewitching the children but also set the stage for New England's largest witch-hunt four years later.

On the other hand, cases of possession, especially those that occurred after many similar cases had been reported, could lead to greater caution in the handing of witchcraft prosecutions. The disclosing of counterfeit possessions, the recognition that the symptoms of possession might have had natural causes, and the realization that the devil was unlikely to obey the command of a witch all contributed to a decline in witch-hunting. As we have seen, the acquittal of the two witches accused by the demoniac Anne Gunter at Abingdon in 1605 marked a turning point in the history of English witch-hunting. Scepticism regarding the authenticity of numerous possessions in France contributed to the reluctance of the parlement of Paris to prosecute witches in the early seventeenth century.[80] In New England the change in judicial attitude came during the Salem trials, when the clergy and the judges realized that they could not trust the claims that the afflicted girls could see the spectres of the witches who were afflicting them. Shortly thereafter witch-hunting in New England came to an end.

The judicial response to the cases of Scottish demonic possession in the late seventeenth and early eighteenth centuries reveals a similar growth of judicial caution. The first case of possession linked to witchcraft, that of Christian Shaw, resulted in the execution of seven people at Paisley in 1697. It appeared, therefore, that the new phenomenon of demonic possession would lead to a renewed intensification of Scottish witch-hunting, even at this late date. At the same time, however, the privy council's refusal to authorize the prosecution of a number of witches named in this witch-hunt indicates that they considered some of the evidence taken in the precognition of witnesses to be unsatisfactory.

Scepticism in the wake of the Paisley trials also found expression in a letter from James Johnston, the former Scottish secretary of state, who heard about the trials while in London. Reflecting on the French response to cases of possession and witchcraft earlier in the century, Johnston observed that 'the parliaments of France and other judicatories who are persuaded of the being of witches never try them now because of the experience they have had that it's impossible to distinguish possession from nature in disorder'.[81] There may have been other compelling reasons why the French did not try witches in 1697, but Johnston's explanation at the very least shows how the evidentiary problems associated with possession could lead to a state of judicial paralysis in witchcraft cases.

The privy council came closer to the position taken by the parlement of Paris in 1699, when the demoniacs Margaret Murdoch and Margaret Laird accused witches of causing their possessions. This time the council allowed John Maxwell of Pollok to take precognitions of the persons she and others had named, but never to try any of those whom they had examined. In responding to the possession of Patrick Morton at Pittenweem in 1704, the council went even further, refusing to delegate any functions to local authorities. After examining some of the accused witches in Edinburgh, they set them at liberty. The judicial scepticism of the privy council, which the accusations made by demoniacs had fostered, contributed to the decline in the number of Scottish witchcraft prosecutions. After 1704 Scottish courts tried witches only occasionally, and executed very few of them.

If the cluster of cases of demonic possession contributed to greater caution in the prosecution of witches, it did not do anything to erode the belief in the reality of witchcraft. Quite to the contrary, the physical evidence of bodily contortions, fits, and other afflictions suffered by Christian Shaw, Margaret Murdoch, Margaret Laird, and Patrick Morton confirmed the belief that evil spirits and the witches who made pacts with them did in fact exist and that in Scotland, where Satan 'shows the greatest malice and where he is hated and hateth most', the reign of Satan was nearing to an end.[82]

8   The decline and end of Scottish witch-hunting

During the late seventeenth and early eighteenth centuries, prosecutions and executions for witchcraft in Scotland declined in number and eventually came to an end. The decline was marked by a reduction in the number of trials, a rise in the number of acquittals, and a drop in the execution rate. The decline began in the early 1660s in the wake of the largest witch-hunt the country had ever experienced, but it took more than 50 years for the trials to end altogether. The decline did not follow a linear path. After the hunt of 1661–2, there were brief local panics in 1678 in East Lothian and again in 1697 at Paisley. The overall trend, however, was unmistakable. The witch-hunts that occurred after 1662 claimed far fewer lives than those of the 1590s or of the mid-seventeenth century, and the number of individual prosecutions was gradually reduced to a trickle. The last executions recorded in the central records of the country took place in 1706, while the last trial, one of questionable legality, occurred in 1727, a mere nine years before the British parliament repealed the Scottish witchcraft law of 1563. The British statute of 1736 officially determined that witchcraft in Scotland, as well as in England, was no longer a crime.

The main purpose of this chapter is to account for this decline in the number of Scottish witchcraft prosecutions and executions after 1662. In so doing it will establish the extent to which the decline of Scottish witch-hunting conformed to a broader European pattern. This type of investigation has yet to become a central concern of witchcraft scholars. Historians of witchcraft have traditionally given much more thought to the question why the trials began than why they came to an end. We have only a few surveys of the process throughout Europe[1] and a handful of local and national studies exploring the issue.[2]

The persistence of belief

Until recently, most of the scholars who addressed this question, usually in passing, attributed the decline in one way or another to the emergence of modern rationalism, the rise of science, or an even vaguer dispelling of ignorance and 'superstition'.[3] This interpretation arose during the

Enlightenment, and it became the backbone of late nineteenth- and early twentieth-century liberal and Whig historiography. Historians writing in this tradition focused mainly on the content of published witchcraft treatises and the theological and philosophical controversies to which those treatises contributed. They assumed that the decline of witchcraft prosecutions had been caused by a decline in the witch beliefs of the educated classes and therefore made little distinction between the two developments. The little that has been written on the decline of Scottish witchcraft conforms to this pattern.[4] The end of the trials thus became synonymous with the enlightened rejection of the demonological ideas that had provided the intellectual foundations of witch-hunting. Only recently have alternative approaches to the decline and end of European witchcraft prosecutions, based on either changes in judicial administration or economic and social factors, begun to take its place.[5]

An explanation of the decline of European witchcraft prosecutions in intellectual terms is highly problematic. The main problem is that the expression of sceptical ideas, especially those that denied the possibility of the crime of witchcraft, either had little impact among the intellectual elite or took place after witchcraft prosecutions had already begun to wane. There were, to be sure, sceptical voices throughout the entire period of witch-hunting, the most famous in the sixteenth century being those of Johann Weyer and Reginald Scot. These men did not, however, put an end to the prosecutions. Not only did their ideas experience a cool reception in intellectual circles and elicit some vigorous responses,[6] but their scepticism itself was of a limited nature. Neither Weyer nor Scot, for example, took the extreme position that witchcraft was an impossible crime.[7] A group of late seventeenth- and early eighteenth-century sceptics, which included the Dutch Cartesian minister Balthasar Bekker and the Saxon jurist Christian Thomasius, came much closer to that radical position, but their scepticism emerged at a time when most western European countries had already begun to end the trials. The views of Bekker and Thomasius, moreover, took even longer to be disseminated among the judges, magistrates, and clergy who actually controlled the prosecutions. It will never be clear exactly when European ruling elites lost their belief in witchcraft, but we can be confident that very few of them did so until the trials were almost completely over.[8]

The problem of explaining the decline of witchcraft prosecutions in terms of a rejection of learned witch beliefs becomes insurmountable when we focus on Scotland. There are few countries in Europe where a philosophical or intellectual opposition to witch-hunting had a weaker voice or commanded less widespread support than in Scotland. To put the matter in its simplest terms, Scotland did not have any counterparts of either Weyer and Scot in the late sixteenth century or of Bekker and Thomasius a century later. Scotland did have its critics of witch-hunting, most notably the jurist Sir George Mackenzie, but Mackenzie refused in any way to lend support even to Weyer's moderate position. Among Scottish judges, magistrates, and clergy there was not even a hint of the argument that witchcraft was an impossible crime until long after decriminalization, which took place in 1736.

Mackenzie, both in his defence of the accused witch Maevia and in his book on Scots criminal law, took pains to establish the existence of witches, even if those witches did not appear to be as numerous as many contemporaries claimed.[9] The furthest Mackenzie would go in challenging contemporary witch beliefs was to deny the possibility of witches' flight and their metamorphosis.[10] The same reluctance to challenge the intellectual foundation of witch-hunting can be seen in the vigorous defence of the Paisley witches mounted by the advocate James Robertson in 1697. Robertson made a strong case for the innocence of his clients, but he never challenged the firm witch beliefs of the prosecuting advocates, James Stewart and Francis Grant.[11] Even in 1730, three years after the last Scottish witch-trial, the jurist William Forbes, in his authoritative summary of Scots criminal law, insisted upon the reality of witchcraft.[12]

A religiously inspired rejection of the belief in witchcraft, based on biblical scholarship, also failed to gain support in Scotland. In the sixteenth century biblical scholars began to use the techniques of humanist philology to show that the references to witchcraft in the Bible used to justify the harsh treatment of witches, most notably Exodus 22:18 ('Thou shalt not suffer a witch to live'), did not refer to the type of person who was being prosecuted as a witch in early modern Europe. The Lutheran Johann Weyer and Reginald Scot, who was a member of the Family of Love, devoted entire sections of their witchcraft treatises to these differences, noting that the Hebrew word *kaskaph* meant a diviner or a poisoner rather than a maleficent magician who made a pact with the devil.[13] The English political theorist Robert Filmer, whose opposition to the Maidstone trials of 1652 was discussed in Chapter 6, wrote an entire pamphlet exposing these differences.[14] In the late seventeenth century the Dutch Calvinist minister Balthasar Bekker deployed massive biblical scholarship to show that Satan could not have exercised any power in this world and that therefore the prosecution of witches should cease.[15]

It is somewhat surprising that this body of Protestant biblical scholarship made no apparent inroads in Scotland during the seventeenth or eighteenth century. Biblical references to witchcraft figured prominently in Scottish demonological treatises, but the authors tended to rely on the traditional literal interpretation of the key texts rather than to have recourse to the increasingly large volume of humanist scholarship that would present an alternative interpretation.[16] It was not until 1815, long after the prosecution of witches had ceased in Scotland and in all of Europe, that a Scottish theologian, James Paterson, presented the sceptical interpretation in his book, *A Belief in Witchcraft Unsupported by Scripture*.[17] One could easily lament that such a point a view came too late.

The growth of judicial scepticism

The decline of Scottish witchcraft prosecutions, therefore, took place within the context of a general belief in the reality of the crime. This persistence of learned belief forces us to consider alternative explanations for the reduction in the number of prosecutions and executions. In particular it encourages us to take a legal approach, to focus on the judicial process itself and the concerns of the judges, lawyers, and magistrates who were responsible for the operation of the judicial machinery. In the most general terms it encourages us to study the growth of a judicial rather than a philosophical scepticism, an outlook that does not question the reality of witchcraft but does question whether specific individuals, and ultimately whether *any* individuals, could be proved guilty of this crime at law. Judicial scepticism in its various forms, especially the insistence on following due process in proceeding against witches, has been shown to have been highly instrumental in reducing the number of trials and executions in Spain after 1614, northern France after 1624, Würzburg after 1629, England after 1646, Italy after 1655, Sweden after 1676, New England after 1692, and Hungary after 1750. It was also instrumental in reducing the intensity of Scottish witch-hunting after 1662.

The episode that gave rise to this demand for legal caution was the great Scottish witch-hunt of 1661–2. That hunt was so large, involving a total of 664 named witches in four counties, and the death toll so great, that it almost inevitably called attention to the procedural irregularities that characterized it. The abuses identified specifically in the records of the privy council were the unauthorized arrest of suspects, the torture and pricking of suspects without proper warrant, and the use of other illegal means to extract confessions. The determination of the central government to prevent these abuses from recurring, which found expression in the proclamation of April 1662 discussed in Chapter 5, marks the turning point in the entire history of Scottish witch-hunting.[18]

The impact of the witch-hunt of 1661–2 on the way in which subsequent witchcraft prosecutions were handled in Scotland can be seen in three different ways. First, after 1662 there was a significant increase in the percentage of trials that were conducted, or more closely supervised, by central judicial authorities, a development that resulted in a higher number of acquittals. Second, as a result of this increased control from the centre, there was a reduction in the incidence of judicial torture and the more frequent dismissal of cases in which it had been used illegally. Finally, in all witchcraft trials there was a more careful weighing of the evidence and greater adherence to strict standards of judicial proof. Taken together, these three developments go a long way towards explaining the reduction in the number of convictions and executions. They also explain, in an indirect way, the reduction in the number of trials.

The role of the central government

The first and most important of these changes concerns the role of central governmental authorities in the trial of witches. In Scotland, as in virtually all countries in Europe, the main pressure to prosecute witches came from local communities. This is not to say that central governments did not from time to time initiate or at least encourage witch-hunts. Certainly they had done so in Scotland in 1590, just as they had in Bavaria in 1587 and were to do at Køge in Denmark in 1612. But for the most part central governments responded to requests from local authorities either to have the witches tried in the central courts or to give those same local authorities permission to try the witches in their own communities. At that point central judicial officials could either facilitate or impede the success of the trials. This meant that the intensity of witch-hunting in a particular area depended to a great extent upon the way in which the central government responded to these local initiatives.

Prior to 1662 the Scottish government had not followed a consistent policy in this regard. King James VI himself had encouraged, if he had not actually inspired, many of the prosecutions in 1590–1, but during the large witch-hunt of 1597 the privy council had taken steps to reduce the intensity of witch-hunting. In that year noblemen and local officials, operating under commissions of justiciary to apprehend and try any persons suspected of witchcraft, had used their judicial power to settle personal disputes, thereby placing 'honest and famous persons' in great danger. In order to prevent these abuses from recurring, the council revoked the commissions that had been granted to those men and required that any local authorities who wished to prosecute witches petition the council for new commissions, which would include at least three or four members operating conjointly.[19] After this time the council reviewed all requests for commissions of justiciary on a case-by-case basis, and they resisted pressure from local clerical and secular authorities to issue standing commissions to try witches. These policies contributed to a significant decline in the total number of witchcraft trials during the next 30 years.

The practice of requiring conciliar approval of all commissions to conduct local witchcraft trials did not always keep witch-hunting under control. At four critical junctures in the seventeenth century – 1628, 1643, 1649, and 1661 – major witch-hunts took place. There were two main reasons for these breakdowns in the system. The first was that the government from time to time granted commissions without carefully considering whether a local trial was warranted or whether due process had been followed in the arrest and interrogation of the accused. Especially during the periods of intense prosecution, it issued commissions almost routinely in response to local requests. Under these circumstances the government could not possibly have taken the time to evaluate the evidence carefully enough to see if a commission of justiciary was warranted.

Once these commissions were granted, there was little likelihood that the witches would be spared. As we have seen, the commissioners entrusted with the task of assembling an assize were almost always legally untrained local lairds, magistrates, or elders of the parish, rather than lawyers or justice deputes from Edinburgh. These men, according to Mackenzie, were 'not exactly acquaint with the nature of this crime'.[20] They also were in many cases the same men who had already interrogated the accused witches, gathered evidence of their guilt and sent a petition to Edinburgh requesting the trials. In these cases the juries that were assembled to decide the guilt of those who had been accused almost always confirmed the suspicions of the commissioners. Until the late seventeenth century most witches tried on the basis of these commissions, unlike those tried in Edinburgh, did not have access to counsel.[21] In one of the few instances when counsel was present, in the trial of Margaret Barclay discussed in Chapter 2, the lawyer appeared too late in the proceedings to make a difference in the outcome. Even in the trial of the Paisley witches in 1697, when the witches did have the benefit of counsel, all seven of the accused were convicted and executed. As we have seen, this was the fate of the vast majority of witches tried before local assizes.

The harm done by the privy council's delegation of judicial authority to untrained amateurs was compounded when the government encouraged the local identification and prosecution of witches. The most notorious of such witch-hunts began in 1628, as part of broader governmental initiative, encouraged by the church, to punish crime, especially crimes of a religious nature. In that year the privy council instructed specially appointed commissioners to collect charges against people for more than 70 different crimes, with witchcraft close to the top of the list.[22] In 1643–4 and again in 1649–50 privy council and parliament supported the prosecution a number of moral crimes, including adultery and witchcraft. In these witch-hunts the central government catered to, if it did not take steps to stimulate, local demand for prosecution. At the same time local pressure to prosecute, often inspired or reinforced by religious fervour, intensified.

In 1662 this episodic pattern of recurrent witch-hunts, fuelled either by the neglect of the council or its active support, came to an end, leading to the decline in prosecutions and their eventual end in 1727. In that year members of the council, the lord advocate and the judges of the justiciary court succeeded in imposing effective checks on local witch-hunting. They did this in three different ways. First, they reduced the number of conciliar or parliamentary commissions while at the same time taking steps to funnel local cases into the justiciary court at Edinburgh. Whereas more than 1,150 witches had been tried by conciliar or parliamentary commissions of justiciary before 1662, the total number of such cases heard between 1662 and 1727 dropped to 97. These trials still resulted in a high percentage of executions, at least among those trials whose outcomes are known (23 out of 24 cases), but the dramatic reduction in the number of trials goes a long way towards accounting for the overall pattern of decline. By contrast, the percentage of cases that were heard before the justiciary court (officially established as the High Court of Justiciary in 1672) increased after 1662, and more than two-thirds of those cases resulted in acquittals.[23] In some cases the justices deliberately denied requests for a local trial and ordered the cases to be heard in the justiciary court.[24] In others the justices ordered the release of witches who had been imprisoned by local authorities on the grounds that no one had insisted, that is, continued to act as the private accuser and prosecutor of the imprisoned witch.[25]

This policy of reducing the number of trials conducted by local magistrates reflected a broader effort of the Scottish government in the late seventeenth century to centralize and rationalize the criminal justice system. This meant first of all insisting that all trials, especially those of witchcraft, be conducted by properly constituted authority. This was the import of the council's order of April 1662 and its frequent reiteration after that date. The government's policy became evident in 1674, for example, when the judges of the justiciary court dropped the charges against an accused witch after it was discovered that justices of the peace had brought her to trial. At that point the judges made it clear that 'no inferior judge, much less justices of the peace, were competent to the crime of witchcraft'.[26] Only central justices or those who were properly commissioned by them could bring witches to trial. Sir George Mackenzie, the lord advocate from 1677 to 1686, became the most vocal proponent of this policy. In 1680, for example, he secured the acquittal of the accused witch Bessie Gibb, mainly on the grounds that the magistrates and the bailie of the burgh of Bo'ness, who had originally proceeded against her, were not competent to try her.[27] Mackenzie's position on this question conformed to his broader objective to take criminal trials out of the hands of men who did not have legal training and to entrust the entire process, including the determination of guilt, to professional lawyers and judges.[28]

The second means by which central authorities restrained the excesses of local witch-hunting was through the successful implementation of an effective circuit court system after 1671. This system, the heir to the old medieval justice ayres and the Scottish counterpart to the English assizes, had been proposed from time to time in the sixteenth and seventeenth centuries, especially as part of the legal reforms of 1587, but the plan had never really got off the ground.[29] Only during the Cromwellian occupation of the 1650s did the circuit courts operate as intended. After 1670, however, these courts began to function in a more regular fashion, and an increasingly large number of witchcraft cases were brought before them. These local trials, presided over by judges from Edinburgh, yielded far more acquittals than those in which local commissioners acted as judges. Between 1671 and 1709 only two witches are known to have been executed by circuit courts.

The third step that the council took was to exercise tighter control over those witchcraft trials conducted by conciliar commissions. As we have seen, one of the main problems with these commissions before 1662 was that there was no central involvement in, or supervision of, the actual trial. In a number of commissions after 1662, however, the council insisted that a justice depute from Edinburgh be included among the commissioners, thereby guaranteeing the presence of central authority at the trial.[30] Another tactic was to insist on conciliar review of the commissioners' sentences. The privy council did this in a commission granted to the Aberdeen burgh council in February 1669, and it followed a similar course of action in a commission granted in 1699 to try nine accused witches from Ross-shire. In this last instance the council appointed a special committee to decide whether the sentences of the commission should be carried out. As a result of this action, two witches who had confessed were given non-capital punishments, and the others were set at liberty.[31] This review of the commissioners' sentences is reminiscent of the way in which continental European countries, most notably France, Sweden, and Russia, instituted the practice of submitting all sentences in witchcraft cases to appellate review. Scotland did not have an appellate structure of judicial administration, but this review of sentences by an ad hoc committee served the same purpose. In this case, moreover, it appears to have had the desired effect, since the trials did not result in executions.

Reduction in the use of torture

The second change in the conduct of witchcraft trials after 1662 was the reduction in the use of torture. Torture played a central role in the prosecution and conviction of witches in many European countries. Its use allowed magistrates and prosecutors to secure the confessions that were necessary for conviction when witnesses were not forthcoming, and it also allowed them to obtain the names of alleged accomplices. By the same token the critiques of torture that developed throughout Europe in the seventeenth century played a vital role in reducing the number of convictions and executions. A group of early seventeenth-century treatises condemning the procedure, the most influential being that of the German Jesuit Friedrich Spee, was followed by the more comprehensive and systematic works of Augustin Nicolas, Michael Sassen, and Christian Thomasius in the late seventeenth and early eighteenth centuries.[32] Scottish writers did not produce any formal treatises of this sort, but they did formulate a critique of the use of torture in witchcraft cases, and that critique played a crucial role in the decline of Scottish witchcraft prosecutions.

The essence of this Scottish critique was not that torture was *ipso facto* wrong or illegal but that it was being applied without proper authority. In Scotland torture could be administered only when specifically warranted by the council or parliament. In that regard it was essentially the same as the law of torture in England, which also prohibited the use of torture without the approval of the council. (The same law was also in force in Sweden, where the right to torture formed part of the royal prerogative.) There was therefore a striking difference between Scottish practice in this regard and the practice of countries that followed a fully inquisitorial system of justice. In those countries torture could be applied by judges when sufficient evidence, usually the testimony of one witness or the equivalent in circumstantial evidence, created a presumption of guilt.

As discussed in earlier chapters, local burgh authorities often did not observe the strict requirement that Scottish torture required a warrant from the privy council. Prior to 1662, however, the council made only sporadic efforts to prosecute local officials who violated this rule.[33] The turning point came in the wake of the great witch-hunt of 1661–2. During that panic the council noted that 'pricking, watching, keeping of them from sleep and other torture' had been responsible for the execution of innocent persons.[34] Shortly thereafter the council issued its proclamation prohibiting the use of torture in witchcraft cases without its specific permission. This prohibition was also included in some of the justiciary commissions granted during the next few years.[35]

The council's prohibition of torture in witchcraft cases was not completely successful. Reports of illegal torture continued to reach the council, especially during the East Lothian trials of 1678. In September of that year Katherine Liddell of Prestonpans, who had been arrested and imprisoned for witchcraft, petitioned the council to take action against those who 'did most cruelly and barbarously torment and torture' her 'by pricking of pins in several parts of her body to the great effusion of her blood and whereby her skin is raised and her body highly swelled and she is in danger of her life'. Liddell herself was set free, while one of her tormentors, the pricker David Cowan, was imprisoned 'for presuming to torture or prick any person without warrant from the council'.[36] Even this action failed to put an end to the practice. In 1680 five witches whose confessions were shown to have been the product of 'several types of torture' were set at liberty.[37] There is evidence that local authorities continued to administer torture illegally into the early eighteenth century.[38] Nevertheless, the prohibition by the council did help to reduce the frequency with which torture was applied and thus the number of convictions and executions in witchcraft cases.

The person who had recommended the release of the five witches of 1680 was Sir George Mackenzie, acting in his capacity as lord advocate. Mackenzie's primary concern in making this recommendation was to prevent the conduct of judicial business by men who were not competent to do so. It was not torture as such to which Mackenzie, the persecutor of covenanters, objected: he defended his own use of the practice in treason trials on the basis of reason of state and claimed that its use was sanctioned by the law of nations.[39] But he insisted that its use be restricted to the council and the judges of the justiciary court, a policy similar to that adopted by the parlement of Paris in 1624.[40] Only in this way could the procedure be used properly. It is noteworthy that, even while recommending the use of a new instrument of torture, the thumbkins, in 1684, the council insisted that any use of the device should be approved 'by their order'.[41]

A conflict between the burgh council of Aberdeen and the privy council provides us with the best illustration of the late seventeenth-century policy of the council regarding torture and also how it was connected to the issue of granting commissions of justiciary. In May 1669 the Aberdeen council apprehended three suspected witches on the basis of common fame and evidence that they had committed various malefices. The burgh council then wrote to the privy council, requesting a commission that would include the 'power of torture in the ordinary manner in like cases'.[42] The privy council responded that it would not grant the commission unless the burgesses submitted a confession of the witches and that under no circumstances would they grant them a warrant to put the witches to the torture. The burgesses responded by claiming that they needed a commission forthwith, since otherwise the witches, being old and kept in prison at the expense of the town, would likely die 'without trial or confession'. They offered to submit a statement of a presumption against the witches upon which a commission could be granted, and they renewed their request for the power to torture, 'which it hath been the ordinary way of former commissions without something whereof they will not confess'.[43]

On 11 June the Aberdeen council reported that they were still waiting for a commission and that the council had indicated that it would not grant such a warrant to the Aberdeen magistrates alone, insisting that they be joined by 'some able persons'. The burgesses protested that they were as trustworthy and had carried themselves as legally and deliberately as any magistrates of any burgh in the kingdom.[44] Only when the Aberdeen council offered to pay the expenses of a justice depute from Edinburgh, John Preston, to travel north and sit with the Aberdeen magistrates, did the council relent and grant the commission on 15 July.[45] The outcome of the trial of the three witches, together with a fourth who was named in the commission, is not known, although there was a reference in the records of the privy council in August 1670 that several witches had been executed at Aberdeen on an unspecified date.[46]

This long jurisdictional conflict between Aberdeen and the council illustrates three important developments. First, the council after 1662 was determined not to grant torture warrants to local magistrates and was not at all receptive to the transparently false claim of the burgesses that such warrants had been granted on a regular basis in the past.[47] Second, the council had been reluctant even to grant the commission, on the apparent ground that they did not trust the magistrates to conduct a fair trial. Only after adding a justice depute from Edinburgh did they grant the commission, with specific instructions to conduct the trial according to the laws of the realm.[48] Third, even though the Aberdeen council did not receive permission to torture the accused, they apparently did secure the witches' eventual conviction and execution. Since the verdict was determined by a jury of local Aberdonians, that result should not surprise us. All in all, the episode reveals that the council, and in particular the lord advocate and justice clerk, were making a conscious effort to control the local prosecution of witches, even if in this case they did not prevent the witches from perishing.

The evaluation of evidence

A third major reason for the decline in the number of convictions and executions in witchcraft cases was the greater care with which evidence was evaluated at witchcraft trials and the adherence of judges to increasingly rigorous evidentiary standards. In Scotland this development was closely associated with the greater participation of lawyers in witchcraft trials. Although Scottish criminal trials were similar to those in England in that the outcome was decided by lay juries, they differed from English trials in that the accused had a right to counsel. Representation consisted mainly in the submission of written pleadings by an advocate on behalf of the accused. In these pleadings the advocate would challenge the relevance of particular pieces of evidence to the libel, which is the proposition stating the reasons for the defendant's guilt. This process, which resembled continental European criminal procedure more than that of England, often resulted in long exchanges between the prosecutors and the advocates for the accused. These debates on relevancy took place before the evidence was presented to the jury, and the judge's decision on these points of law could effectively lead to acquittals.

Until the late seventeenth century, very few Scottish witches could afford the cost of legal representation, and those who could usually were tried in the justiciary court in Edinburgh. Towards the end of this period, however, advocates represented witches more frequently and even appeared in some of the local cases heard by commissioners of justiciary, such as in the trial of the Paisley witches in 1697.[49] Lawyers could have a dramatic impact on the course of a witchcraft trial. They could raise doubts regarding the supernatural causes of alleged *maleficia* and impeach the credibility of witnesses who might not have been allowed to testify in the trial of ordinary crimes. They could point out the insufficiency of the evidence, especially when it was hearsay, and the irrelevancy of the evidence to the libel. They could identify procedural irregularities upon which the judges would discontinue proceedings or have the trial moved to Edinburgh, such as when the advocate for Margaret Clark showed the High Court of Justiciary in 1674 that the justices of the peace in the sheriffdom of Banff had proceeded summarily and illegally against her and had behaved most partially and unjustly.[50] In an earlier case David Williamson, who represented the accused witch Mary Cunningham, succeeded in having the case moved to Edinburgh when he showed that the procurator fiscal who prosecuted her in Culross, a man 'who had no skill of law', could not answer his defence.[51] Finally, lawyers could influence the jury to bring in acquittals. It is not surprising, therefore, that the growing number of acquittals during the late seventeenth century coincided with the greater frequency of legal representation.

The more careful evaluation of evidence in witchcraft trials can be seen, first and foremost, in a growing reluctance of lawyers and judges to accept confessions, traditionally regarded as the queen of proofs, as sufficient proof of guilt. In the East Lothian trials of 1678 the judges released a group of witches who were about to implicate 'sundry gentlewomen and others of fashion', attributing their confessions to 'malice, or melancholy, or the devil's deception'.[52] In his summary of Scottish criminal law Mackenzie, who was responsible for a large number of acquittals in such cases, argued that confessions to witchcraft (or any other crime) were valid evidence only if such confessions were in no way extorted, if they contained nothing that was impossible or improbable, and if the person confessing was not either melancholic or suicidal.[53]

A second and even more frequent expression of the new judicial scepticism was the argument of lawyers that events attributed to supernatural agency might have had natural causes. This argument was particularly relevant to charges of *maleficium*, according to which it was claimed that witches had inflicted harm by supernatural, that is, diabolical, means. The sceptical response to such allegations, frequently adopted when lawyers defended witches against such charges, was that the misfortune had natural causes, and that in order to convict a person of the crime, the possibility of natural causation had to be ruled out. The burden of proof was on the prosecution; all that was necessary to secure acquittal was evidence that natural causation was *possible*. In a number of trials in Scotland in the late 1620s, advocates for the witches had gone to great lengths to prove that malefices might not have been the product of supernatural intervention.[54] Later in the century Mackenzie, in defending the witch Maevia, argued that his client could not be proved to have caused her neighbour's madness, since 'distraction was a very natural disease'. The distraction, moreover, could have been caused by fear, of which Maevia was only the occasion, not the cause.[55] A similar argument regarding natural causation was made by James Robertson, the advocate for the seven Paisley witches accused of causing the demonic possession of Christian Shaw in 1697.[56]

Robertson was unable to bring about his clients' acquittal in this trial. Perhaps the prosecutor's speech to the jury, threatening them that if they should acquit the witches they would be 'accessory to all the blasphemies, apostacies, murders, tortures and seductions, etc., whereof those enemies of heaven and earth shall hereafter be guilty when they get out' frightened them into returning a guilty verdict.[57] Robertson had succeeded, however, in raising serious doubts about the possibility of actually proving the crime of witchcraft at law. James Johnston raised similar doubts when he claimed that it was impossible to determine whether the fits of demoniacs were of natural or supernatural origin.[58] By 1704, when another case of possession led to local demands to prosecute a cluster of alleged witches at Pittenweem, the arguments of Robertson and Johnston seem to have prevailed. The council refused in this case to authorize a local trial.

The end of prosecutions

The fact that seven of the Paisley witches were executed even after their counsel had presented a compelling defence reveals that the scepticism of lawyers and judges regarding the guilt of witches could not by itself bring an end to witchcraft executions in a country where guilt or innocence was still ultimately determined by lay juries. The same was true in England, where during the late seventeenth century judges had not always been able to prevent the conviction and in some cases the execution of witches who they believed were innocent. In both countries entrusting the determination of guilt or innocence to juries guaranteed that the decline of witchcraft prosecutions would proceed more gradually than in those countries where judges exercised more immediate control over the judicial process.[59] In the long run, however, the scepticism of Scottish lawyers, judges, and advocates prevailed. Not only the convictions and the executions but even the trials themselves came to an end. The decline in the number of prosecutions can most reasonably be attributed to the difficulty local communities had securing commissions of justiciary and to the rising frequency of acquittals and dismissals. As George Nicholson of Aberdeen wrote in 1669, if the privy council did not support the burgh council's efforts to prosecute, the burgh would be much less likely to administer justice or petition the council for new commissions in the future.[60]

Even when the government stopped authorizing local prosecutions and when local magistrates stopped asking them to do so, pressure from the local community, especially from the clergy, continued. Under these circumstances towns and villages that wished to take action against witches had three options. The first was to become reconciled to the fact that witches would now be able to live amongst them and to give up any hope of removing them. This is the decision that villagers and townspeople throughout Europe ultimately made, although not until the nineteenth and even the twentieth centuries in some parts of Europe. The second was to lynch the suspected witches. This of course had always been an option when the cost of proceeding against witches was too high, when the government refused to authorize a trial, or when an accused witch was acquitted. It became an even more viable option in the eighteenth century, when the number of acquittals and dismissals rose. Perhaps the most notorious witch-lynching in Scotland took place at Pittenweem in 1705, after the privy council dismissed charges of witchcraft that had been levelled against six women and one man for causing the possession of a teenage boy. The local community responded by crushing her to death under heavy weights. The government was never able to bring the murderers to justice.[61]

The third option was to encourage *local* officials to take unauthorized action against the witches. This seems to be what happened in the very last recorded witchcraft prosecution in Scotland, at Dornoch in 1727, when a sheriff depute of Sutherland proceeded against two women, a mother and daughter, for witchcraft. The daughter escaped, but the mother, who had been accused among other things of riding her daughter after she had been transformed into a pony, suffered death by being burned in a barrel of pitch. In this case the sheriff depute was not acting on the basis of any legal authority, nor is it clear whether he was observing due process. It is even uncertain whether the mother was convicted in court or whether she was lynched after the trial.[62] When witchcraft prosecutions took this form it is difficult to make a distinction between a trial and a lynching. Whatever we may call it, it was clearly a procedure that was initiated and executed entirely by the residents of that village, and it received no support whatsoever from the central government.[63] Witch-hunting in Scotland, even in its last gasp, remained a local affair that the central government tried to control, regulate, and eventually eliminate, but not always with complete success.

9 Witch-hunting and witch-murder in early eighteenth-century Scotland

In January 1705, a woman from the Scottish fishing burgh of Pittenweem in Fife, Janet Cornfoot, was brutally murdered by a crowd of people who were convinced that she was a witch. Having fled from the burgh after her prosecution for witchcraft had failed, Cornfoot was forcibly taken from the nearby village of Leuchars and returned to Pittenweem by two armed men. When she arrived in the town she was brought to the minister's house and then, since he was not present, to that of one of the bailies. The bailies of the burgh were, however, unable to protect Cornfoot from a group of at least ten people who seized her and apparently set out to swim her. Cornfoot was suspended from a rope extending from a ship's mast to the shore. From this rope she was swung from side to side while people in the crowd threw stones at her. After being cut loose, she was dragged along the shore by her heels. At that point a man placed a door on her chest while her assailants piled stones on top of the door, crushing her to death in a popular version of the English (but not Scottish) judicial procedure known as *peine forte et dure*, which was used to force an accused criminal to enter a plea. According to one report, which may not be accurate, a man then drove his horse and sledge over Cornfoot's corpse several times.[1]

The murder of Janet Cornfoot was carried out by the people of the burgh, but it succeeded only with the tacit compliance of the burgh elite, including the local presbyterian minister, Patrick Cowper. Witch-lynchings of this sort were not uncommon in eighteenth-century Europe, most notably in Poland, where apparently hundreds took place, but there had been very few in Scotland before this date and even fewer south of the border in England, which had executed its last witch in 1685.[2] The lynching of Cornfoot was even more exceptional in that the Scottish privy council in Edinburgh, which had taken steps to prevent her prosecution, was apparently unable to bring the murderers to justice.

This tragic episode in the history of Scotland poses a series of questions. First, how did the original charges of witchcraft against Janet Cornfoot arise? Second, why did so many people in Pittenweem, especially the burgh elite, believe that she was guilty of witchcraft and promote her prosecution? Third, why did the official prosecution against Cornfoot fail, leading members of the community to take illegal action against her? Fourth, why did the Scottish government, after demanding that her murderers be held of account for this crime, fail to bring them to trial?

The possession of Patrick Morton

The case of Janet Cornfoot began when Patrick Morton, a 16-year-old blacksmith apprentice in Pittenweem, began to exhibit behaviour that was identified by members of the community as demonic possession. Unlike some of the more famous demoniacs on the European continent, Morton's symptoms did not include speaking in foreign languages he had never heard, or vomiting pins, or levitation. But he did allegedly exhibit the fits and contortions that other demoniacs throughout Europe were reported to have experienced. His countenance and neck became distorted; the bones of his back and chest were so distended that they rose to a prodigious height before collapsing; his stomach swelled up, and his breathing sounded like the blowing of a bellows. His arms and legs became so stiff and firm that no effort could move them. His head could turn towards the back of his body. Since physicians were unable to present a natural explanation for these symptoms, the members of the community quickly came to the conclusion that he was possessed by the devil.

Whenever cases of demonic possession have been discussed, either by sceptical contemporaries or modern scholars, an effort has been made to explain the behaviour of demoniacs as either the effects of mental or physical disease or as deliberate hoaxes intended by subordinate members of society to attract attention or to wreak revenge on their enemies. Unfortunately, however, these efforts to explain what was 'really' happening when a person fell into fits and convulsions of this sort ignore the fact that demoniacs were following a script that was an important part of their religious culture. It does not matter whether Morton was suffering from the disease then called melancholy, as was suggested by the bailie William Bell in 1710.[3] Nor does it matter whether he was consciously engaged in fraudulent behaviour, as was claimed by one observer who said that the boy had been exposed as a cheat.[4] Both claims may have some validity. The important consideration is that his affliction followed a script that was a part of late seventeenth-century Calvinist religious culture.

In this case we know how Morton learned this script, because Patrick Cowper, the minister who coached the boy every step of the way, actually read him an account of another Scottish possession just before his own afflictions began.[5] This account was a published narrative of the possession of Christian Shaw, an 11-year-old girl in the household of the laird of Bargarran in Renfrewshire, in 1697. As discussed in Chapter 7, Shaw's possession had triggered a witch-hunt when the girl named seven women as the cause of her possession, and all seven were executed at Paisley. The narrative of Christian Shaw's possession was in turn modelled on Deodat Lawson's narrative of the possession of a group of young girls in Salem, Massachusetts, in 1692, an even more famous case of demonic possession that had led to the execution of 19 people as witches.[6] The similarity between these two possessions, as well as that of Richard Dugdale, a teenage gardener from Lancashire known as the Surey demoniac, whose possession narrative was published in 1697,[7] suggests that there was a common Calvinist culture of possession around the turn of the eighteenth century.[8] Calvinist beliefs regarding demonic possession linked puritan households in New England, presbyterian communities in Scotland, and dissenting presbyterian congregations in England in the same way that their belief in the doctrine of predestination gave rise to similar religious experiences as they sought to discover whether they were among the elect.

The early modern Calvinist culture of possession not only gave unity to the afflictions experienced by these young people but it also linked those afflictions to witchcraft. As we have seen in Chapter 7, all the cases of demonic possession in Scotland during the period from 1697 to 1704, which are in fact the only documented cases of possession in Scottish history, did in fact lead to accusations of witchcraft. This included the possession of Patrick Morton, who accused Beatrix Laing, a woman of ill repute who had been excluded from the Lord's table (communion) and who had long been suspected of being a witch, of causing his possession by witchcraft. The incident that triggered this accusation was Morton's refusal to do some work for Laing, for the apparently legitimate reason that he was already committed to making nails for one of the local fishing boats.[9] Rebuffed in this way, Laing went away cursing the boy. Shortly thereafter, Morton began to experience fits and contortions, and he also stopped eating. Recognizing the opportunity afforded by this boy's misfortune, Cowper not only read him the narrative of Christian Shaw's possession, thus giving him a script to act out, but urged him to identify Laing as the witch who was responsible for sending the devil to torment him. Cowper also suggested the names of four others whom he suspected of witchcraft and whom Morton then dutifully named as co-conspirators: Janet Cornfoot, Lillie Wallace, Nicolas Lawson, and Isobel Adam – all of them residents of Pittenweem or the surrounding area.[10] Later testimony before the presbytery of St Andrews indicated that that Morton had also named Janet Horseburgh as one of the women's accomplices.[11]

Two of the six women named by Morton as the cause of his possession appeared to be fairly well off. Beatrix Laing, described in one of the pamphlets as a 'very poor woman' who had 'married meanly', was in fact married to William Brown, a tailor who had served as the town treasurer.[12] The fact that she had asked Morton to do some work for her also suggests that she was hardly poverty-stricken. On the other hand, Laing was not wealthy. At one point she reportedly said, 'If they burn me, both ladies in coaches and sedans must burn also.'[13] The other witch who occupied a fairly high niche in the town's social hierarchy, Janet Horseburgh, was clearly among the town's elite. She was married to Thomas White, a mariner who later served as one of the bailies of the burgh. After her husband died, she had sufficient financial resources to take legal action against those who had imprisoned her in 1704.[14] Little is known about the social status or wealth of the other women, including Janet Cornfoot, except that Nicolas Lawson was married to Alexander Young, a farmer, and was reported to have been shearing bear (harvesting barley) in 1704.[15]

Four of the women had been suspected of witchcraft before Morton accused them. Lawson's reputation as a witch was so well established that a fellow worker, Jean Durkie, had asked her to 'learn her to be a witch so that she could wreak vengeance on the magistrates for sending her husband to Flanders'.[16] Janet Cornfoot, who was described as 'a woman of very bad fame', was a charmer and had a penchant for threatening people who disagreed with her. Like Lawson, she was widely reputed to be a witch.[17] Beatrix Laing had been cited before the kirk session in 1696 for charming, while a contemporary pamphlet asserted that her husband had suspected her of witchcraft before her arrest and imprisonment.[18] Her husband's personality could easily have led him to be suspected of witchcraft as well, for he was once fined 500 marks (more than £27 sterling) for speaking 'opprobrious words' against the town clerk.[19]

The most contentious personality was that of Janet Horseburgh, who in 1686, during the tenure of the episcopalian minister Andrew Bruce (before his expulsion for drunkenness in 1692), had become involved in a bitter dispute with one of the bailies, Alexander Griege, over retaining her seats in church for use by her daughters while her husband was at sea.[20] On this point Horseburgh refused to yield, and the failure to reach a compromise led her husband on his return to have the seats destroyed and new ones built. As a result of this dispute Horseburgh brought a slander suit against Griege for calling her a witch. Griege defended himself against the change, but there is little doubt that Horseburgh had a reputation of being a witch who became involved in disputes with other members of the town elite.[21] The incident also confirms reports dating from the period of Bruce's incumbency that Horseburgh contributed to a spirit of disaffection in the parish. The incident also reflected the religious divisions in the town that had led to an attempt by Jacobites to prevent the admission of Cowper as minister in 1692.[22] By all indications Cowper, who had been imprisoned three times for his covenanting activities in the 1670s and 1680s and who had little tolerance for either Jacobites or witches, inflamed these divisions. The accusations against both Laing and Horseburgh and the lawsuits they initiated after the trials against certain bailies of the town apparently reflected the perpetuation of those factional disputes.

The concern of the residents of Pittenweem with the war against France, which began in 1700, might also have contributed to a mood that encouraged witch-hunting. As part of the war effort an unknown number of soldiers had been quartered in the town, and these men presented new challenges to the maintenance of a godly discipline. In particular, soldiers were involved in a number of flagrant and violent attacks on women. In July 1703 James

Stewart, a dragoon (an infantry soldier who moved about on horseback) under the command of Captain Douglas in the marquis of Lothian's regiment, was accused of raping a woman in the town.[23] In January 1704 a dragoon attempted to rape Margaret Strang, and when she resisted and cried for help he stuffed her mouth with straw and dung, and 'did blood her grievously'.[24] Three months later, just before the witch-hunt began, Robert Varner, later to be discovered as a married man, had impregnated Isobel Courie but escaped the censure of the kirk by embarking on a man-of-war, presumably for military service.[25] The following year two soldiers quartered in Pittenweem were declared guilty of fornication with Isobel Bruce on the highway, an incident that today would be referred to as gang rape.[26]

These problems were aggravated by the fact that the residents of the town were reported to have been drinking with the soldiers during the time of the sermon on Sunday. What is more, some of the soldiers refused to recognize the authority of the kirk session unless commanded to do so by their superior officer.[27] Above and beyond the effect the soldiers may have had on the town's moral discipline, the experience of the war itself may have directly contributed to the fear of witchcraft within the community, just as the impact of the Indian war in 1692 had contributed to the concern with witchcraft at Salem.[28] It may not be a coincidence that the only other recorded prosecutions of witches at Pittenweem took place in 1643, during the civil war.[29]

The prosecution of the Pittenweem witches

The initial charge against Beatrix Lang was the practice of *maleficium* or harmful magic, which in this case had allegedly caused Morton's fits and convulsions. In this respect Laing's prosecution began in the same way as the overwhelming majority of witchcraft prosecutions throughout Europe – with an accusation brought by the witch's neighbour that she had caused harm or misfortune through some sort of preternatural, supernatural, mysterious or occult means. The charge that this magical power came from making a pact with the devil – an idea developed by medieval theologians and jurists in the fifteenth century – was usually not introduced until the accused witch was brought before judicial or ecclesiastical authorities.[30]

To confirm Morton's accusation Laing and her alleged accomplices were brought into Morton's bedroom, where he, although blindfolded, nonetheless sensed that his tormentors were in the room and named them all as the source of his affliction. In this ritual Morton was carefully following the script followed originally by the Salem girls and repeated by Christian Shaw, all of whom personally identified the witches responsible for tormenting them. At this point Bettie Laing confessed to being a witch and having made a pact with the devil, of having renounced her baptism, and of having offered her daughter and then, when the devil refused the daughter, her 6-year-old granddaughter to the devil's service.[31] She also implicated the other four women as confederates in her diabolical work. In the course of her confession she indicated the methods of her *maleficum*: throwing a hot coal into a bowl of water and forming a wax image of the intended victim and sticking it with pins – a use of image magic that was based on the assumption that a secret sympathy prevailed between a person and his or her image.[32]

Three of Laing's alleged accomplices – Adam, Cornfoot, and Lawson – also produced confessions, the most elaborate being that of Isobel Adam, who gave details of her pact with the devil, including having sexual intercourse with him, receiving his mark (which she described as being a very painful branding), and conspiring with the others to murder one McGregor in his house. This plan was foiled when McGregor awoke and blessed himself, driving away the group of prospective assailants together with the piper who accompanied them. The reference to the piper in Isobel Adam's confession reveals that local elements were often inserted into standard accounts of the witches' sabbath. Janet Cornfoot, the future victim of her neighbours' wrath, also confessed, but she later told a group of two noblemen and two lairds who visited her in the tollbooth where she was imprisoned that everything she had confessed regarding either herself or her neighbours were lies and that she had confessed only after the minister beat her with his staff. The lies, so she said, were intended to please the minister and the bailies.[33] Beatrix Laing later made a similar statement regarding the untruth of her forced confession.[34]

Cornfoot's claim that she had been beaten by Cowper raises the question to what extent torture was used to extract the confession of the Pittenweem witches. An abundance of evidence confirms that they were subjected to a variety of physical abuses, including the repetitive pricking of them by 'drunken fellows' (apparently under the guise of searching for the devil's mark), depriving them of sleep for several days and nights, and brutal beatings.[35] As one Mr Miller wrote in a letter to a correspondent in Edinburgh later that year, 'The ministers have used a great deal of barbarous severities to extort confessions from those unhappy creatures.'[36]

It should come as no great surprise that torture was used to extract confessions from Bettie Laing and Janet Cornfoot. They were hardly the first Scottish witches to have been subjected to such treatment. It is somewhat surprising, however, that this incident occurred so late in the history of Scottish witch-hunting. By this time it was widely known that this type of physical abuse of suspected criminals was patently illegal, as one of the pamphlets published at the time of this witch-hunt indicated.[ak] It was also widely known that the privy council had on numerous occasions in the past taken action against local officials who had tortured witches without warrant. The fact that Laing and Cornfoot were nonetheless treated in this manner testifies to the determination of their interrogators to secure their confessions and the confidence of these same men that the council would not hold them responsible for their actions.

On 29 May, at the request of the burgh magistrates, the Pittenweem kirk session examined Adam, Laing, Lawson, and Cornfoot, all of whom confirmed the confessions they had previously made, and admitted having made pacts with the devil, renouncing their baptism, and meeting with the devil in the loan of Pittenweem. The four confessing witches also repeated their implication of 'several others', but the minutes of the session did not mention their names because they had not yet confessed. The session then asked Cowper to ask the presbytery of St Andrews, of which he was moderator *pro tempore*, to meet in Pittenweem to examine those imprisoned for witchcraft.[38]

Before this meeting took place, the burgh magistrates and minister took the first steps towards obtaining a commission from the privy council to try the witches 'in this part of the country'. On 1 June they had sent a delegation to Edinburgh to ask Sir Thomas Moncrieff, the justiciar within the regality of St Andrews, to help them obtain such a commission. The same day they agreed to meet with the presbytery, which was now scheduled to hold its meeting at Pittenweem on 14 June, to 'crave their advice anent the persons charged with witchcraft'. Two days before the presbytery met, the burgh appointed one of the bailies and one of the burgh council members to meet with the commission of the general assembly to advise the privy council how best to bring them to trial so that they 'may suffer punishment according to the laws of God and this nation'.[39]

The presbytery met on 14 June and began its investigation by interrogating Janet Horseburgh, who had been implicated by Cornfoot and Lawson as well as being named by 'the lad Patrick Morton'. Horseburgh acknowledged that the boy 'had said such things to her hearing, and that it was the devil that spoke of her name', but she denied the sin of witchcraft. She testified further that neither Cornfoot nor Lawson had any malice or prejudice towards her. Horseburgh was followed by Lillie Wallace, who likewise denied being a witch and also challenged Cornfoot's accusation that she had been at the loan of Pittenweem on the fateful night of the alleged assembly. Attempts by two of the members of the presbytery to persuade her to confess were of no avail.[40]

The examination of Beatrix Laing produced mixed results. While confirming her earlier confession regarding the bewitchment of Patrick Morton, she denied that she had ever seen the wax picture referred to in previous testimony. She also, quite remarkably, denied that she had made a pact with the devil, but said that she had seen him only once on Ceres Moor, when he appeared in the shape of a black dog. On that occasion she had stroked this canine spirit on his back, leaving some hair on her hand. Asked how she knew it was the devil, she answered because it changed its shape. Even though she denied making a pact with the devil, she admitted that the devil on this one occasion had caused her to renounce her baptism.[41]

The examinations of Cornfoot and Adam were more productive. Adam confirmed that she had not only renounced her baptism but had also made a pact with the devil, and she produced the first recorded reference to the seventh accused witch, Thomas Brown, who she claimed had joined the other witches and the devil at McGregor's house. Cornfoot likewise confirmed her former confession but added that the devil had also appeared to her in the tollbooth and said that if she confessed he would 'tear her to pieces' but if she did not confess, she would only have to lie awhile in prison.[42] The author of *A Just Reproof* used Cornfoot's confirmation of her original confession to undermine her claim that she had confessed the first time only to please the minister and bailies. It is clear, however, that Cornfoot was still trying to please the presbytery by confessing, declaring her repentance, and showing how she had rejected the devil's command. It should be remembered that the primary concern of the presbytery was still the reintegration of the offender into the Christian community, not civil action against the accused.

Nicolas Lawson was not examined until at a second meeting of the presbytery on 28 June. Her interrogation was undertaken in connection with the examination of Jean Durkie for having asked Lawson to teach her to be a witch. Durkie's position was that she had made the remark in jest and recounted it as beginning with the proposition that 'If I were a witch as you are ...' Lawson denied that she knew of any compact that Durkie had made with the devil but was never asked to confirm her own.[43] The meeting concluded with professions by Cornfoot and Adam that they wished to renew their vows of baptism, but the presbytery was not satisfied that they had a sufficient 'sense of guilt' and therefore referred the matter to a committee that was instructed to meet at Pittenweem to decide the issue. Cowper later reported that it was inconvenient for the committee to have met at that location.[44]

Two days after the second meeting of the presbytery, the burgh council and the minister and elders of Pittenweem submitted a formal petition to the privy council to grant a commission to such 'gentlemen and others that live in and about the place' to try the four witches who had confessed, as well as the three others (Thomas Brown, Janet Horseburgh, and Lillie Wallace) who had been accused but had not yet confessed.[45] In their petition of 12 July the burgh officials claimed that confessions of the four witches and the physical harm inflicted on Morton constituted the *corpus delicti* – the body of evidence that a crime had in fact been committed and upon which a trial could proceed.[46]

The burgh council requested that the trial be held in the town rather than before the justiciary court in Edinburgh because of the expense of transporting witnesses to the capital. The more plausible reason was that there was a much greater likelihood of conviction in a trial before local magistrates and lairds who knew the witch and her reputation than before the more impartial judges in Edinburgh. Those same judges in the capital were also far more likely to adhere to proper legal procedure, making acquittals more likely. We don't know the fates of many of the witches tried by ad hoc commissioners of justiciary, but fragmentary evidence suggests that the conviction rate was very high. The case of Margaret Barclay in 1618, discussed in Chapter 2, provides one of the best examples of what usually happened when local officials received permission to try witches in their own burghs.

The privy council was certainly aware of the procedural irregularities that often took place when local authorities were given permission to try witches by themselves. Sir George Mackenzie had called attention to these irregularities in his book on Scots criminal law, where he complained about entrusting the trial of witches to ignorant, legally untrained country men. It should have come as no surprise, therefore, that on 13 June the privy council ordered the trial to be held in Edinburgh and instructed the lord advocate, Sir James Stewart of Godtrees, to initiate a process against the witches. Stewart was no friend of witches, but he dutifully ordered the earl of Rothes, the sheriff of Fife, to transport the witches to Edinburgh.[47] The prospect of an Edinburgh examination and trial dampened the zeal of the burgh officials. The privy council made arrangements to cover the expenses of transporting the accused to Edinburgh, but the delay in the proceedings meant that the costs of keeping the suspects in the tollbooth would be burdensome. This financial situation probably explains why on 12 August, two months after the decision of the privy council, the burgh council released five of the six female suspects on bail (Cornfoot apparently excepted) pending their examination in Edinburgh.[48] The bail money of 500 marks was provided by the women's friends.

The fact that these women's friends were able to raise the bail bond money suggests that the accused had a significant measure of support from within the community, which was not always the case in European witch-hunts. It is perfectly plausible that such assistance would be forthcoming in this instance, however, since none of the original charges had come from women in the community; they had all come from Patrick Morton and his clerical coach, Patrick Cowper. The amount of the bail money also suggests that these friends were fairly well off and had sufficient assets at their disposal. As we have seen, the witches themselves, especially Janet Horseburgh, were far from destitute, and their friends may have occupied an even higher social bracket. It is even possible that these friends were 'some of the most considerable men's wives in the town' whom Morton wanted to name but whom the minister and bailies were reluctant to imprison. They certainly were more prosperous than most Scottish witches and a large majority of English witches, who relied on the charity of the community to survive.

The entire prosecution of the witches began to unravel in September when the privy council, on the recommendation of Rothes, ordered Morton to appear before the privy council, at which time the boy's symptoms of possession quickly disappeared, and he recovered his former health.[49] In October the prosecution suffered another blow when Isobel Adam was brought to Edinburgh for questioning by the privy council, which ordered her to be set at liberty. The other witches apparently were examined a month later, and they too were released, although a contemporary pamphlet contends that they were required to pay a fine of £8 Scots each upon their release.[50]

Unfortunately, the case did not unravel quickly enough to spare the life of Thomas Brown, the only man accused by Morton, who died during his imprisonment in the tollbooth. The charge that he was starved to death – a fate that many witches faced when they were imprisoned for long periods of time – was challenged by the author of *A Just Reproof*, who claimed that Brown's daughter had brought him provisions faithfully.[51] Nor did the release of the women end the predicament of Janet Cornfoot, whom the minister had placed in solitary confinement after she had retracted her confession in the presence of two lawyers, one Mr Ker of Kippilaw, a writer to his Majesty's signet, and Mr Robert Cook, an advocate. The keeper of the prison, however, placed Cornfoot in a cell with a very low window in order to facilitate her escape. She fled to the nearby village of Leuchars, eight miles from Pittenweem, where she was discovered and apprehended by the minister of that parish, Mr George Gordon. Enticed by a reward of £10 Scots for her capture, Gordon arranged for Cornfoot to be taken back to Pittenweem.[52] Her murder took place the night she arrived in the town.

Like many accused witches who were lynched, Cornfoot fell victim to a community that remained convinced she was guilty but was denied the satisfaction of having her convicted by a legitimate legal tribunal. When the opportunity arose to return her to Pittenweem, her assailants were waiting to give her the rough popular justice they believed she deserved. The responsibility for her murder did not lie entirely with 'the rabble' that strung her up in the harbour. Just as responsible were the members of the town's ruling elite who promoted her prosecution in the first place and then either facilitated or condoned her lynching. It was, after all, the bailies of the burgh who failed to protect her from the furious mob. Not surprisingly, when the privy council investigated this gross miscarriage of justice, they recommended the initiation of legal proceedings against the magistrates of the burgh as well as the people who pelted her with stones and pressed her to death.[53]

Witch beliefs in eighteenth-century Pittenweem

The question then arises why the members of this burgh elite – ministers and bailies alike – believed that Patrick Morton was possessed by demons; that his possession was caused by the Beatrix Lang and her associates, and that these witches had not only practised *maleficium* but had also made pacts with the devil and had entered his service. If this witch-hunt had taken place in the late sixteenth century, at the height of witch-hunting in Europe, when the weight of learned opinion endorsed the reality of witchcraft, there would have been no need even to ask that question. But this was the first decade of the eighteenth century, a time when witchcraft prosecutions had entered a precipitate decline in western Europe and even the belief in witchcraft was beginning to be called into question. The growing conviction among educated people that the natural world followed immutable laws of nature, the biblically based belief that the devil could not influence the course of human events after Christ had chained him to hell, and the insistence that the only effective type of magic was what Neoplatonic philosophers termed natural magic had created a growing conviction that witches could not in fact perform the deeds attributed to them.

What is lost sight of in discussing the decline of witch-hunting is that these sceptical attitudes, articulated by a small group of Cartesian philosophers and biblical scholars, did not succeed in undermining witch beliefs among the majority of educated people. Indeed, those ideas proved to be remarkably resilient, persisting in various contexts well into the eighteenth century. Many of the people who criticized the process of prosecuting witches, including the English jurist William Blackstone, still believed that witchcraft existed because it was based on the revealed word of God.[54] In Scotland such attitudes were pervasive within all educated circles. Even the jurist Sir George Mackenzie of Rosehaugh went to great lengths to refute the sceptical views of the sixteenth-century physician Johann Weyer.

Elites in Pittenweem not only accepted the reality of witchcraft but also were engaged in a broader campaign to use the evidence of witchcraft and possession in their communities to prove the reality of the supernatural world. To this extent they were involved in a major philosophical enterprise that developed in England, Scotland, and New England in the late seventeenth century to refute the so-called sadducees who, like their biblical Jewish predecessors, denied the reality of spirits.[55] Frightened that this denial would lead inevitably to atheism, the protagonists in this undertaking went to great lengths to find empirical evidence of demonic presence in the world. This they found in confessions of witchcraft, in stories of people who had witnessed poltergeists and monsters, and most of all, in the visual evidence that demons had taken control of the bodies of human beings. As we saw in Chapter 7, the most significant contribution to this literature was Richard Baxter's *The Certainty of the Worlds of Spirits*, published in 1691. The book was replete with tales of witchcraft and possession, including stories of demoniacs vomiting pins, geese, and chamber pots of blood. Baxter's treatise, however, was only one of many publications – almost all of them from Protestant dissenters in England, presbyterians in Scotland, and puritan congregationalists in New England – intended to refute these latter-day sadducees. This literature was inspired by an apocalyptic belief that the devil was loose on earth and that the last days were near, a belief expressed in a sermon given by Cotton Mather on Revelation 12:12 during the Salem witchcraft trials, which was published in *Wonders of the Invisible World* both in Boston and London in the early months of 1693.[56]

This Calvinist determination to prove the existence of spirits underlay the series of spectacular cases of possession and witchcraft that erupted in Scotland in the closing years of the seventeenth century and the opening years of the eighteenth. The evidence for this ulterior theological motive comes mainly from the literature intended to justify the execution of the witches who were blamed for the possession of Christian Shaw and from the pamphlets written about the witch-hunt at Pittenweem.[57] The title of the most apologetic of the Pittenweem pamphlets could not have been more explicit: *A True and Full Relation of the Witches at Pittenweem, to which is added by way of preface, an essay for proving the existence of good and evil spirits, relating to the witches of Pittenweem, now in custody, with arguments against the sadducism of the present age.*[58]

The narrative of the events that had taken place at Pittenweem continued to serve the purposes of anti-sadducism into the late eighteenth century, long after witchcraft prosecutions had come to an end. This was most evident in the publication of a new edition of George Sinclair's *Satan's Invisible World Discovered* in 1780. In the first edition of this work, which represented the first significant Scottish contribution to the debate on sadducism, Sinclair had relied mainly on accounts of witchcraft and supernatural wonders to prove the existence of spirits. In the amended revision of the book, however, the editor included accounts of Christian Shaw's possession, the case of possession and witchcraft in Antrim in Ireland discussed in Chapter 7, and the episode at Pittenweem. Witch-hunting was dead by 1780, but not the theological and philosophical campaign to prove the existence of the spirits from whom witches had allegedly received their powers.[59]

In light of this effort to prove the existence of spirits, the cultivation and exploitation of Patrick Morton's affliction and the prosecution of the witches of Pittenweem can be attributed in large part to the determination of presbyterian clergy and elders to defend their innermost religious beliefs. The central role of the minister, Patrick Cowper, in coaching Morton would support this theory, as would the active part that both the kirk session and the presbytery played in the process. Even more persuasive evidence that the ministry was exploiting this case for its religious purposes comes from Mr Miller, who in the previously quoted letter wrote: 'Our presbyterian ministers are showing great zeal in discovering witches and they think they have fallen luckily on a cluster of them in Pittenweem.'[60]

The question remains however how these 'lucky' ministers were able to influence the legal process that was set in motion by the appeal to the privy council in July. In England any such efforts could not have come to fruition in the late seventeenth or early eighteenth century for the simple reason that English clerics, unlike their Scottish counterparts, played no role in the administration of criminal justice. In England there was a clear division of jurisdiction between the ecclesiastical courts and the common law courts, and by 1660 the common law courts at Westminster had secured the unrestricted right to define those jurisdictional boundaries by issuing writs of prohibition against cases brought into the church courts. What is more, English ecclesiastical courts had lost their criminal jurisdiction in 1641 and never regained it, leaving them only with a civil jurisdiction over marriage and wills. In the few witchcraft cases still being prosecuted in the common law courts the clergy apparently played no part. Nor could the sermons preached by clerics at the assizes have had a bearing on the trial of witches. The sermon delivered by the English minister White Kennet in the wake of the Jacobite rebellion of 1715, *The Witchcraft of the Present Rebellion*, struck a familiar rhetorical note, but it had nothing to do with witchcraft prosecutions.[61] The most prominent English cleric to write about witch-hunting in the early eighteenth century was Francis Hutchinson, who used the opportunity to castigate those who had conducted the trials.[62]

In Scotland the situation was very different. There the kirk sessions still cooperated with the secular courts, referring cases of witchcraft and other crimes to the civil magistrate.[63] The kirk sessions, moreover, performed many of the functions that the justices of the peace exercised in England. James VI had introduced the justices to Scotland in 1609, but they had never gained the respect, prestige, and jurisdiction of their English counterparts.[64] A further form of cooperation between Scottish clergy and civil magistrates became apparent when ministers and lay elders participated in the civil functions of the burghs, as when Patrick Cowper joined the burgh council to petition the privy council for a commission to try Beatrix Laing and her alleged confederates locally rather than in Edinburgh.[65] In England there would never have been an occasion for such a petition, since all English trials were initiated by an indictment approved by a grand jury consisting entirely of laymen. Scotland did not have a grand jury, forcing them to rely upon indictments by the lord advocate to try cases in the justiciary court or commissions from the privy council to try them in the localities. There were, to be sure, many similarities between English and Scottish criminal justice, but as we have seen, the procedure for formally initiating prosecutions were very different indeed.[66]

The aftermath of the murder

If differences between English and Scottish criminal justice account for the greater role of Scottish ministers in the prosecution of witches, the greater difficulty the Scottish government had exercising control over criminal justice in the localities explains the failure to bring Janet Cornfoot's murderers to justice. The privy council was not negligent in this regard. Two weeks after the murder the council commenced an investigation of the murder. It appointed a committee of five noblemen, including the sheriff of Fife, to interrogate the magistrates of the town and determine why they did not protect Cornfoot and maintain the public peace. The committee submitted its report on 14 February, placing much of the blame on Bailie Cook, whose house was the site of the first assault on Cornfoot, and identifying the people who had committed the murder or were accessory to it. The three 'principal actors', all of whom had fled, were Robert Dalzell, identified as a skipper's son, a man named Groundwater from Orkney, and an unidentified man from Burntisland. Four other 'actors', including a schoolboy and two

Englishmen, were also reported to have fled. Four residents of Pittenweem who had dragged Cornfoot around the town and who had witnessed the murder but had not informed Cook that it had taken place were also named. Altogether the bailies had imprisoned four men who had been present at the murder.[67] Upon receiving the committee's report on 15 February the council instructed the lord advocate to initiate legal proceedings against the burgh magistrates for 'suffering such tumults and rabbles and other such outrages to be committed within their burgh' and against five named persons and any others who had a hand in or were accessory to the murder. These prisoners were ordered to be sent to Edinburgh for trial.[68]

This order was never obeyed. Instead of transporting the prisoners to Edinburgh, the burgh council paid the expenses of the magistrates to make the trip to clear their names and the reputation of the burgh. One of the bailies later reported that they had spent £194. 11s. Scots (£16. 4s. 3d. sterling) for that purpose.[69] While they were away, Patrick Cowper, the witch-hunting minister, freed the prisoners by his own authority, leading one contemporary to observe that Cowper 'exercised more of the civil authority than any of the bailies'.[70]

The release of Cornfoot's assailants did not end this witch-hunt. In May 1705 Beatrix Laing petitioned the privy council for protection against the threats of her neighbours. After recounting her torture, pricking, and solitary confinement for five months, she reported that she had recently returned to her home in Pittenweem but that 'the rabble there' threatened to treat her as they had Janet Cornfoot, forcing her to leave her home. She asked the council to provide for her protection. The council responded by ordering the bailie and council to put up a bond to protect Laing.[71] This the Pittenweem burgh council unanimously refused to do, on the grounds that Laing might be murdered at night without their knowledge.[72]

On the same day that it accepted Laing's petition, the privy council also appointed a second committee, consisting of three noblemen, to inquire into the murder of Janet Cornfoot.[73] The committee was ordered to meet at Pittenweem on 9 May, but apparently it did not, for five months later the privy council once again asked the committee to prepare and submit a report regarding the murder.[74] There is no record of the council's reception of that report or any evidence that Janet Cornfoot's murderers were ever punished.[75] That failure can be attributed to the persistence of a belief in witchcraft among all social groups in Pittenweem, the disappointment expressed by members of the town's leadership that the privy council had never granted a commission for judging the 'wretches' who had escaped punishment,[76] and the inability of the central Scottish government, despite its best intentions, to control local justice.

The only justice that any of the witches of Pittenweem ever received was that of Janet Horseburgh, who sued two of the bailies, William Bell and Robert Vernour, for wrongous imprisonment in 1710. The suit was based on an act passed by the Scottish parliament in 1701 that in effect gave

Scottish subjects the same protection afforded English subjects by the writ of habeas corpus.[77] Horseburgh's suit resulted in financial compensation and an acknowledgement by William Bell in 1710 that he had acted rashly and had defamed an innocent person. He asked for God's pardon and hers.[78] Bell's admission that justice had miscarried, which recalls the recantation of the Salem jurors in 1693, may have dealt a final blow to intense witch-hunting in Scotland, as there were no attempts to prosecute entire groups of witches, only individuals, after that date. Nevertheless, the features of Scottish criminal justice that had become apparent in the prosecution of the Pittenweem witches and in the murder of Janet Cornfoot did not disappear when she won her suit.

Nor did these features disappear when the kingdoms of England and Scotland were united in 1707. The main reason for this was that articles 18 and 19 of the union treaty left the legal systems of the two countries separate, as they remain today.[79] But in the long run the union did contribute to the end of witch-hunting in the northern kingdom. Since the treaty did bring about a union of the parliaments of England and Scotland, the new British parliament had the authority to bring the 'the laws concerning public right, policy and civil government' into conformity throughout the new United Kingdom. This meant that the criminal law of Scotland, unlike private law, was always open to amendment and reform.

The most significant change in Scots criminal law came with the elimination of the Scottish privy council, which was not provided for in the union treaty but nonetheless came suddenly in 1708, much to the chagrin of the Scottish political nation. This denial of Scottish administrative autonomy within the union eliminated the institution that had stood at the very centre of witchcraft prosecutions throughout the period of witch-hunting. To be sure, the privy council had done far more to restrict than promote witch-hunting in the late seventeenth century, but two years after the Pittenweem episode a commission from the privy council to try two men for witchcraft in Inverness had nonetheless resulted in their execution. The abolition of the privy council meant that this type of conciliar justice, in which local gentry and magistrates could prosecute witches without central judicial supervision, could no longer operate. In the year of the council's abolition, a new circuit court system in which judges would ride the northern, southern, and a newly established western circuit at least once each year, was finally put into place. Unlike earlier initiatives, most notably in 1587 and 1652, this attempt to establish a regular system of circuit courts, similar to the English assizes, finally came to fruition. The records of these courts date from 1708 and continue to the late twentieth century.

The permanent establishment of a circuit court system had a bearing on the last gasp of witch-hunting in Pittenweem. In October 1708 charges of witchcraft were once again brought against Beatrix Laing and Nicolas Lawson at the instance of Patrick Cowper and William Wadroper, the minister from Anstruther East.[80] When the circuit court justices visited Perth later that month they released the two women on caution but ordered them to appear at the next session of the circuit court.[81] Their accusers would not give up. In April 1709 a new arrest warrant put Laing and Lawson back in prison, with their trial set for 20 May.[82] On that day the justices sitting in Perth set the two witches at liberty, together with more than 150 people charged with adultery, about the same number accused of fornication, and others accused of crimes ranging from blasphemy to beating and cursing one's parents to being a vagabond.[83] The accused were released on the basis of an act of indemnity granted by Queen Anne in the wake of the Jacobite rebellion of 1708.[84] Such acts of indemnity had been passed after earlier rebellions and disturbances, the most comprehensive being in 1662.[85] This act 'acquitted, pardoned, released, and discharged' subjects for all offences committed before 19 April 1709 except those indicated in the statute. Since witchcraft was not excepted, Laing and Lawson were thereby pardoned. It is significant that the pardon of these two witches – the last two whose names appear in the central judicial records of Scotland – took place in a circuit court, before judges from Edinburgh.

Two parliamentary statutes passed after the union also had a bearing on Scottish witch-hunting. The first, which became law in 1708, prohibited the use of torture in the northern kingdom. This act, which was intended mainly to eliminate torture in the prosecution of treason, provided a statutory remedy against the use of torture in all Scottish courts, even if the torture was administered without warrant.[86] The second act was the repeal of the witchcraft statutes of the two kingdoms: the English statute of 1604 and the Scottish act of 1563. The act of repeal was passed in 1736, long after witchcraft had been a matter of serious debate in England. Its purpose, in addition to giving statutory force to a *de facto* decriminalization of witchcraft that had already taken place, was to ensure that witch-hunting did not continue in Scotland. This was of no little concern, since a witch had been executed a mere eight years before in Dornoch. Politically astute Scots recognized immediately that the bill was directed against them, and the Scottish nobleman, James Erskine, Lord Grange, attacked the bill as an affront to Scottish religious and legal independence within the union.[87] Grange, who was known to have an unrivalled collection of books on demonology in his library, also abhorred the separation of secular and religious justice that had become axiomatic in England but had not yet been achieved in Scotland.[88] The treaty of union was in his eyes an attempt to bring England and Scotland into greater legal conformity, in this case regarding the prosecution of witches.

A final footnote to witch-hunting in Scotland was written in 1743 when the associate presbytery of Edinburgh, in a confession of 'national and personal sins', declared that the repeal of the witchcraft statutes six years before was 'contrary to the express law of God'.[89] In this belated but futile protest the presbytery confirmed the persistence of the attitude that had inspired the attempted prosecution of the Pittenweem witches and the 'horrid and barbarous murder' of Janet Cornfoot. Witch-hunting finally came to an end in Scotland in the early eighteenth century, but witch beliefs persisted, not just among the illiterate but also among some of the most learned men in the kingdom.

Glossary

Assize   a Scottish jury.

Assizes   the English system of circuit courts.

Bailie   an officer of a Scottish burgh who exercised a number of administrative and judicial functions.

Charming   acts of white magic, often used for healing.

Delate   to accuse someone of a crime in Scotland.

Dittay   a document enumerating the grounds of a charge against someone accused of a crime; similar to an English indictment.

Indemnity   an act passed after a rebellion or disturbances releasing all individuals accused of certain crimes.

Indictment   In England the formal charge approved by the grand jury against someone accused of a crime.

Information   the mode of initiating a criminal prosecution for a misdemeanour in England.

Justice depute   one of the judges in the justiciary court at Edinburgh who could be assigned to hear cases in a locality.

Justice of the peace   an officer of an English or Scottish county entrusted with administrative and judicial powers.

Libel   in Scots law the proposition that a witch is guilty of a crime. Evidence was found to be relevant or not relevant to this proposition.

Malefice   the word used by Scots to identify a harmful deed allegedly caused by magic; (*maleficium* in Latin).

Panel   a Scottish criminal defendant.

Porteous roll   the portable roll listing the persons accused of a crime to be heard before a circuit court.

Witches' sabbath [or sabbat]   the alleged meeting of witches to worship the devil.

Notes

1 Witch-hunting in Scotland and England

1 J. Goodare *et al.*, 'The Survey of Scottish Witchcraft, 1563–1736', www.arts.ed.ac.uk/witches/ has identified 3,837 Scots accused of witchcraft.

2 C. Larner, *Enemies of God*, Baltimore, MD: Johns Hopkins University Press, 1981, p. 63 estimated that only 1,000 witches were executed. This estimate however was based on a figure of 3,014 accusations given in *Source-book*. 'Survey of Scottish Witchcraft' suggests that the figure could have been as high as 2,000, but the exact figure will never be known.

3 *Mercurius Politicus* 10 (10 Aug. 1650).

4 See W. Behringer, *Witches and Witch-hunts: A Global History*, Cambridge: Polity Press, 2004, ch. 4; W. Monter, 'Witch Trials in Continental Europe, 1560–1660', in B. Ankarloo *et al.*, *Witchcraft and Magic in Europe*, London: Athlone Press, 2002, pp. 12–16.

5 Larner, *Enemies*, p. 197.

6 For a discussion of the historiography of these comparisons, see J. Sharpe, 'Witch-hunting and Witch Historiography', *SWHC*, pp. 182–9.

7 B.P. Levack, *The Witch-hunt in Early Modern Europe*, 3rd edn, London, 2006, pp. 80–8.

8 See for example the banishment of Katherine Black, Elizabeth Black, and Elizabeth Crocket and the whipping of Isobel Bennet by the circuit court at Stirling, 24 March 1659. JC 10/1, fol. 244v.

9 [R. Filmer], *An Advertisement to the Jury-Men of England, Touching Witches*, London, 1653, p. 2.

10 S. Clark, 'King James's *Daemonologie*', in S. Anglo (ed.), *The Damned Art*, London: Routledge & Kegan Paul, 1976, pp. 156–81.

11 Filmer, *Advertisement*, sig. A3v.

12 See pp. 26–7.

13 See for example the conflict between the bailies of Cunningham and the presbytery of Irvine in 1649. CH2/197/1/24-5.

14 M.B. Wasser and L.A. Yeoman (eds), 'The Trial of Geillis Johnstone for Witchcraft, 1614', *Miscellany XIII*, Edinburgh: SHS, 2004, pp. 83–114.

15 L. Yeoman, 'Hunting the Ritch Witch in Scotland: High Status Witchcraft Suspects and their Persecutors, 1590–1650', *SWHC*, pp. 106–21.

16 The accusations were first made by Lady Pittathron. See R. Chambers, *Domestic Annals of Scotland*, vol. 2, p. 187. *APS* (31 July 1649).

17 K. Thomas, *Religion and the Decline of Magic*, New York: Scribner, 1971, pp. 553–9.

18 P. Elmer, 'Towards a Politics of Witchcraft in Early Modern England', in. S. Clark (ed.), *Languages of Witchcraft*, Basingstoke: Macmillan, 2001, pp. 101–18. Conversely, witchcraft accusations tended not to arise in well established regimes.

19 On the revival of witchcraft ideology in England after 1660 see I. Bostridge, *Witchcraft and its Transformations c.1650–c.1750*, Cambridge: Cambridge University Press, 1997.

20 J. Goodare, 'The Scottish Witchcraft Act', *Church History* 74 (2004), 39–67. The act did not, however, make any reference to the pact with the devil, except implicitly in its condemnation of necromancy, i.e. ritual magic. The act did, however, condemn witchcraft as 'heavy and abominable superstition', which in the sixteenth century meant corrupted or erroneous religion, not irrational belief or practice. It is telling that the clergy, and in particular John Knox, were mainly responsible for these phrases in the act.

21 S. Macdonald, 'In Search of the Devil in Fife Witchcraft Cases, 1560–1705', in *SWHC*, p. 36, shows that the devil was mentioned by name in only 20 per cent of the trial records for that shire. Even this low figure is four times higher than the corresponding percentage of cases in Essex in England.

22 JC26/13, Bundle B, 1649.

23 Ibid. Accusations against Jean Craig, spouse to William Steel in Tranent.

24 *Justiciary Cases*, vol. 3, pp. 812–15. The trial was held on 27 April.

25 S. Clark, 'Protestant Demonology: Sin, Superstition, and Society (*c.*1520–*c.*1630)', in B. Ankarloo and S. Clark (eds), *Early Modern European Witchcraft*, Oxford: Clarendon Press, 1990, pp. 45–81.

26 Goodare, 'Scottish Witchcraft Act of 1563'.

27 J. Miller, 'Devices and Directions', in *SWHC*, p. 91.

28 Larner, *Enemies*, pp. 67–8.

29 G. Neilson, 'A Sermon on Witchcraft in 1697', *SHR* 7 (1910), 390–9.

30 A. Macfarlane, *Witchcraft in Tudor and Stuart England*, New York, Harper & Row, 1970, p. 25.

31 'The Examination of John Walsh or Welshe, 1566', in M . Gibson (ed.), *Witchcraft and Society in England, 1550–1750*, Ithaca, NY: Cornell University Press, 2003, pp. 20–4.

32 Thomas Potts, *A Wonderfull Discovereie of Witches in the Countie of Lancaster*, London, 1613, sig. C2v–C3.

33 See for example *A True Relation of the Araignment of Eighteen Witches*, London, 1645, p. 5.

34 Henry Holland, *A Treatise against Witchcraft*, Cambridge, 1590; William Perkins, *A Discourse of the Damned Art of Witchcraft*, Cambridge, 1608; Alexander Roberts, *A Treatise of Witchcraft*, London, 1616; Richard Bernard, *A Guide to Grand-Jury Men … in Cases of Witchcraft*, London, 1627. See also the manuscript treatise on witchcraft, written *c.*1630, in Beinecke Library, Yale University, Osborne Shelves, fb 224.

35 D. Oldridge, *The Devil in Early Modern England*, Stroud: Sutton, 2000; N. Johnstone, *The Devil and Demonism in Early Modern England*, Cambridge: Cambridge University Press, 2000.

36 Macdonald, 'In Search of the Devil in Fife', p. 46, has argued that 'the Devil and belief in the demonic pact can no longer be used to explain the severity of the Scottish witch-hunt'. That may be true, but charges of collective devil worship lie at the very centre of such explanations.

37 CH2/197/1/24-5. Sometimes ministers took it upon themselves to persuade a suspected witch to confess. Andrew Reid, the minister at Kirkleen, testified in 1709 that for fifteen years Janet Hairstones, a reputed witch, 'frequently called at his house but he could never deal with her confession'. JC40/11.

38 CH2/121/7, fol. 55.

39 Henry Goodcole, *The Wonderful Discoverie of Elizabeth Sawyer a Witch, Late of Edmonton, her conviction and condemnation and death*, London, 1621.

40 C.H. Firth (ed.), *Scotland and the Commonwealth*, Edinburgh: SHS 18, 1895, pp. 367–8.

41 G. Waite, *Heresy, Magic and Witchcraft in Early Modern Europe*, Basingstoke: Palgrave, 2003.

42 J. Goodare, 'The Scottish Witchcraft Panic of 1597', *SWHC*, pp. 52–3.

43 W. Behringer, 'Weather, Hunger and Fear', *German History* 13 (1995), 351–77.

44 Macfarlane, *Witchcraft in Tudor and Stuart England*, p. 160, calculates that 92 per cent of the witches in Essex were female. In the East Anglian witch-hunt of 1645–7, 87.5 per cent of the witches prosecuted were female. J. Sharpe, 'The Devil in East Anglia', in J. Barry *et al.* (eds), *Witchcraft in Early Modern Europe*, Cambridge: Cambridge University Press, 1996, p. 240. In Scotland 84 per cent of witches named in the records were female. Survey of Scottish Witchcraft', introduction.

2 Witchcraft and the law in early modern Scotland

 1 Sir Walter Scott, *Letters on Demonology and Witchcraft*, London: G. Routledge, 1884, pp. 255–64, considers the case illustrative of the barbarity and irrationality of the time.
 2 *Trial, Confession and Execution of Isobel Inch, John Stewart, Margaret Barclay and Isobel Crawford for Witchcraft at Irvine. Anno 1618*, Ardrossan and Saltcoates, Herald Office, 1855, p. 4.
 3 Ibid., pp. 5–6.
 4 Ibid., pp. 7–9.
 5 *RPCS*, vol. 11, pp. 366–7. The four commissioners were the former provost of Irvine, two bailies, and one former bailie. The commission was dated 2 June 1618.
 6 *Trial, Confession and Execution of Isobel Inch*, p. 11.
 7 Ibid.
 8 Ibid., p. 14.
 9 Occasionally Scottish witches were burned alive. See J. Dalyell, *The Darker Superstitions of Scotland*, Edinburgh: Waugh & Innes, 1834, p. 686; E. Henderson (ed.), *Extracts from the Kirk-Session Records of Dunfermline*, Edinburgh, 1865, p. 28, n. 22; idem, *The Annals of Kinross-shire*, pt 1, Kinross: Fossoway Council, 1990, p. 27.
10 *RPCS*, vol. 11, p. 401.
11 Thomas Craig, *De Unione Regnorum Britanniae Tractatus*, ed. S. Terry, Edinburgh: SHS, 1909.
12 Ibid., pp. 305–6. Craig argued that the jury derived from Roman law, not ancient custom.
13 B.P. Levack, 'Judicial Torture in Scotland during the Age of Mackenzie', in *Miscellany IV*, Edinburgh: Stair Society, 2002, vol. 49, pp. 185–98.
14 See I.D. Willock, *The Origins and Development of the Jury in Scotland*, Edinburgh: Stair Society, 1966, pp. 144–7. In giving examples of the affinity between English law and Scots law, the union proclamation of 1604 erroneously listed grand juries as well as trial juries. The proclamation reported that the information came from those skilled in the laws of England. Obviously these men's knowledge of Scots law was limited. F. Larkin and P. Hughes (eds), *Stuart Royal Proclamations*, vol. 1, Oxford: Clarendon Press, 1973, pp. 95–6.
15 J.H. Baker, 'Criminal Courts and Procedure at Common Law, 1550–1800', in J.S. Cockburn (ed.), *Crime in England, 1550–1800*, Princeton: Princeton University Press, 1977, p. 19.
16 *APS*, vol. 3, p. 45, c. 54.
17 National Archives, SP 14/27/43.
18 J.I. Smith, 'Criminal Procedure', in *An Introduction to Scottish Legal History*, Edinburgh: Stair Society, 1958, pp. 429–30.
19 See Baker, 'Criminal Courts and Procedure', p. 19.
20 National Archives, STAC 8/4/10. See B.P. Levack, 'Possession, Witchcraft and the Law in Jacobean England', *Washington and Lee Law Review* 52 (1996), 1613–40.
21 National Archives, STAC 8/200/27. A further attempt by Lowes to prosecute Cooke for slander in King's Bench was unsuccessful. See M. Gaskill, *Witchfinders: A Seventeenth-Century English Tragedy*, Cambridge, MA: Harvard University Press, 2005, p. 140.
22 T.B. Howell (ed.), *State Trials*, vol. 14 (1816), p. 640.
23 JC26/38.

24 The justiciary court released Laidlawe and three other witches (Marie Somervail, George Guislet, and John Scot) in the summer of 1671 on the grounds that no accuser had insisted against them. JC 2/13, 3 July, 10 July, and 20 July. See also *Justiciary Records*, vol. 2, pp. 56–7.

25 J.I. Smith (ed.), *Selected Justiciary Cases*, vol. 3, Edinburgh: Stair Society, 1974, p. 628. The privy council ordered the trial at the request of the witch herself, who complained that her private prosecutors would neither try her nor set her free. The council had the case tried in the justiciary court on indictment, in which case the lord advocate was the sole prosecutor.

26 Robert Filmer was correct, then, in claiming that Englishmen were 'tied to a stricter or exacter rule in giving their sentences then others are, for all of them must agree in their verdict, which in a case of extreme difficulty is very dangerous'. *An Advertisement to the Jury Men of England Touching Witches*, London, 1653, sig. A4.

27 In 1659 Catherine Black and Elizabeth Black were convicted by the narrowest plurality of 8 to 7. See their petition to the commissioners for the administration of justice, JC26/26/3, item 2. In 1661 Janet Cock and Isobel Ramsay were convicted by a plurality. JC26/27/1, Duddingston witches process papers. There are also some examples of acquittal by a plurality.

28 *Newes from Scotland*, Edinburgh, 1591, pp. 9, 12, 27–8; Bulstrode Whitelocke, *Memorials of the English Affairs*, London, 1652. p. 522. D. Purkiss, *The English Civil War*, London: HarperPress, 2006, p. 377. For the criticism of the Scottish propensity to torture, see the pamphlet by the Whig reformer James Welwood, *Scotland's Inquisition* (1689), cited in C. Jackson, 'Judicial Torture, the Liberties of the Subject, and Anglo-Scottish Relations, 1660–1690', in T.C. Smout (ed.), *Anglo-Scottish Relations from 1603 to 1900*, Oxford: Proceedings of the British Academy, 2005, p. 75. Many of these reports were intended for English audiences.

29 Sir George Mackenzie claimed that torture was allowed 'not only by the law of our nation but of all nations except England'. *A Vindication of the Government of Scotland*, Edinburgh, 1691, p. 11. Lord Fountainhall, however, stated that torture 'is agreeable to Roman law but does not suit the genius of our nation, which looks upon the torture of the boots as a barbarous remedy'. Sir John Lauder of Fountainhall (ed.), *The Decisions of the Lords of Council and Session*, Edinburgh, 1759–61, vol. 1, p. 42. A paper drafted *c.*1604 regarding the admission of witnesses to the defendant states categorically: 'In Scotland causes are not governed by the Civil Law.' National Archives, SP 15/36/93.

30 J.T. Rutt (ed.), *Diary of Thomas Burton, Esq., Member of Parliaments of Oliver and Richard Cromwell from 1656 to 1659*, London, 1828, vol. 1, p. 16.

31 The only court in the kingdom that was permitted to use torture, presumably to quell the violence in the region, was the Council in the Marches of Wales, which was established as an offshoot of the Court of Star Chamber during the reign of Henry VIII. See P. Williams, *Council in the Marches of Wales under Elizabeth I*, Cardiff: University of Wales Press, 1958, pp. 49, 55. The court was deprived of this power by an act of parliament in July 1607. A summary of grievances against the court for the period of 1631–42, however, includes the allegation that it 'tortured the bodies of the king's subjects for bare suspicion of felony'. C.A.J. Skeel, *The Council in the Marches of Wales*, London: H. Rees, 1904, p. 140.

32 On the connection between torture and the Roman law tradition in Scotland see Levack, 'Judicial Torture', pp. 185–98. Sir Thomas Hope argued in the seventeenth century that Scottish municipal law in respect of torture was different from that of the civil [i.e. Roman] law. NLS, Advocates MS 25.3.15, fol. 350.

33 The English torture warrants for the period 1540–1640, which number 81, are listed in J. Langbein, *Torture and the Law of Proof*, Chicago: Chicago University Press, 1976, pp. 94–123. A total of 34 Scottish warrants for the years 1590–1689 appear in *RPCS*. An additional five warrants were granted by parliament, Levack, 'Judicial Torture', p. 191. Mackenzie was correct therefore when he claimed that torture was 'seldom used' in

Scotland. Mackenzie, *Laws*, p. 543. In general see R.D. Melville, 'The Use and Form of Judicial Torture in Scotland', *SHR* 2 (1905), 225–48.

34 Langbein, *Torture and the Law of Proof*, pp. 94–123. The torture of Samuel Peacock, a schoolmaster, for practising sorcery on King James in 1620, was a case of treason by means of ritual magic and was not defined as witchcraft. Ibid., p. 120. William Perkins, *A Discourse on the Damned Art of Witchcraft*, Cambridge, 1608, p. 187, argued that torture could be used lawfully and in good conscience but not in all cases. In the 1630s an anonymous English treatise recommended the use of torture on a recalcitrant witch 'providing the law will permit'. Unpublished tract on the nature, extent, and prosecution of witchcraft, Beinecke Library, Osborne Shelves fb 224, fol. 27.

35 *RPCS*, vol. 4, p. 680. The commissioners were given the power to examine and torture 'all and sundry persons' who had been, or would be, accused of witchcraft. On the limited nature of this commission see J. Goodare, 'The Framework for Scottish Witch-hunting in the 1590s', *SHR* 81 (2002), 242. The warrrant did not delegate the authority to administer torture to any other individuals besides the six commissioners.

36 *RPCS*, vol. 9, p. 83.

37 *Newes from Scotland*, p. 15.

38 The incident became known during the prosecution of John Stewart, Patrick's brother, in 1596. R. Pitcairn (ed.), *Criminal Trials in Scotland*, 3 vols, Edinburgh: William Tait, 1833, vol. 3, pt 2, pp. 374–7.

39 J. Goodare, 'The Scottish Witchcraft Panic of 1597', *SWHC*, p. 55.

40 S. Macdonald, *The Witches of Fife*, East Linton: Tuckwell, 2002, p. 173.

41 *RPCS*, 2nd ser., vol. 4, p. 473.

42 Examination of Johnstone at Musselburgh 28 July 1661. Johnston claimed he knew 'nothing of witchcraft more than the childe in his mother's womb'. JC 26/27/2, Musselburgh witches processes.

43 *RPCS*, 3rd ser., vol. 1, pp. 237–8.

44 See p. 150.

45 *Two Terrible Sea-Fights … Likewise the Tryal of Six Witches at Edenborough in Scotland*, London, 1652, pp. 3–4. The pamphlet attributed these 'cruel and bloody proceedings' to the Scottish kirk. See also Whitelocke, *Memorials of the English Affairs*, p. 522.

46 On the different grades of torture and for examples of these procedures see S. Macdonald, 'Torture and the Scottish Witch-hunt', *Scottish Tradition* 27 (2002), 95–114.

47 W. Stephen, *History of Inverkeithing and Rosyth*, Aberdeen, 1921, p. 437, considers the pricking instruments the main instrument of torture in witchcraft cases. For an example of how pricking for the mark could lead to a confession, see the report of the confession of Janet Thomson on 27 Nov. 1660, JC 26/26, Tranent witches processes.

48 R. Chambers, *Domestic Annals of Scotland: From the Reformation to the Revolution*, 3 vols, Edinburgh: W. & R. Chambers, 1858–61, vol. 2, p. 279.

49 *RPCS*, 3rd ser., vol. 1, p. 25.

50 Ibid., p. 210.

51 Sir John Lauder, *The Decisions of the Lords of Council and Session from June 6th 1678 to July 30th 1712*, Edinburgh, 1759–61, vol. 1, p. 16.

52 Ibid. Cowan was accused of 'pricking of pins in several parts of her body to the great effusion of her blood and whereby her skin is raised and her body highly swelled'. *RPCS*, 3rd ser., vol. 6, p. 13.

53 *An Answer of a Letter from a Gentleman in Fife* (Edinburgh, 1705), p. 2.

54 *RPCS*, 3rd ser., vol. 1, p. 210; vol. 6, p. 645.

55 During the seventeenth century six prisoners were tried by a jury after withstanding torture and not confessing. NLS, Advocates MS 25.3.15. See Levack, 'Judicial Torture', p. 192.

56 *Aberdeen Council Letters*, vol. 4, p. 394.

57 See Mackenzie, *Laws*, p. 88.

58 B.P. Levack, *The Witch-hunt in Early Modern Europe*, 3rd edn, London: Longman, 2006, pp. 84–8.

59 R. Kieckhefer, *European Witch Trials: Their Foundations in Popular and Learned Cultures, 1300–1500*, London: Routledge & Kegan Paul, 1976, ch. 5.

60 *RPCS*, vol. 5, pp. 409–10.

61 See for example the petition of officials in east Lothian in 1649 *RPCS*, 2nd ser., vol. 8, p. 205.

62 Goodare, 'Scottish Witchcraft Panic of 1597', p. 51.

63 Larner, *Enemies*, pp. 71–2, 200.

64 Larner, *Witchcraft and Religion*, pp. 77–8.

65 For this reason it is misleading to claim that 'most Scottish witch-hunting was remarkably centralized'. Goodare, 'Framework', p. 248. The only aspect of Scottish witch-hunting that was centralized was the process of obtaining a commission. The discovery of witches, their pretrial examinations, and most trials were conducted locally.

66 *APS*, vol. 7, appendix, p. 78.

67 The percentages are calculated on the basis of the figures in *Source-book*, p. 237, table 2. In each calculation I have considered only those cases whose outcomes are known. I have also excluded those cases classified as 'miscellaneous', since they were never fully tried, the accused having escaped or died in gaol. One reason why the conviction and execution rates for the circuit courts are especially low is that courts heard witchcraft cases only very late in this period, when there were fewer convictions in all courts.

68 Ibid. In this calculation all cases have been included, even if their outcomes are not known.

69 Mackenzie, *Laws*, p. 88.

70 See below, Ch. 9.

71 L. Taylor (ed.), *Aberdeen Council Letters*, London, 1954, vol. 4, p. 398. See below, Ch. 8.

72 K. Thomas, *Religion and the Decline of Magic*, New York: Scibner, 1971, pp. 458–9.

73 J.S. Cockburn, *A History of English Assizes, 1558–1714*, Cambridge: Cambridge University Press, 1972, p. 98.

74 Macfarlane, *Witchcraft in Tudor and Stuart England*, p. 37.

75 Whitelocke, *Memorials*, p. 545.

76 *Source-book*, p. 238, table 4.

77 *RPCS*, 3rd ser., vol. 1, p. 198.

78 For the general effect of the civil war on the assizes see Cockburn, *English Assizes*, p. 241. The crucial question is not whether the assizes were held but whether the justices were in attendance.

79 On the role of Grimstone see Malcolm Gaskill, *Witchfinders* (London, 2005).

80 See Kieckhefer, *European Witch Trials*, esp. pp. 10–18; E. Peters, *The Magician, the Witch and the Law*, Philadelphia: University of Pennsylvania Press, 1978, pp. 110–37.

81 G. Henningsen, *The Witches" Advocate: Basque Witchcraft and the Spanish Inquisition, 1609–1614*, Reno, NV: University of Nevada Press, 1980, pp. 44, 168, 170, 180. During this hunt local authorities often 'took the lead by sanctioning acts of violence, imprisonment, and torture'. Ibid. 208–9.

82 Ibid., pp. 357–86.

83 A.F. Soman, 'The Parlement of Paris and the Great Witch Hunt (1565–1640)', *Sixteenth-Century Journal* 9 (1978), 36.

84 Ibid., pp. 37–42.

85 Langbein, *Prosecuting Crime*, pp. 167–209.

86 The intense witch-hunting that took place in the German ecclesiastical territory of Ellwangen was at least partially the result of that territory's virtually complete territorial autonomy. See H.C.E. Midelfort, *Witch Hunting in Southwestern Germany, 1562–1684*, Stanford, CA, 1972, pp. 98–100.

87 Monter, *Witchcraft in France and Switzerland*, pp. 105–6. See also R.H. Robbins, *The Encyclopedia of Witchcraft and Demonology*, New York: Crown Publishers, 1959, p. 215. See also Robischeaux on the way in which the code could discourage prosecutions.

88 For examples of the role of presbyteries see Pitcairn, *Criminal Trials in Scotland*, vol. 3, p. 600; report of the presbytery of Irvine, 2 Feb. 1658, JC 26/24; A.G. Reid (ed.), *The Diary of Andrew Hay*, Edinburgh: SHS, 1901, pp. 145 n., 195, 243; *Selected Justiciary Records*, vol. 3, p. 628. Macdonald, *Witches of Fife*.

89 *Trial, Confession and Execution of Isobel Inch*, p.12.

90 About 10 per cent of the cases in the archdeaconry of Essex involved charges of *maleficium*. In the church courts at York only 4 of 37 prosecutions for witchcraft involved charges of cursing or black magic. Macfarlane, *Witchcraft in Tudor and Stuart England*, p. 72; P. Tyler, 'The Church Courts at York and Witchcraft Prosecutions 1567–1640', *Northern History* 4 (1969), 97.

91 Ibid., p. 93.

92 See B.P. Levack, *The Civil Lawyers in England, 1603–1641*, Oxford: Clarendon Press, 1973.

93 J.H. Gleason, *The Justices of the Peace in England, 1558 to 1640*, Oxford: Clarendon Press, 1969, pp. 49–51.

94 C. Holmes, 'Popular Culture? Witches, Magistrates and Divines in Early Modern England', in S.L. Kaplan (ed.), *Understanding Popular Culture*, New York: Mouton, 1984, p. 92, claims that the clergy could 'interfere at any and every stage of the judicial process'. The interventions referred to in the sources cited, however, were far from vigorous. George More, *A True Discourse concerning the certain possession and dispossession of 7 persons in one family in Lancashire*, London, 1600, pp. 18–19, reported that preachers caused a man to be apprehended as a witch because he could not say the Lord's Prayer. John Davenport, *The Witches of Huntingdon*, London, 1646, p. 2, reported only that a minister was present at the examination of a witch by two lay justices of the peace. Richard Bernard, a 'country minister', gave only written advice, acquired from reading accounts of witchcraft trials and learned treatises, to judges in the western circuit in *A Guide to Grand-Jury Men ... in Cases of Witchcraft*, London 1627, sig. A3–4. In the prosecution of Susanna Edwards and Mary Trembles at Devon in 1682, Revd Hann tried to obtain a further confession from the witches. C.L. Ewen, *Witchcraft and Demonianism*, London: Heath Cranton, 1933, pp. 369–72. In 1566 Dr Thomas Cole, the archdeacon of Essex, participated in the examination of the Chelmsford witches but did not preside at their trial, as claimed in Macfarlane, *Witchcraft in Tudor and Stuart England*, pp. 73, 79.

95 Mackenzie, *Laws*, pp. 495–7. In the eighteenth century Scottish judges acquired the power to either accept or reject jury verdicts.

96 J.I. Smith, *Selected Justiciary Cases, 1624–1650*, vol . 2, Edinburgh: Stair Society, 1972, p. x. Smith argues that the operation of a system of written evidence and the general regard that Scots law had for the 'ascertainment of the facts as the principal object of criminal procedure' meant that there operated in Scotland 'an Inquisitorial system bearing most of the hallmarks of the mature inquisitorial systems of Europe. ... The tribunals were concerned with ascertaining facts, not with providing rules whereby two sides might, more or less decorously, sublimate a trial by combat in words.' For a detailed analysis of the Marian statutes that dealt with pre-trial procedure see J. Langbein, *Prosecuting Crime in the Renaissance*, Cambridge, MA: Harvard University Press, 1974, pp. 21–34.

97 See for example the presumptions and proofs for convicting a witch in William Perkins, *A Discourse of the Damned Art of Witchcraft*, Cambridge, 1608.

98 An Act Concerning Pirates and Robbers of the Sea, passed by the English Parliament in 1536, replaced the civil law procedure used to try pirates and others who committed felonies on the high seas with that of the common law. The statute complained that the requirement of the civil law for conviction (either a confession or the testimony of eyewitnesses) was allowing pirates, thieves, robbers, and murderers on the high seas to

escape unpunished, noting that would not confess 'without torture or pains'. 27 Henry VIII, c. 4; 28 Henry VIII, c. 15.

99 R. Godbeer, *The Devil's Dominion: Magic and Religion in Early New England*, Cambridge: Cambridge University Press, 1992, p. 177. See also the statement by the puritan cleric Samuel Fairclough in 1645. Samuel Clark, *The Lives of Sundry Eminent Persons in this Later Age*, London, 1683, p. 172.

100 J.D. Mackie and W.C. Dickinson, 'Relation of the Manner of Judicatores of Scotland', *SHR* 19 (1922), 271. *A True Account of the Forms Us'd in Pursuits of Treason According to the Laws of Scotland*, Edinburgh, 1691, p. 29. For an example of the use of counsel see *Justiciary Cases*, vol. 3, pp. 627–60. English courts would allow legal representation on a matter of law but not in the conduct of the trial proper. See J. Langbein, 'The Criminal Trial before the Lawyers', *University of Chicago Law Review*, 45 (1978), 307–16. For the appointment of such counsel in a witch-trial see Cockburn, *English Assizes*, p. 121.

101 *Justiciary Cases*, vol. 2, pp. xxii–xxiii, 602, 613, 815. Larner, *Enemies*, p. 175, attributes the higher acquittal rate in the justiciary court to the availability of counsel there.

102 L. Yeoman and M. Wasser (eds), 'The Trial of Geillis Johnstone for Witchcraft in 1613', in *Miscellany XIII*, Edinburgh: SHS, 2004.

3   King James VI and witchcraft

1 H. Stafford, 'Notes on Scottish Witchcraft Cases, 1590–91', in N. Downs (ed.) *Essays in Honor of Conyers Read*, Chicago: Chicago University Press, 1953, pp. 96–118, 278–84; E.J. Cowan, 'The Darker Vision of the Scottish Renaissance: The Devil and Francis Stewart', in I.B. Cowan and D. Shaw (eds), *The Renaissance and Reformation in Scotland*, Edinburgh: Scottish Academic Press, 1983, pp. 125–40; J. Wormald, 'The Witches, the Devil and the King', in D.T. Brotherstone and D. Ditchburn (eds), *Freedom and Authority: Scotland c.1050–c.1650*, East Linton: Tuckwell, 2000, pp. 165–80. S. Clark, 'King James's *Daemonologie*: Witchcraft and Kingship', in S. Anglo (ed.), *The Damned Art*, London: Routledge & Kegan Paul, 1977, pp. 56–81; C. Larner, *Witchcraft and Religion*, Oxford: Basil Blackwell, 1984, pp. 3–22; J. Goodare, 'The Scottish Witchcraft Panic of 1597', *SWHC*, pp. 51–72; P.G. Maxwell-Stuart, *Satan's Conspiracy*, East Linton: Tuckwell Press, 2001.

2 *Newes from Scotland*, London, 1591, pp. 8–9.

3 *CSPS*, vol. 10, pp. 165–6.

4 *WEMS*, document 1. The report of this examination is not dated.

5 *Newes from Scotland*, pp. 12–13, reports that Sampson refused to confess in an initial examination before the king but that she confessed after she was tortured and the devil's mark was found 'upon her privities'. The judicial record makes no mention of the torture but records a mixture of denials and admissions on the morning of that day and a full confession before the king that afternoon. JC 26/2/12. The English ambassador reported on 7 December that the king had elicited the confession by his 'own special travail', and six months later the king told the jurors in the case of Barbara Napier that he had secured the confession 'by me myself', *CSPS*, vol. 10, pp. 430, 524. The most compelling evidence that Sampson was tortured comes from the fact that when she was examined in January, she first denied the convention at North Berwick but then confessed to it again. The application of torture provides the most likely explanation of such rapid reversals in her testimony. *WEMS*, p. 15.

6 Reports of the number of witches varied. In her initial confession Sampson set the figure at more than 100, with only six being men. *WEMS*, p. 147. *Newes from Scotland*, p. 13, reports that there were more than 200 witches at the North Berwick assembly.

7 JC 26/12/3; *WEMS*, document 2. Sampson also confessed to performing maleficent magic in the attempt to destroy David Seton and his goods.

8 *WEMS*, p. 149.

9 Ibid., p. 148. When asked whether the king would have bairns, the devil replied that he would first have lads and then lasses. The devil also told her that the ministers would destroy the king and Scotland, but if he would use his counsel, he would destroy them.

10 *CSPS*, vol. 10, p. 524.

11 *WEMS*, p. 41.

12 *WEMS*, p. 136.

13 J. Melville, *Memoirs of His Own Life by Sir James Melville of Halhill*, Edinburgh: Bannatyne Club, 1827, p. 395.

14 *WEMS*, documents 5–9. The depositions taken early in 1591 made reference to an image in the possession of Agnes Sampson at an assembly of witches, but only Donald Robson had testified that the image was that of the king.

15 *WEMS*, document 22. According to *Newes from Scotland*, pp. 15–16, Sampson confessed that 'by the devil's persuasion' she had intended to bewitch the king to death by placing the venom of a toad in a piece of the king's clothing.

16 In reporting Napier's trial to Lord Burghley on 9 May, Robert Bowes, the English ambassador, said that Napier had been arraigned for attempting the destruction of the king at Bothwell's instigation. *WEMS*, p. 211.

17 Ibid., p. 267

18 Ibid., p. 272.

19 *Newes from Scotland*, p. 15.

20 *WEMS*, p. 208.

21 In *Newes from Scotland*, p. 17, the witches allegedly raised a stiff wind that affected only the king's ship (and not the others in the royal convoy) as he and his bride returned from Denmark in April 1590. According to the pamphlet, which was intended to show the folly of witchcraft and rebellion, this wind would have also caused the king's death if it had not been for his strong faith in God.

22 *WEMS*, p. 218.

23 Larner, *Witchcraft and Religion*, p. 11, claimed that James accepted the reality of these ideas as a result of conversations with the Danish philosopher and demonologist Nils Hemmingius, author of a treatise on superstition and magic, at his residence in Roskilde.

24 J. Goodare, 'The Scottish Witchcraft Act of 1563', *Church History* 74 (2005), 62–4.

25 *Newes from Scotland*, p. 9; *WEMS*; Richard Bannatyne, *Memorials of Transactions in Scotland, AD 1559–1573*, ed. R. Pitcairn, Edinburgh: Bannatyne Club, 1836, p. 233. Maxwell-Stuart, *Satan's Conspiracy*, p. 61.

26 Lammas marked the halfway point between the summer solstice and the autumn equinox, whereas All Hallows' Eve marked the halfway point between the autumn equinox and the winter solstice. These were originally Celtic pagan festivals that were transformed into important days on the Christian liturgical calendar. Witches allegedly gathered on those days not because they were pagans but because the church wished to represent them as having rejected Christian culture.

27 Maxwell-Stuart, *Satan's Conspiracy*, ch. 6, has conjectured that this assembly at North Berwick church did actually take place. He also suggests that Sampson and Fian might not have been tortured, as claimed in *Newes from Scotland*; for this reason their confessions would have more credibility. Impartial evidence of the torture of the North Berwick witches comes from Robert Bowes in a letter to Burghley, *CSPS*, vol. 10, p. 502. Even if torture had not been used in these prosecutions, the acceptance of the confessions of the witches at face value, without an analysis of the way in which their testimony was filtered by interrogators, judges, and scribes, including the king himself, makes the claim that a meeting actually took place difficult to sustain.

28 *WEMS*, p. 257.

29 Pierre de Lancre, *Tableau de l'inconstance des mauvais anges et demons*, Paris, 1613.

30 *WEMS*, p. 42.

31 A.I. Cameron (ed.), *The Warrender Papers*, vol. 2, Edinburgh: SHS, 1932, p. 168.

32 *Daemonologie*, pp. 54–5.

33 *RPCS*, vol. 4, p. 680. In *Daemonologie*, p. 21, James, reflecting on his own difficulties obtaining the confession of Agnes Sampson, admitted that 'experience daily proves how loath they are to confess without torture, which witnesses their guiltiness'.

34 D. Calderwood, *The History of the Kirk of Scotland*, Edinburgh: Wodrow Society, 1842–9, vol. 5, pp. 685–7.

35 Bowes to Burghley, 15 Aug. 1597. *CSPS*, vol. 3, pt 1, p. 73. Although Bowes's letter is dated three days after the order of the privy council, the date of Anderson's examination is not given. It is not known, therefore, whether James continued to examine witches after 12 August.

36 J. Goodare, 'Scottish Witchcraft Panic', p. 62.

37 *CSPS*, vol. 13, p. 73.

38 *Daemonologie*, p. 6.

39 Ibid., p. 22. He discusses some of the different fashions in Book II, ch. 3, pp. 24–6.

40 Ibid., Book III, ch. 3.

41 Ibid., pp. 25–6.

42 Ibid., p. 56.

43 Catholic demonologists, however, had no difficulty emphasizing the importance of the devil's mark as well. See J. Fontaine, *Discours des marques des sorciers*, Paris, 1611. Fontaine had examined the French witch Father Louis Gaufridi and had found the incriminating marks on his body.

44 *Daemonologie*, p. 25. This same emphasis on the mark as an inversion of the baptismal seal appears in the manuscript treatise by John Bell, 'A Discourse of Witchcraft' (1705) ''Tis but rational to think that the devil, aping God, should imprint a sacrament of his covenant.' Quoted in C.K. Sharpe, *A Historical Account of the Belief in Witchcraft in Scotland*, London: Hamilton, Adams & Co., 1884, p. 208.

45 *Daemonologie*, p. 56.

46 Ibid., book II, ch. 4.

47 M. Summers (ed.), The *Malleus Maleficarum of Heinrich Kramer and James Sprenger*, London: John Rodker, 1928, pp. 104–9.

48 *Daemonologie*, pp. 42–3.

49 Ibid., p. 43.

50 Ibid., p. 49.

51 Ibid., pp. 44, 165.

52 *WEMS*, pp. 228, 229, 410 n.

53 National Archives, STAC 8/4/10, fol. 201 *et passim*. The fits began shortly after midsummer 1604.

54 STAC 8/4/10, fols 95v, 96, 105, 140v, 156.

55 See B.P. Levack, 'Possession, Witchcraft and the Law in Jacobean England', *Washington and Lee Law Review* 52 (1996), 1622, n. 34.

56 STAC 8/4/10, fol. 18, refers to her 'being supported on either side and behind her with some of her friends and scholars of Oxford'. A number of the fellows of Exeter later gave testimony in the Star Chamber *ex parte* Brian Gunter. See also the deposition of Susanna Holland, STAC 8/4/10, fol. 207.

57 C. Karlsen, *The Devil in the Shape of a Woman*, New York: W.W. Norton, 1987, p. 231, discusses possession as 'cultural performance' in which shared meanings were communicated by the demoniacs, the ministers, and the audience. For a discussion of exorcism as theater see S. Greenblatt, *Shakespearean Negotiations*, Berkeley, CA: University of California Press, 1988, pp. 96–114.

58 STAC 8/4/10, fol. 21, deposition of John Harding. Harding and Holland were both members of the commission that prepared the King James version of the Bible.

59 Examination of Murray by Lord Ellesmere, 29 July 1607, Huntington Library, Ellesmere MS 5955/2.

60 STAC 8/4/10, fols 2b, 167v, 178.

61 Ibid., fol. 178. See also deposition of William Sawyer, fol. 168.

62 Ibid., fols 160, 196, 226.

63 Ibid., fols 88, 106.

64 The depositions of Thomas Hinton and Alexander Chokke in the later trial of Anne and Brian in the Star Chamber, STAC 8/4/10, fols 9–18, remain the only source for this proceedings of this trial. The assize records for the Oxfordshire circuit are no longer extant.

65 Examination of Alexander Chokke, STAC 8/4/10, fol. 18v.

66 G.N. Clark, *A History of the Royal College of Physicians of London*, Oxford: Clarendon Press, 1964, vol. 1, p. 198. William Harvey, then a candidate of the college and a friend of one of Anne's examiners, later used this case in his Anatomical Lectures of 1616 to illustrate how a person could make herself insensitive to pain. *The Anatomical Lectures of William Harvey*, ed. G. Whitteridge, Edinburgh: E. & S. Livingstone, 1964, pp. 46–7. R. Hunter and Ida MacAlpine, 'A Note on William Harvey's "Nan Gunter" (1616)', *Journal of the History of Medicine* 12 (1957), 512–15, suggest that Anne may have first drawn Harvey's attention to patients who showed disturbances of sensation accompanying mental illness. Harvey did not, however, claim that Anne was mentally ill but simply that she made herself insensitive to pain.

67 STAC 8/4/10, fols, 3v, 20v, 23, 100.

68 STAC 8/4/10, fols, 151v, 163. Brian Gunter brought his daughter to Oxford again at this time with the specific purpose of securing James's interest in the case.

69 The first interview was at Oxford on 27 Aug., while two more took place at Finchingbrooke, near Windsor, on 9 and 10 Oct. The date of the meeting at Whitehall is uncertain. H.N. Paul, *The Royal Play of Macbeth*, New York: Macmillan, 1950, p. 122, claims that it occurred in Sept., at which time the king referred the girl to Edward Jorden. Thomas Guidott reports this meeting, without a date, in the preface to Edward Jorden, *Discourse of Natural Baths*, 3rd edn, London, 1669. Edward Jorden later testified that Anne 'came from court' within a month after being committed to Harsnett's custody, thus suggesting some time in Sept. as the date of the meeting at Whitehall. Anne refers to all these interviews, but without dates, in STAC 8/4/10, fol. 128v. James requested yet another meeting at Ware on 30 Oct., but Dr Richard Neile claimed that Anne could not be delivered to him at that time. Neile to the earl of Salisbury, 30 Oct. 1605, *Calendar of the Manuscripts of … the Marquis of Salisbury Preserved at Hatfield House*, vol.17, London: Historical Manuscripts Commission, 1938, pp. 471–2.

70 On this campaign see M. MacDonald (ed.), *Witchcraft and Hysteria in Elizabethan London*, London: Routledge, 1990, pp. xix–xxvi.

71 C.L. Ewen, *Witchcraft in the Star Chamber*, privately printed, 1938, p. 36.

72 *Calendar of Salisbury Manuscripts*, vol. 17, pp. 471–2.

73 R. Johnston, *Historia Rerum Britannicarum*, Amsterdam, 1655, claimed that Harsnett deliberately sued Ashley 'to entice the girl into love' and that Anne, 'inclined to lust', revealed all of her tricks to him. Paul, *Royal Play of Macbeth*, pp. 125–6.

74 Paul, *Royal Play of Macbeth*, pp. 120–1, claims that the king referred the girl directly to Jorden in Sept., but Jorden's deposition in Star Chamber refers to examination one month after the girl was committed to Harsnett's custody, and that commitment probably did not take place until early Sept. STAC 8/4/10, fol. 57.

75 Edward Jorden, *A Briefe Discourse of a Disease Called Suffocation of the Mother*, London, 1603.

76 Deposition of Edward Jorden, STAC 8/4/10, fol. 57. Jorden's testimony was given *ex parte* Gunter.

77 James I to the earl of Salisbury, 10 Oct. 1605, *Calendar of Salisbury Manuscripts*, vol. 17, pp. 450–1.

78 Walker, *Unclean Spirits*, pp. 80–1.

79 BL, Additional MS 12,497, fol. 197v.

80 STAC 8/4/10, fol. 75.

81   Ibid., fols 97, 103. For the swearing her to secrecy see fols 104, 124, 128.
82   The king allegedly gave Anne a marriage portion after she confessed to him on 10 Oct. 1605. Thomas Guidott, preface to Edward Jorden, *Discourse of Natural Baths*, 3rd edn, London, 1669.
83   G.L. Kittredge, *Witchcraft in Old and New England*, Cambridge, MA: Harvard University Press, 1929, p. 326.
84   Samuel Harsnett, *A Declaration of Egregious Popish Impostures*, London, 1603.
85   Harsnett referred to those persons who have 'their fancies distempered with the imaginations and apprehensions of witches, conjurers, and fairies and all that lymphatical chimera', and he cited Chaucer's opinion that 'all these brainless imaginations of witchings, possessings, house-haunting and the rest were the forgeries, cosenages, impostures and legerdemain of crafty priests and lecherous friars'. Ibid., p. 309.
86   Kittredge, *Witchcraft in Old and New England*, pp. 322–3. The boy was sent to Lambeth Palace for examination.
87   *CSPD 1611–1618*, p. 398.

4   Witch-hunting in revolutionary Britain

1   On this political theory see E. Kantorowiz, *The King's Two Bodies*, Princeton: Princeton University Press, 1957.
2   Scottish commissioners consented to the union in 1652, but an act of union was not passed by parliament until 1656. Scottish representation in the parliament of the protectorate was established by ordinance in 1654.
3   C. Carlton, *Going to the Wars*, London: Routledge, 1992, pp. 201–29. These deaths were more numerous, when figured on a percentage basis, than the number of people killed in the American civil war.
4   J. Morrill, *The Nature of the English Revolution*, London: Longman, 1993, ch. 2.
5   *Source-book*, p. 239.
6   J.R. Young, *The Scottish Parliament, 1639–1661*, Edinburgh: John Donald, 1996, p. 41.
7   *APS*, vol. 6, pt 1, p. 197.
8   *RPCS*, 2nd ser., vol. 8, pp. 204–5. The names of two of the confessing witches, Nicoll Stillie and Isobel Stillie, were deleted in the final version of the commission. The anticipated penalty was routinely included in commissions granted in 1649. See for example the commission to try Robert Maxwell, PA 11/8, p. 63.
9   *RPCS*, 2nd ser., vol. 8, p. 205.
10   PA 7/9/1, 2 May 1661.
11   The committee gradually took shape between 1639 and 1640. See D. Stevenson (ed.), *The Government of Scotland under the Covenanters, 1637–1651*, Edinburgh: SHS, 1982, pp. xix–xx. The committee also operated from 1660 to 1661. *RPCS*, 3rd ser., vol.1, p. v.
12   The commissions are included in the registers of the committee, PA11/8 and 11/9. Five additional commissions appear in the warrant book for 1650, PA12/5. I am grateful to Paula Hughes for calling my attention to these additional commissions.
13   PA11/8, fol. 49.
14   *APS*, vol. 6, pt 2, *passim*.
15   Ibid., p. 538.
16   J. Gilmore, 'Witchcraft and the Church of Scotland', unpublished Ph.D. thesis, University of Glasgow, 1948, pp. 32–4, 41. *APS*, vol. 6, pt 1, p. 197.
17   E. Henderson, *Annals of Dunfermline and Vicinity*, Glasgow, 1879, pp. 319–20.
18   A. Mitchell and J. Christie (eds), *Records of the Commissions of the General Assemblies of the Church of Scotland ..., 1648 and 1649*, Edinburgh: SHS, 1896, p. 414.
19   Act concerning the passing of commissions against witches, PA12/5, 2 April 1650.
20   *APS*, vol. 6, pt 2, pp. 563–4, 565, 566.
21   PA12/5, 2 April 1650.

22 S.R. Gardiner (ed.), *Letters and Papers Illustrating the relations between Charles the Second and Scotland in 1650*, Edinburgh: SHS, 1894, p. 136. The name of the parish in the letter mistakenly reads 'Wadington'.

23 E. Henderson, *Extracts from the Kirk-Session Records of Dunfermline*, Edinburgh, 1865, p. 27. CH2/592/1, fol. 76. Henderson, *Annals of Dunfermline*, p. 317.

24 Irvine presbytery records, 29 Oct. 1622, Glasgow University Archives, MS. DC1/39, p. 4.

25 PA11/8, p. 189. George Sinclair, *Satan's Invisible World*, Edinburgh, 1780, pp. 73–80.

26 Glasgow University Archives, MS DC/1/139, p. 138.

27 J. Paterson, *History of the County of Ayr*, Ayr, 1847, vol. 3, pp. 263–4. Paterson records their executions in March rather than April, but this was probably an error in transcription.

28 CH2/197/1/25.

29 The last name of this Margaret is omitted in the transcription of the records of the presbytery but she is likely the Margaret Cooper referred to in the *Statistical Account of Ayshire*, pp. 632–3.

30 CH2/197/1/27.

31 CH2/197/1/27–8. The minutes read that the petition was to be submitted to 'the lords of the privy council for committee of estates', suggesting some uncertainty which body might respond to the request.

32 CH2/197/1/29.

33 Of the 128 witchcraft cases tried during the Cromwellian occupation 97 were tried in circuit courts; the remaining 31 were tried before the English commissioners in the court of justiciary. L. Smith, 'Scotland and Cromwell: a study in early modern government', D.Phil. thesis, University of Oxford, 1979, p. 163.

34 The trial record reports that the ministers and bailies of Dumbarton had also heard his confession. JC 6/5, 5 Feb. 1656.

35 Of the 23 witches tried by the English commissioners in the circuit courts between 1654 and 1656, only one, Patrick Barnett, was accused of demonic activity, which in his case was consulting with Satan. JC17/1, Perth fugitive list, p. 5. All the others were prosecuted for charming.

36 Lamont, *Diary*, p. 47.

37 J. Nicoll, *A Diary of Public Transactions and other Occurrences, chiefly in Scotland*, Edinburgh, 1836, p. 106; JC 10/17.

38 Smith, 'Scotland and Cromwell', pp. 187–8, 181. The justices of the peace had been established by an act of parliament in 1609, but they had not functioned properly. The decision to appoint justices on the English model was made in 1654 but the plan was not implemented until Dec. 1655. F.D. Dow, *Cromwellian Scotland*, Edinburgh: John Donald, 1979, pp. 176–87. The JPs had little influence on witch-hunting until 1657.

39 In 1658 the Scots gained a majority of the commissioners for the administration of justice, but only the English judges continued to try criminal cases. Dow, *Cromwellian Scotland*, pp. 121–2.

40 JC 26/24, 19 July 1658, testimony by the justices of the peace that the witches were not tortured at Alloa, This statement was a response to charges that they had in fact subjected witches to torture.

41 In response to this request, the presbytery of Irvine identified four confessing witches, including a 10-year-old girl. The presbytery also appointed two people to present the persons to the justices. JC 26/24, process at Irvine, 2 Feb. 1658.

42 Kincaid found four marks on the body of Janet Bruce in Tranent. JC 26/22, depositions against Janet Bruce, 23 June 1657. Kincaid testified one week later that the four marks were diabolical. For Kincaid's activity in 1659 see JC 26/26, processes against Tranent witches.

43 JC 26/26, processes against Stenton witches, 2 March 1659.

44 Henderson, *Annals of Dunfermline*, pp. 319–20.

45   Glasgow University Library, MS. DC/ 1/139, pp. 3–14. The month and day of the order are not given.

46   W. Ross, *Aberdour and Inchcolme*, Edinburgh: David Douglas, 1885, pp. 324–43; Stephen, *Inverkeithing*, pp. 440–6. JC 26/13.

47   PA 11/8, pp. 62–3. In anticipation of a guilty verdict the committee also decreed that he should suffer death if found guilty and even prescribed the method of execution by strangling and burning.

48   *CSPD 1649–50*, p. 215. The original commission granted by the privy council in 1644 had been found inadequate, so Crooks requested that 'a competent number of others' be added to the commission. *RPCS*, vol. 8, pp. 133–4. The petition was granted on 29 June. *APS*, vol. 6, pt 1, p. 453b; National Archives, SP 46 (pt X)/129, fol. 188.

49   BL, Egerton MS 2879, fol. 1.

50   JC26/26. In 1583 the general assembly protested about the failure to punish incest, adultery, witchcraft, murder, and other crimes, that sin was increasing daily and that this 'provoketh the wrath of God against the whole country'. D. Calderwood, *The History of the Kirk of Scotland*, Edinburgh: Wodrow Society, 1842–9, vol. 3, p. 736.

51   *Justiciary Cases*, vol. 3, pp. 610–13.

52   Glasgow University Archives, MS DC/1/139, p. 140 *et passim*.

53   S. Macdonald, *The Witches of Fife*, East Linton: Tuckwell, 2002, p. 183.

54   See for example the commissions granted by the committee of estates in 1649, PA 11/8. They included one case of 'double adultery' and one of bestiality. John Nicoll observed the startling increase in cases of bestiality and incest during the period of the English occupation. Nicoll, *A Diary of Public Transactions*, p. 202.

55   CH2/523/1, fol. 191v., 17 March 1650.

56   Lamont, *Diary*, p. 47.

57   JC 26/13. This James Wilson should not be confused with another sexual offender by the same name who was convicted and executed for bestiality in Feb. 1649. This James Wilson was convicted of copulation with various animals, most notably a black cow twelve times and a grey mare six times, 'twice in the daytime and four times at night'. JC 26/13, 5 Feb. 1649.

58   The link was even closer in the prosecution of Janet Anderson in March 1658 for 'sundry adulteries and fornications and for having copulation with Satan'. Nicoll, *A Diary of Public Transactions*, pp. 213–14.

59   Larner, *Enemies*, pp. 73–5. *Acts of the General Assembly of the Church of Scotland, 1638–1842*, Edinburgh, 1843, pp. 44, 216–17.

60   *WEMS*, document 20.

61   *Justiciary Cases*, vol. 3, pp. 597–602.

62   See the petition of the presbytery of Linlithgow to the synod of Lothian and Tweeddale in April 1644 seeking advice on how to curb the excessive use of charming. CH2/242/3. I am grateful to Paula Hughes for this reference.

63   *Justiciary Cases*, vol. 3, pp. 597–8.

64   A. Mitchell and J. Christie (eds), *Records of the Commissions of the General Assemblies of the Church of Scotland ... 1646–1647*, Edinburgh: SHS, 1892, p. 123. On the general assembly's lobbying of parliament for legislation against charming see J.R. Young, 'The Scottish Parliament and Witch-hunting in Scotland under the Covenanters', *Parliaments, Estates and Representation* 26 (2006), 56–8. Parliament passed a witchcraft act in 1649, but it dealt mainly with those who consulted with witches and did not mention charmers.

65   CH2/265/2, p. 165.

66   C.L. Ewen, *Witch-hunting and Witch Trials*, London: Kegan Paul, 1929, pp. 117–245. Contemporaries support this contention. One letter-writer claimed that more witches had been indicted during the 1640s than at any other time in English history. See J. Jacobs (ed.), *Epistolae Ho-Eliane: The Familiar Lettres of James Howell*, London, 1890, pp. 506, 515. See also K. Thomas, *Religion and the Decline of Magic*, New York: Scribner, 1971, p. 455 and sources in n. 4.

67 J. Sharpe, 'The Devil in East Anglia', in J. Barry *et al.* (eds), *Witchcraft in Early Modern Europe*, Cambridge: Cambridge University Press, 1996, p. 238.

68 In addition to the 16 executions at Newcastle on 21 Aug. 1650, there were further trials and executions at Alnick in that year. The number of executions at Berwick and Gateshead is not known. The Gateshead parish books for 1649 reported paying the justices to examine the witches, money for a witch's grave, and £1. 5s. for trying the witches. The Gateshead witches were sent to Durham for trial. Richardson, *The Local Historian's Table*, London, 1841, p. 283.

69 M. Gaskill (ed.), *The Matthew Hopkins Trials (The English Witchcraft Trials, 1560–1736,* vol. 3), London: Pickering & Chatto, 2003, pp. 455–6. Warburton petitioned parliament to reprieve three of the six convicted witches, but they were executed before action could be taken. The examinations of some of the Maidstone witches, including Wilman Worcester, had taken place in 1651. See Kent Archives Office, Q/SB/2/12–14.

70 *A Prodigious and Tragicall History of the Arraignment, Tryall, Confession, and Condemnation of Six Witches at Maidstone in Kent*, London, 1652. There was pressure to have the witches' bodies burned, reflecting the emphasis on the spiritual or heretical nature of their crime, but the judge ensured that the traditional sentence of execution by hanging would be administered.

71 Warburton's doubts concerning the guilt of the accused were reinforced by Sir Robert Filmer in *An Advertisement to the Jury-Men of England*, London, 1653, sig. A2.

72 The effect of this caution was evident almost immediately in Kent, where six witches, including Elizabeth Wood, a single woman, were acquitted in 1653. Kent Archives Office, Q/SB4/54; Q/SMc1, 4 Oct. 1653.

73 B.P. Levack, *The Witch-hunt in Early Modern Europe*, 3rd edn, London: Longman, 2006, pp. 180–2. The only case of English witchcraft related directly to the war was the parliamentary seizure and execution of the witch of Newbury, who was suspected of being a royalist spy. *A Most Certain, Strange and True Discovery of a Witch*, London, 1643.

74 G. Durston, *Witchcraft and Witch Trials*, Chichester: Barry Rose Law Publishers, 2000, pp. 191–2.

75 Ibid., p. 199.

76 *The Examination, Confession, Triall, and Execution of Joane Williford, Joan Cariden, and Jane Holt: who were executed at Feversham in Kent*, London, 1645.

77 R. Howell, *Newcastle upon Tyne and the Puritan Revolution*, Oxford: Clarendon Press, 1967, pp. 232–3.

78 Samuel Clark, *The Lives of Sundry Eminent Persons in this Later Age*, London, 1683, p. 172.

79 The vacancy ended on 30 Aug. 1645 when Richard Lane was appointed lord keeper. Commissioners of the great seal had taken their place and were authorized in Aug. 1645 to grant special commissions to whomever they wished. *Journals of the House of Commons*, vol. 4, p. 247; *Journals of the House of Lords*, vol. 6, pp. 683, 687, 688.

80 See M. Gaskill, *Witchfinders*, Cambridge, MA: Harvard University Press, 2005, pp. 150–5, for a discussion of this witch-hunt in Suffolk. The comparison with Salem is strengthened by the fact that in both cases the gaols were filled with accused witches.

81 Samuel Clark, *Lives of Sundry Eminent Persons*, p. 172. See also Increase Mather, *Cases of Conscience Concerning Evil Spirits Personating Men*, Boston, 1693.

82 Matthew Hopkins, *The Discovery of Witches*, London, 1647, p. 5.

83 Gaskill's discussion of the treatment of the Suffolk witches, including the effects of forced sleeplessness, *Witchfinders*, pp. 89–90, leaves little doubt that they were subjected to torture by any definition.

84 Ibid., epilogue.

85 John Cotta, *The Trial of Witch-craft*, London, 1616, pp. 107–9; Beinecke Library, Osborne Shelves, fb 224, p. 8.

86 Ibid., pp. 158, 167.

87 W.N. Neill, 'The Professional Pricker and his Test for Witchcraft', *SHR* 19 (1922), 205–13. Two prickers known to have been active in 1649 were John Kincaid of Tranent and

Alexander Bogs, who searched Elizabeth Graham for the mark in August of that year. G. Sinclair, *Satan's Invisible World Discovered*, Edinburgh, 1780, p. 74. The pricker John Balfour of Corshouse was active as early as 1632. *RPCS*, 5th ser., 4 (1632), 427, 432. For the prickers known by name see S.W. McDonald, 'The Devil's Mark and the Witch-Prickers of Scotland', *Journal of the Royal Society of Medicine* 90 (1997), 509.

88 Tyne and Wear Archives Office, Newcastle Common Council Books 1645–1650, County Council Records 589/4, fol. 328v.

89 Richardson, *Local Historian's Table*, pp. 281–2. The account is taken from J. Brand, *The History and Antiquities of the Town and County of the Town of Newcastle upon Tyne*, London, 1789, pp. 477–8.

90 J. Fuller, *The History of Berwick upon Tweed*, Edinburgh, 1799, pp. 155-6.

91 Richardson, *Local Historian's Table*, pp. 281–3. The account of the execution of the pricker cannot be verified in Scottish records.

92 *Prodigious and Tragicall History*, p. 5.

93 Ralph Gardiner, *England's Grievance Discovered in Relation to the Coal Trade*, London, 1796, p. 117.

94 K. Thomas, *Religion and the Decline of Magic*, New York: Scribner, 1971, p. 501.

95 The case for Hopkins's puritanism, while largely circumstantial, is made persuasively by Gaskill, *Witchfinders*, ch. 1.

96 Ibid., p. 36. On Grimstone's career in Essex, see W. Hunt, *The Puritan Moment*, Cambridge, MA: Harvard University Press, 1983.

97 J. Sharpe, *Instruments of Darkness*, London: Hamish Hamilton, 1996, pp. 141–2.

98 W. Lamont, *Godly Rule*, London: Macmillan, 1969, pp. 99–100, claims that Hopkins was the natural successor to the English millenarian Thomas Brightman.

99 *The Lawes against Witches and Conjuration*, London, 1645, title page.

100 John Stearne, *A Confirmation and Discovery of Witchcraft*, London, 1648, p, 60. Stearne writes that for the time being, however, the devil 'is busy in deceiving nations'.

101 N. Homes, *Daemonologie and Theologie*, London, 1650. For millenarianism in English demonological treatises see S. Clark, *Thinking with Demons*, Oxford: Clarendon Press, 1997, p. 325.

102 Macfarlane, *Witchcraft in Tudor and Stuart England*, p. 141. See also Gaskill, *Witchfinders*, pp. 22, 45.

103 Howell, *Newcastle on Tyne*, pp. 232–3.

104 Perkins, *Damned Art of Witchcraft*, pp. 173–80. See also the assertion of an anonymous Protestant author in the 1630s who wrote 'All witches, white or black, good or bad (as they term them), are both bad.' Beinecke Library, Osborne Shelves, fb. 224, p. 19.

105 John Downame, *Annotations upon all the Books of the Old and New Testament*, London, 1645, sub Exod. 22:18. See also Gaskill, *Witchfinders*, p. 138.

106 Stearne, *Confirmation and Discovery of Witchcraft*, sig. A2.

107 *The Book of the General Laws and Liberties concerning the Inhabitants of the Massachusets*, Cambridge, MA, 1648.

108 William Prynne, *Diotrephes Catechised: Or Sixteen Important Questions touching the Ecclesiastical Jurisdiction*, London, 1646, p. 4.

109 Sharpe, 'Devil in East Anglia', p. 238.

110 Some of these are described in Hopkins, *Discovery of Witches*, p. 2.

111 Sharpe, 'Devil in East Anglia'.

112 Ibid., p. 248.

113 D. Purkiss, *The English Civil War*, London: HarperPress, 2006, p. 383.

114 A further connection between Scotland and English witch-hunting in the 1640s was that the anti-Calvinist pastor John Lowes, who was tried and executed as a witch in 1645, had frequently preached against the Scottish nation. Gaskill, *Witchfinders*, p. 139.

115 H.F., *A True and Exact Relation of the Severall Informations, Examinations and Confessions of the Late Witches Arraigned and Executed in the county of Essex*, London, 1645, p. 2.

116 John Gaule, *Cases of Conscience touching Witches and Witchcraft*, London, 1646, p. 92.

117 Gaskill, *Witchfinders*, p. 77.
118 Ibid., p. 192.
119 Ibid., pp. 194–5.
120 Ibid., pp. 184–5.
121 Hopkins, *Discovery of Witches*, p. 3.
122 *The Tryall and Examination of Mrs. Joan Petereson … also the tryal, examination and confession of Giles Fenderin*, London, 1652.
123 Filmer, *An Advertisement to the Jury-Men of England*, pp. 9–24.
124 I. Bostridge, *Witchcraft and its Transformations, c.1650–c.1750*, Oxford: Clarendon Press, 1997.

5 The great Scottish witch-hunt of 1661–2

1 This number includes not only individuals tried for witchcraft and those for whom trials were commissioned, but also those who were merely named as witches in the course of proceedings against others. Many of the names can be located in the *Source-book*. A total of 38 names not included in the *Source-book* can be found in the National Archives of Scotland. JC 26/27 (justiciary court processes), CH (kirk session records), and PA7 (records of parliament).

2 *RPCS*, 3rd ser., vol. 1, p. lv. F. Legge, 'Witchcraft in Scotland', *The Scottish Review* 18 (1891), 274, estimates that about 450 witches were executed during the period 1660–3. There is in fact hard evidence for only 65 executions and one suicide (Patrick Cathie, PA7/23/1) during the two-year period 1660–2. It is likely, however, that a great majority of those tried by local authorities upon receipt of a commission from the privy council or parliament were executed.

3 The number of persons formally accused at Salem is 165. See J. Demos, 'Underlying Themes in the Witchcraft of Seventeenth-Century New England', *American Historical Review* 75 (1970), 1314. P. Boyer and S. Nissenbaum, *Salem Possessed* (Cambridge, MA: Harvard University Press, 1974), p.190, work with only 142 accusations. It should be recognized, however, that the prosecutions at Salem were confined to a much smaller geographical area than the Scottish prosecutions of 1661–2.

4 For the treatment of the prosecutions of 1661–2 as part of a larger, four-year witch-hunt see P.G. Maxwell-Stuart, *An Abundance of Witches*, Stroud: Tempus, 2005.

5 C.K. Sharpe, *A Historical Account of the Belief in Witchcraft in Scotland*, London: Hamilton, Adams & Co., 1884, pp. 125–6.

6 R. Chambers, *Domestic Annals of Scotland*, Edinburgh: W. & R. Chambers, 1858–61, vol. 2, p. 277; W.L. Mathieson, *Politics and Religion*, Glasgow: James Maclehose and Sons, 1902, vol. 2, pp. 182–3; H.R. Trevor Roper, 'Scotland and the Puritan Revolution', in *Religion, the Reformation and Social Change*, New York: Harper & Row, 1967, pp. 440–1.

7 Articles against Andrew Laidlawe, 1671, JC 26/38. Laidlawe was set at liberty. JC 2/13.

8 C.H. Firth, *Scotland and the Commonwealth*, Edinburgh: SHS, 1895, pp. 367–8; Chambers, *Domestic Annals*, vol. 2, p. 220.

9 Lamont, *Diary*, p. 47.

10 JC 26/16, confession of John Bayne, 4 Jan. 1654.

11 *Source-book*, pp. 15–16, 53–5, 209–10.

12 Ibid., pp. 16–25, 55–7, 211–14. Seven of the witches executed in 1659 are listed more than once.

13 D. Laing (ed.), *The Letters and Journals of Robert Baillie, A.M.*, Edinburgh: Bannatyne Club, 1841–2, p. 436. This letter was dated 31 Jan. 1661, but the first half of it was written in 1659, as both internal evidence and the author himself indicate. See p. 437.

14 JC 26/26, extracts from the records of the kirk of Tranent, 25 Nov. 1660.

15 The minute books reveal that the commissioners actually sat until 5 July 1659, JC 6/5. The English parliament attempted to resolve this crisis, see *Journals of the House of Commons*, vol. 7, pp. 659, 775. A bill of union was introduced shortly after the Long Parliament

was recalled in July 1659, but parliament was dissolved before the third reading. In October commissioners were instructed to see that Scots had justice administered to them, but there is no record of actual legal proceedings. See BL, Egerton MS 1048, fol. 177.

16 *Letters of Baillie*, vol. 3, p. 430.

17 C.H. Firth (ed.), *Scotland and the Protectorate*, Edinburgh: SHS, 1899, pp. 391–2.

18 *APS*, vol. 7, appendix, p. 31.

19 G.F. Black, *A Calendar of Cases of Witchcraft in Scotland, 1510–1727*, New York: New York Public Library, 1938, p. 65.

20 Petition against Christian Wilson, 6 June 1661, PA 7/9/1, and proceedings against Wilson, GD 103/2/3/11, item 1. See also G.F. Black, *Some Unpublished Scottish Witchcraft Trials*, New York, 1941, pp. 36–7.

21 Janet Wilson, Janet Watt, Margaret Little, and Janet Fergreive. Newbattle kirk session, 11 and 14 Aug. 1661, CH2/276/4.

22 JC 26/27/1, Janet Millar process papers. See also CH 2/229/2, Kirliston kirk session, 14 Aug. 1659.

23 Thirteen of the witches whose trials had been authorized in 1649 came from East Lothian. They are named in *RPCS*, 2nd ser., vol. 8, pp. 204–5, and were tried again by a parliamentary commission on 2 May 1661, PA 7/9/1. The other five came from the presbytery of Irvine. See *RPCS*, 2nd ser., vol. 8, pp. 133–4, and the parliamentary commission granted on 29 June 1661. SP 46/129, f. 188.

24 Black, *Calendar*, p. 13; Legge, 'Witchcraft in Scotland', pp. 260–9; J.I. Smith, 'The Transition to Modern Law', in *An Introduction to Scottish Legal History*, Edinburgh: Stair Society, 1959, pp. 42–3. See also S. Macdonald, *The Witches of Fife*, East Linton: Tuckwell, 2002.

25 Trevor Roper, 'Scotland and the Puritan Revolution', pp. 440–1.

26 Lay elders were of course only quasi-clerical figures. See G. Donaldson, *The Scottish Reformation*, Cambridge: Cambridge University Press, 1960, pp. 186–7. Irrespective of how one labels them, they formed part of the clerical organization that Black and others consider to have been the main source of witchcraft prosecutions.

27 CH2/84/3, fol. 17v. For similar proceedings at Dalkeith before the hunt began see CH2/84/2, fols 29, 44v.

28 CH2/283/2, fols 56v–57.

29 Ibid., fol. 55; CH 2/531/1, Inveresk kirk session, 4 June 1661.

30 See for example the report of the presbytery of Irvine, 2 Feb. 1658, JC26/24; A.G. Reid (ed.), *The Diary of Andrew Hay of Craignethan 1659–1660*, Edinburgh: SHS, 1901, pp. 145n., 195, 243.

31 Pitcairn, *Criminal Trials in Scotland*, vol. 3, p. 690.

32 CH 2/424/4.

33 Neither the kirk session of Newton nor that of Edmiston would take action against Agnes Johnston, although the elders of Edmonston did express a hope that the civil authorities would proceed against her for witchcraft. CH2/283/2, fols 55v–57, Newton kirk session, 4 Aug. and 15 Sept. 1661.

34 The complaint that the council received on 1 April regarding the torture of Margaret Dron was directed against the minister and 14 laymen, many of them local landowners. Maxwell-Stuart, *An Abundance of Witches*, p. 206.

35 See for example the minutes of the Humbie kirk session, 7 July 1661, CH2/389/1.

36 Inveresk kirk session, 5 Nov. and 3 Dec. 1661, CH 2/531/1.

37 *APS*, vol. 7, appendix, p. 31; vol. 7, p. 123. For the confused judicial situation in Jan. 1661 see Sir John Lauder, *Historical Notices of Scottish Affairs*, ed. J. Laing, Edinburgh: Bannatyne Club, 1848, vol. 1, pp. 1, 3.

38 *RPCS*, 3rd ser., vol. 1, pp. 11–12.

39 *APS*, vol. 7, appendix, p. 78.

40 RPCS, 3rd ser., vol. 1, pp. 11–12. Since the judges were being asked to leave their ordinary place of judicature to administer justice in the country, they were given 'the first end' of the fines and escheats of any witches they should happen to convict. John Preston, bailie of the regality of Musselburgh for the earl of Lauderdale, was granted permission to sit with the three justice deputes. JC 2/10, 29 July 1661.

41 PA 7/9/1, no. 26, 3 April 1661. On 16 and 20 March Mackenzie had petitioned for the ratification of his appointment, against the claim of Thomas Henderson, on the basis of a prior signature of the late king, i.e. Charles I. Ibid., no. 21.

42 *APS*, vol. 7, appendix, p. 78.

43 JC 26/27, *passim*. Newbattle kirk session, 23 June 1661, CH 2/276/4. Although these records include numerous charges of *maleficia* made in 1661, there is no record of the specific malefices allegedly perpetrated at Samuelston.

44 *APS*, vol. 7, appendix, p. 31.

45 JC 26/27/2, 29 July 1661, examination of Agnes Loch.

46 Mackenzie, *Laws*, p. 91.

47 CH 2/276/4, 7 Aug. 1661. In her defence Lyle claimed that she only heard others make this claim.

48 J.G. Dalyell, *The Darker Superstitions of Scotland*, Edinburgh: Waugh & Innes, 1834, p. 643.

49 Ibid., p. 640. At Newbattle Janet Wilson, Janet Watt, and Isobel Fergusson all asked for the pricker. Newbattle kirk session, 3 July and 21 Aug. 1661, CH 2/276/4.

50 For the activities of the prickers before 1659 see the prosecution of Janet Bruce in 1657, JC 26/22 and JC 6/5.

51 Kincaid, using a 'great long pin', searched Christian Cranstoun, Janet Thomson, Barbara Cochrane, Marion Lynn, Helen Simbeard, and Marion Guild, and it is almost certain that he searched the other Tranent witches as well. Tranent witches process papers, 1659, JC 26/26. Kincaid was practising his trade as early as 1649. Pitcairn, *Criminal Trials*, vol. 2, p. 599.

52 For Kincaid's activity in Midlothian see Black, *Unpublished Witchcraft Trials*, pp. 38–45.

53 See Maxwell-Stuart, *An Abundance of Witches*, pp. 20–2, 73–5, *et passim*.

54 Newton kirk session, 4 and 11 Aug. 1661, CH2/283/2, fols 55v–56.

55 Ibid., 15 Sept., fols 56v–57.

56 Ibid., fols. 55v–57.

57 JC 26/27/2, Musselburgh witches processes, 29 July 1661.

58 Newton kirk session, 5 Jan. 1662, CH 2/283/2, fol. 59.

59 Sharpe, *Witchcraft in Scotland*, pp. 128–30. In one instance she laid the decapitated head of a dog on a sick child.

60 JC 26/27, Duddingston witches process papers.

61 JC 2/10, p. 218; Inveresk kirk session, 17 July 1655, CH 2/531/1. Cass claimed that the English soldiers had come to her house at midnight to buy clothes and left at 2 a.m. On 24 June the session decided that, since she was a 'notorious whore', the bailies should ask the master of the house of correction to take her in.

62 Dalkeith kirk session, 16 Nov. 1658, CH2/84/2, fol. 39v.

63 Inveresk kirk session, 4 June 1661, CH 2/531/1.

64 Helen Cass's confession, for example, included the admission that the devil had carnal dealing with her. JC 26/27/7, Duddingston witches processes, 10 Aug. 1661.

65 Black, *Unpublished Witchcraft Trials*, p. 36.

66 JC 26/27/3, dittay against Cock, 18 June 1661; Black, *Unpublished Witchcraft Trials*, p. 36.

67 JC 26/27/9, dittay against Margaret Allen, 14 Nov. 1661.

68 Mackenzie, *Laws*, p. 86.

69 Ibid, p. 87. JC 26/27/2, no. 6. The other possibility is that the poor woman was Janet Daill, aged 63, who was married to George Bell, a collier. I am grateful to Anne Cordey for suggesting this latter option.

70 JC 26/27/3, dittay against Cock, 11 Nov. 1661. This was the third dittay against Cock. She was accused of threatening Lithgob that he would not have the power to stand, after which he was bedridden for three months.

71 Millar was also held responsible for killing James Wilkie's horse by witchcraft when he refused to lend the horse to her for a shilling. JC 26/27, Janet Millar and Duddingston witches process papers.

72 Macfarlane, *Witchcraft in Tudor and Stuart England*, pp. 147–56, 173–6, 205–6; Boyer and Nissenbaum, *Salem Possessed*, pp. 209–16. Both authors argue that witchcraft accusations arose at a 'critical stage' in the emergence of an individualistic ethic. It should be noted, however, that at Salem those villagers who wished to preserve the old order accused their more entrepreneurial antagonists as well as some members of their own group, whereas in Essex, England, the situation was reversed.

73 Boyer and Nissenbaum, *Salem Possessed*, pp. 32–3; H.C.E. Midelfort, *Witch-hunting in Southwestern Germany, 1562–1684*, Stanford, CA: Stanford University Press, 1972, p. 194.

74 Numerous implications are recorded in JC 26/27. In East Lothian, Helen Deanes and Anna Pilmore, both of whom had been named in the earl of Haddington's petition of 3 April 1661, implicated a total of 14 persons on 24 April, the day that the commission established by parliament sentenced seven witches to death. PA 7/23/1. Of these 13 had been named as witches together with Deanes and Pilmore in 1649 but had not been convicted, mainly because a sufficiently empowered commission had not been granted. Compare the names in PA 7/9/1 and PA 7/23/1 with *RPCS*, 2nd ser., vol. 8, p. 205. In place of Janet Wast, accused in 1649, Helen Wast was named. Commissions to try seven of these individuals were granted on 9 May and 6 June 1661. *RPCS*, 2nd ser., vol. 8, pp. 199, 248.

75 See for example the case of Janet Stoddart, Inveresk kirk session, 5 Nov. 1661, CH 2/531/1. In Nov. 1661 the earl of Haddington asked that Agnes Williamson, who had been kept in prison eight months at the charge of himself and his tenants, be either tried or set at liberty. *RPCS*, 3rd ser., vol. 1, p. 78.

76 Mackenzie, *Laws*, p. 104. See also W.G. Scott-Moncrieff (ed.), *The Records of the Proceedings of the Justiciary Court, Edinburgh, 1661–1678*, vol. 1, Edinburgh: SHS 1905, p. 34.

77 Cock was acquitted on 10 Sept. but the minister and kirk session of Dalkeith petitioned that she not be put at liberty and presented new dittays against her. The council accordingly refused to set her free. JC 26/27/3, warrant for witnesses against Janet Cock, signed by Sir George Mackenzie, 11 Nov. 1661. For the dittays against Cock see JC 26/27/3, 18 June 1661, 11 Nov. 1661; Black, *Unpublished Witchcraft Trials*, p. 36. For those against Hutchinson, see Black, *Calendar*, p. 66; *Justiciary Court Proceedings*, vol. 1, pp. 11–13, 19

78 CH2/229/1, Kirkliston kirk session, 14 Aug. 1659.

79 JC 26/27/1, Janet Millar process papers.

80 *Justiciary Court Proceedings*, vol. 1, p. 3.

81 There is doubt that the Janet Millar of Kirkliston (*Source-book*, nos. 403, 2812, 2813) is the same person as the Janet Millar tried with the Duddingston witches. Compare the articles in the various dittays and also in the Kirkliston kirk session proceedings, 14 Aug. 1659.

82 JC 26/27/1, Duddingston witches and Janet Millar process papers; JC 2/10.

83 Mackenzie, *Laws*, pp. 80–108. See also Mackenzie, *Pleadings in Some Remarkable Cases*, Edinburgh, 1672, pp. 185–97.

84 There was only one case between 1663 and 1669. See *Source-book*, p. 40.

85 *RPCS*, 3rd ser., vol. 1, *passim*; *Source-book*, pp. 125–42. The privy council met for the first time on 13 July 1661, the day after parliament adjourned.

86 *RPCS*, 3rd ser., vol. 1, p. 198.

87 Ibid., pp. 187, 210.

88 Even in 1658, when local authorities were proceeding against more witches than in the previous few years, they were careful to deny that any torture had been used to extract confessions. See JC 26/24, testification of the justices of the peace, 19 July 1658.

89 Prickers, including one Cowan, a disciple of Kincaid, became active again in 1677, but the council imprisoned him. See W.N. Neill, 'The Professional Pricker and his Test for Witchcraft', *SHR* 19 (1922), 209.

90 See below, Ch. 8.

91 G. Henningsen, *The Witches' Advocate: Basque Witchcraft and the Spanish Inquisition (1609–1614)*, Reno, NV: University of Nevada Press, 1980. Trials continued in the secular courts.

92 Of the 1,802 individuals who confessed, 1,384 were girls under 12 or boys under 14 years of age.

93 Mackenzie, *Pleadings*, p. 185; *Laws*, pp. 81–5.

94 Mackenzie, *Laws*, p. 85.

95 Ibid., pp. 85–6.

96 Ibid., pp. 89–90.

97 Ibid., p. 91.

98 Ibid., p. 105.

99 For specific references to the prosecutions of 1661, see Mackenzie, *Laws*, pp. 87, 90, 93, 97, 104, 105, 106.

100 M. Lee, Jr., *The Cabal*, Urbana, IL: Illinois University Press, 1965, p. 36.

101 The recissory act of 28 March 1661 annulled all the acts of the 'pretended' parliaments of the 1640s and a further act of the same day declared that the recissory act extended to all the pretended parliaments since 1633. On 6 Sept. 1661, Charles ordered the restoration of the Scottish episcopacy by royal proclamation. See G. Davies and P. Hardacre, 'The Restoration of the Scottish Episcopacy, 1660–1661', *Journal of British Studies* 1 (1962), 45–50. It is difficult to determine the popularity of the restoration of the episcopacy. See M. Lee, Jr., 'Comment on the Restoration of the Scottish Episcopacy, 1660–1661', *Journal of British Studies* 1 (1962), 52–3, and I.B. Cowan, *The Scottish Covenanters, 1660–1688*, London: V. Gollancz, 1976, p. 45.

102 Linlithgow apparently was not the site of any witchcraft trials in 1661. In 1648 the privy council had granted a commission to try six witches there. *Source-book*, p. 113.

103 Ramsay was a member of the moderate presbyterian party that had opposed the radical covenanters. He had become minister in 1655, during the Cromwellian occupation. H. Scott (ed.), *Fasti Ecclesiae Scoticanae*, Edinburgh, 1925, vol. 1, p. 216.

104 The text in James Kirkton, *The Secret and True History of the Church of Scotland*, ed. C.K. Sharpe, Edinburgh, 1817, p. 126, transcribed this word as arch, but one of the other two manuscripts, BL Harleian MS 4631, fol. 75, uses 'ark' instead. None of the three manuscript copies of the work was written in Kirkton's hand. The ark of the covenant was the chest containing the Mosaic tablets. This association with the covenant strongly suggests that 'ark' was intended. It is also unlikely that an arch would be positioned on four pillars, as described in the text.

105 Kirkton, *Secret and True History*, ed. Sharpe, p. 126.

6 Absolutism, state-building, and witchcraft

1 S. Leutenbauer, *Hexerei- und Zaubereidelikt in der Literatur von 1450 bis 1550*, Berlin: Schweizer, 1972, p. 109.

2 On the political nature of such inversion see S. Clark, 'Inversion, Misrule and the Meaning of Witchcraft', *Past and Present* 87 (1980), 110–27.

3 W. Perkins, *A Discourse of the Damned Art of Witchcraft*, Cambridge, 1608, pp. 448–9.

4 *A Wonder, A Mercury without a Lye*, London, 1648.

5 G.H. Radford, 'Thomas Larkham', *Reports and Transactions of the Devonshire Association* 24 (1892), 97.

6 Thomas Hobbes, *Leviathan*, ed. C.B. Macpherson, Harmondsworth: Penguin, 1968, p. 374.

7 Ibid., p. 92.

8 *The Parliaments Post* 13(3) (29 July–5 Aug. 1645), 1–3.

9 *A Most Certain, Strange, and True Discovery of a Witch, being taken by some of the Parliament forces*, London, 1643.

10 This definition is based on B.P. Levack, *The Formation of the British State: England, Scotland and the Union, 1603–1707*, Oxford: Clarendon Press, 1987, p. 169, and J. Brewer, *The Sinews of Power: War, Money and the English State, 1688–1788*, Cambridge, MA: Harvard University Press, 1989, p. 252.

11 P. Anderson, *Lineages of the Absolutist State*; London: Verso, 1979; J. Goodare, *State and Society in Early Modern Scotland*, Oxford: Oxford University Press, 1999, ch. 3.

12 B.P. Levack, 'State-Building and Witch Hunting in Early Modern Europe', in J. Barry *et al.* (eds), *Witchcraft in Early Modern Europe*, Cambridge: Cambridge University Press, 1996, pp. 96–115.

13 Larner, *Enemies*.

14 Most notably J. Goodare, 'Witch-hunting and the Scottish State', *SWHC*, pp. 122–45.

15 M.J. Braddick, *State Formation in Early Modern England, c.1550–c.1700*, Cambridge: Cambridge University Press, 2000, pp. 362–3.

16 Larner, *Enemies*, pp. 22, 60.

17 R. Muchembled, 'The Witches of the Cambrésis: The Acculturation of the Rural World in the Sixteenth and Seventeenth Centuries', in J. Obelkevich (ed.), *Religion and the People, 800–1700*, Chapel Hill, NC: North Carolina University Press, 1979, pp. 221–76.

18 Larner, *Enemies*, p. 192.

19 Goodare, *State and Society*, ch. 6.

20 See above, Ch. 2.

21 J. Goodare, 'The Scottish Witchcraft Panic of 1597', *SWHC*, p. 62.

22 W. Behringer, 'Das "reichshündig Exempel" von Trier: Zur paradigmatischen Rolle einer Hexenverfolgung in Deutschland', in G. Franz and F. Irsigler (eds), *Hexenglaube und Hexenprozesse in Raum Rhein-Mosel-Saar*, Trier: Paulinus Verlag, 1995, pp. 436–47; J. Dillinger, *Böse Leute: Hexenverfolgungen in Schwäbisch-Österreich und Kurtrier im Vergleich*, Trier: Spee, 1999, pp. 32–9, 324–7.

23 See for example *RPCS*, vol. 4, p. 680; vol. 5, pp. 296–7. For the operation of such a commission in Burntisland see *RPCS*, vol. 5, p. 405.

24 C. Larner, *Witchcraft and Religion*, Oxford: Basil Blackwell, p. 78.

25 E.W. Monter, *Witchcraft in France and Switzerland*, Ithaca, NY: Cornell University Press, 1976, pp. 88–114.

26 *Acts of the General Assembly of the Church of Scotland*, Edinburgh, 1845, p. 27; *APS*, vol. 6, pt 1, p. 197.

27 Goodare, 'Scottish Witchcraft Panic', pp. 51–72.

28 More than half of all Scottish witchcraft prosecutions were authorized by conciliar or parliamentary commissions. About one-third of the prosecutions occurred in the court of justiciary. The remainder took place in circuit courts, mostly in the late seventeenth century. *Source-book*, p. 237, table 2.

29 See for example the trial of Agnes Finnie, 5 Feb. 1645, in *Justiciary Cases*, vol. 3 Edinburgh: Stair Society, 1974, pp. 627–75.

30 Mackenzie, *Laws*, p. 88.

31 Goodare, 'Witch-hunting and the Scottish State', p. 131.

32 Except during periods of intense Witch-hunting, the prosecution of witchcraft did not account for a very large percentage of prosecutions in the church courts. M.F. Graham, 'Social Discipline in Scotland, 1560–1610', in R.A. Mentzer (ed.), *Sin and the Calvinists*, Kirksville, MO: Sixteenth Century Essays and Studies, 1994, p. 136, tables 1 and 2.

33 *RPCS*, 2nd ser., vol. 2, pp. 437–8. It cannot be determined whether this initiative arose in response to clerical pressure.

34 R. Muchembled, *Popular Culture and Elite Culture in France, 1400–1750*, tr. L. Cochrane, Baton Rouge, LA: Louisiana University State Press, 1978, pp. 235–78.

35 P.S. Gorski, *The Disciplinary Revolution: Calvinism and the Rise of the State in Early Modern Europe*, Chicago: Chicago University Press, 2003, p.158 *et passim*.

36 S. Hindle, *The State and Social Change in Early Modern England, 1550–1640*, London: Palgrave, 2000, p. 137; Larner, *Enemies*, pp. 109–92.

ak *APS*, vol. 2, p. 539.

38 J. Goodare, 'The Scottish Witchcraft Act', *Church History* 74 (2005), 39–67.

39 *APS*, vol. 2, p. 646.

40 The theory of absolutism is evident in *The Trew Law of Free Monarchies* as well as in many of the speeches James gave to his English parliament. C.H. McIlwain (ed.), *The Political Works of James I*, Cambridge, MA: Harvard University Press, 1918.

41 Clark, 'King James's *Daemonologie*'.

42 See Jean Bodin, *Démonomanie des Sorciers*, Anvers, 1586, p. 334.

43 [Robert Filmer], *An Advertisement to the Jury-Men of England Touching Witches, together with A difference between an English and an Hebrew witch*, London, 1653, sig. A3v.

44 Sir George Mackenzie, *Jus Regium: or the just and solid foundations of monarchy in general*, London, 1684.

45 J. Moore and M. Silverthorne, 'Protestant Theologies, Limited Sovereignties: Natural Law and Conditions of Union in the German Empire, the Netherlands and Great Britain', in J. Robertson (ed.), *A Union for Empire: Political Thought and the Union of 1707*, Cambridge: Cambridge University Press, 1995, p. 193.

46 Mackenzie, *Jus Regium*, p. 47.

47 Quoted in T.F. Henderson, 'Sir George Mackenzie', *Dictionary of National Biography*, vol. 12, London: Oxford University Press, 1937–8, p. 587.

48 JC 2/15, fol. 103.

49 Sir John Lauder, who like Mackenzie was a royalist and a conservative despite his later reluctant support for the revolution of 1688–9, took the same position as Mackenzie on this issue by arguing that no inferior judge, much less a baron bailie, had power to incarcerate or detain any of the king's lieges under restraint upon pretence of their being delated or suspected as witches. Sir John Lauder (ed.), *The Decisions of the Lords of Council and Session*, Edinburgh, 1759–61, vol. 1, p. 16.

50 W. Behringer, 'Machiavellianism', in R. Golden (ed.), *Encyclopedia of Witchcraft: The Western Tradition*, Santa Barbara, CA: ABC-Clio, 2004, vol. 3, pp. 688–90.

51 Sir George Mackenzie, *A Vindication of the Government of Scotland during the Reign of Charles II*, London, 1691, p. 25.

7 Demonic possession and witch-hunting in Scotland

1 *A True Narrative of the Sufferings and Relief of a Young Girle*, Edinburgh, 1698, reprinted in *A History of the Witches of Renfrewshire*, Paisley, 1877, p. 93.

2 Ibid., pp. 84–5.

3 Ibid., pp. 71–2.

4 *A Relation of the Diabolical Practices of above Twenty Wizards and Witches of the Sheriffdom of Renfrewshire*, London, 1697, p. 4.

5 Ibid.

6 For these commissions and proceedings see JC10/4 and *Witches of Renfrewshire*, pp. 130–9.

7 Murdoch was the daughter of John Murdoch of Craigtoun in the parish of Govan in Glasgow. Laird, the daughter of John Laird, lived in Paisley.

8 JC 10/4, unfoliated, precognitions taken at Paisley 19–21 April 1699; NLS, Wodrow MS Fol. xxviii, fols 168–74. These precognitions were taken at Glasgow on 22 April 1699.

9 Ibid., especially precognitions 1, 3, 39, 56, 59, 66. Most of these witnesses testified that Margaret Laird had named various people as her tormentors.

10   On Maxwell and the proceedings against witches in both 1697 and 1699 see M. Wasser, 'The Western Witch-hunt of 1697–1700: The Last Major Witch-hunt in Scotland', *SWHC*, pp. 146–65.

11   Henri Boguet, *An Examen of Witches*, tr. E. Ashwin, London: John Rodker, 1929, p. xxxiii.

12   Ibid., pp. 1–14. The author returns to this case in numerous places later in the treatise.

13   Sébastien Michaelis, *Histoire admirable de la possession et conversion d'une pénitente séduite par un magicien*, Paris, 1614.

14   R. Rapley, *A Case of Witchcraft: The Trial of Urbain Grandier*, Montreal: McGill-Queen's University Press, 1998.

15   W. Monter, 'The Catholic Salem; or, How the Devil Destroyed a Saint's Parish (Mattaincourt 1627–1631)', in W. Behringer and J. Sharpe (eds), *Witchcraft in Context*, Manchester: Manchester University Press, forthcoming.

16   R. Decker, *Die Hexen und ihre Henker*, Freiburg: Herder, 1994.

17   P. Boyer and S. Nissenbaum, *Salem Possessed: The Social Origins of Witchcraft*, Cambridge, MA: Harvard University Press, 1974.

18   John Cotta, *The Triall of Witch-craft*, London, 1616, pp. 28–30.

19   H.C.E. Midelfort, 'The Devil and the German People: Reflections on the Popularity of Demon Possession in Sixteenth-Century Germany', in S. Ozment (ed.), *Religion and Culture in the Renaissance and Reformation*, Kirksville, MO: Sixteenth Century Essays and Studies, 11, 1989, pp. 99–119.

20   M. Sluhovsky, 'The Devil in the Convent', *American Historical Review* 107 (2002), 1380. In his study of the possessions at Loudun, Michel Certeau drew a sharp distinction between the appearance of witchcraft in rural areas and concentration of cases of possession in the cities and towns. M. Certeau, *The Possession at Loudun*, tr. M.B. Smith, Chicago: University of Chicago Press, Chicago, 1996, p. 4.

21   C. Worobec, *Possessed: Women, Witches, and Demons in Imperial Russia*, Dekalb, IL: Northern Illinois University Press, 2001.

22   Ibid., p. 31.

23   K. Thomas, *Religion and the Decline of Magic*, New York: Scribner, 1971, p. 478. D. Harley, 'Explaining Salem: Calvinist Psychology and the Diagnosis of Possession', *American Historical Review* 101 (1996), 307–30, distinguishes between cases of possession and those which were caused by witchcraft. One can distinguish between possession and obsession and argue that some of the cases labelled as possession, including that of the Salem girls, were either obsession or simply a demonic assault, but the claim that demonic possession and the effects of witchcraft were mutually exclusive categories cannot accommodate the cases of Christian Shaw, Margaret Laird, and Margaret Murdoch, much less the numerous cases of possession attributed to witchcraft on the continent.

24   Cotton Mather, *Memorable Providences Relating to Witchcrafts and Possessions*, Boston, 1689, p. 3.

25   James makes this point in *Daemonologie*, p. 43.

26   In the Middle Ages it was more common to have the boundary line between the saint and demoniac blurred. See B. Newman, 'Possessed by the Spirit: Devout Women, Demoniacs, and the Apostolic Life in the Thirteenth Century', *Speculum* 73 (1998), 733–70. On the blurred boundary between demonic possession and female charismatic spirituality in seventeenth-century France see S. Ferber, *Demonic Possession and Exorcism in Early Modern France*, London: Routledge, 2004.

27   Midelfort, 'The Devil and the German People', pp. 116–17. Luther, like a number of late medieval demonologists, believed that possession was punishment for sin, sometimes for the sins of the demoniac's father. Ibid, pp. 111–12.

28   C. Karlsen, *The Devil in the Shape of a Woman*, New York: W.W. Norton, 1987, pp. 242–4. See also H.C.E. Midelfort, 'Catholic and Lutheran Reactions to Demon Possession in the Late Seventeenth Century: Two Case Histories', *Daphnis* 15 (1986), 625–8.

29 The two were ultimately convicted of fraud. S. Olli, 'The Devil's Pact: A Male Strategy', in O. Davies and W. de Blécourt (eds), *Beyond the Witch Trials: Witchcraft and Magic in Enlightenment Europe*, Manchester: Manchester University Press, 2004, p. 116, n. 64.

30 The nuns at Loudun were suspected of deceit by many contemporaries, and they still stand accused of feigning their possessions to attract public attention. Rapley, *A Case of Witchcraft*, pp. 90–5.

31 É. Pócs, 'Possession Phenomena, Possession Systems: Some East-Central European Examples', in G. Klaniczay and É. Pócs (eds), *Communicating with the Spirits*, Budapest: Central European University Press, 2005, p. 86.

32 Hugo Arnot made this claim in 1785, and John Millar took the same position in 1877. See *The History of the Witches of Renfrewshire*, pp. xviii, 201–4. For a recent challenge to this interpretation see H. McLachlan and K. Swales, 'The Bewitchment of Christian Shaw: A Reassessment of the Famous Paisley Witchcraft Case of 1697', in Y.G. Brown and R. Ferguson (eds), *Twisted Sisters: Women, Crime and Deviance in Scotland since 1400*, East Linton: Tuckwell Press, 2002, pp. 54–83.

33 S.W. McDonald, A. Thom and A. Thom, 'The Bargarran Witchcraft Trial: A Psychiatric Assessment', *Scottish Medical Journal* 41 (1996), 152–8. Medical explanations hold an important place in the history of possession. As Erik Midelfort has argued, demonic possession is an essential part of the history of mental illness. The most recent analysis of the nuns at Loudun supports the claim of Marescot and of nineteenth-century psychiatrists that the nuns were suffering from hysteria. Some of the reported symptoms of Christian Shaw, Margaret Laird, and Margaret Murdoch, especially the extruded tongue, the bowing of the back, and the crossing of the rigid legs, were all reported by Jean-Martin Charcot in his study of clinical hysteria in Paris in the nineteenth century. See J. Charcot, *Lectures on the Diseases of the Nervous System*, 3 vols, tr. G. Sigerson, London, 1877–9, vol. 1, p. 280.

34 This cultural explanation is compatible with a medical or psychiatric interpretation of possession. Anthropologists and many psychiatrists would argue that psychiatric illness tends to manifest itself in forms that reflect the cultural expectations of the society in which it appears. M. MacDonald (ed.), *Witchcraft and Hysteria in Elizabethan London: Edward Jorden and the Mary Glover case*, London: Routledge, 1990, pp. xxxiv–xxxv and n. 65.

35 L. Yeoman, 'The Devil as Doctor: Witchcraft, Wodrow and the Wider World', *Scottish Archives* 1 (1995), 93–105.

36 Copy of letter sent to the laird of Bargarran from his wife, Christian McGilchrist, 18 Feb. 1697, in *A Relation of the Diabolical Practices of above Twenty Wizards and Witches*, p. 24.

37 NLS, Wodrow MS Fol. xxviii, fol. 170r.

38 *An Answer of a Letter from a Gentleman in Fife to a Nobleman*, 1705, p. 3.

39 Dittay against Dr Fian, 1591, no.12, *WEMS*, p. 229.

40 Mark 3:13–27; Matthew 12:22–9.

41 On Melanchthon and possession see D.P. Walker, *Unclean Spirits: Possession and Exorcism in France and England in the Late Sixteenth and Early Seventeenth Centuries*, London and Philadelphia: University of Pennsylvania Press, 1981, pp. 68, 73.

42 The exorcism took place in the parish church of Wittenberg in 1545. Luther performed it 'in his own manner, not according to the Catholic ritual'. The exorcism was unsuccessful. E. Klingner, *Luther und der deutsche Volksaberglaube*, Berlin, 1912, p. 35.

43 J. Calvin, *Institutes of the Christian Religion*, book 4, ch. 19. On the difference between Calvin and Luther on exorcism see B. Nischan, 'The Exorcism Controversy and Baptism in the Late Reformation', *Sixteenth Century Journal* 18 (1987), 31–51.

44 See above, Ch. 3.

45 G. Mora (ed.), *Witches, Devils and Doctors in the Renaissance: Johann Weyer*, De Praestigiis daemonum, Binghamton, NY: Medieval and Renaissance Texts and Studies, 1991, pp. 304–7. On Weyer's credulousness of possession see C. Baxter, 'Johann Weyer's

De Praestigiis daemonum: Unsystematic Psychopathology', in S. Anglo (ed.), *The Damned Art*, London: Routledge & Kegan Paul, 1977, pp. 63–4. H.C.E. Midelfort, *A History of Madness in Sixteenth-Century Germany*, Stanford, CA: Stanford University Press, 1999, p. 174, shows that Weyer did not believe that most cases of possession were legitimate.

46 B. Bekker, *De Betoverde Weereld*, Amsterdam, 1691–3, book 4, in which he discredits stories about possession and witchcraft.

47 Midelfort, 'The Devil and the German People', p. 118.

48 E.W. Monter, *Witchcraft in France and Switzerland*, Ithaca, NY: Cornell University Press, 1976, p. 60.

49 *Daemonologie*, p. 49.

50 Ibid., pp. 44, 165.

51 B.P. Levack, 'Possession, Witchcraft and the Law in Jacobean England', *Washington and Lee Law Review* 52 (1996), 1626–30.

52 Richard Baxter, who proclaimed the certainty of the existence of spirits, recognized that fraudulent possessions had led people to deny the reality of possession: 'And I confess very many cheats of pretended possessions have been discovered which hath made some weak, injudicious men think that all are such.' Richard Baxter, *The Certainty of the Worlds of Spirits*, London, 1691, p. 2.

53 [Des Niau], *The History of the Devils of Loudun: the Alleged Possession of the Ursuline Nuns and the Trial and Execution of Urbain Grandier*, tr. and ed. E. Goldsmid, Collectanea Adamantea, 21, Edinburgh, 1887, vol. 3, appendix, pp. 31–8. The excerpt comes from Baxter, *Certainty of the Worlds of Spirits*, pp. 82–92. It is also reprinted in C.K. Sharpe, *A Historical Account of the Belief in Witchcraft in Scotland*, London and Glasgow, 1884, pp. 219–29.

54 Probably Sir William Forbes of Monymusk.

55 Weems had been implicated in a false accusation of witchcraft against Katherine Wilson and David Smith at Duns, but it was later disclosed that James Mowat, late deputy clerk for Renfrewshire, had signed a complaint in his name. *RPCS*, 2nd ser., vol. 4, pp. 265–6.

56 *RPCS*, 2nd ser., vol. 2, pp. 604, 608.

57 In making his case for the reality of possession in the face of widespread scepticism, Lauderdale also reported that in the United Provinces of the Netherlands some 30 or 40 years earlier there was another 'unquestionable possession' of a woman who spoke all the languages. He had heard about this case when he lived in the Low Countries. When possessions did actually occur in the Dutch Republic, however, they were either ignored by the authorities or their veracity was called into question. That is what happened when a group of Capuchin monks exorcised a demoniac at Utrecht in 1625. See Baxter, *Certainty of the Worlds of Spirits*, pp. 109–18.

58 W.J. Anderson, 'Narratives of the Scottish Reformation, III: Prefect Ballentine's report, *circa* 1660: Part One', *Innes Review* 8 (1957), 51.

59 Ibid.

60 S. Clark, *Thinking with Demons*, Oxford: Clarendon Press, 1997, ch. 26, establishes the importance of a demonological context in the study of possession.

61 *Daemonologie*, pp. xii, 55.

62 Joseph Glanvill, *Saducismus Triumphatus*, London, 1681; George Sinclair, *Satan's Invisible World Discovered*, Edinburgh, 1685. The translation of François Perreaud, *L'Antidemon de Mascon* (1653) as F. Perrault, *The Devill of Mascon, or, a True Relation of the Chiefe Things which an Unclean Spirit Did, and Said at Mascon*, Oxford, 1658, can be considered part of this discourse. Robert Boyle was responsible for getting Perreaud translated. On Boyle and witchcraft see Clark, *Thinking with Demons*, p. 308.

63 James VI, *Daemonologie*, pp. xii, 55 gives the term the same meaning in stating his opposition to Reginald Scot and Johann Weyer.

64 Henry More, *An Antidote against Atheism*, London, 1655, p. 278.

65 Mather, *Memorable Providences*, pp. 4–5.

66 Clark, *Thinking with Demons*, ch. 27.

67 Deodat Lawson, *A Brief and True Narrative of Some Remarkable Passages relating to Sundry Persons Afflicted by Witchcraft*, Boston, 1693; C. Mather, *Wonders of the Invisible World*, Boston, 1693.

68 *The Surey Demoniack: or, An Account of Satan's Strange and Dreadful Actings in and about the Body of Richard Dugdale of Surey, near Lancashire*, London, 1697, preface.

69 Zachary Taylor, *The Surey Impostor*, London, 1697. See the response by T. Jolly, *A Vindication of the Surey Demoniack*, London, 1698.

70 McLachlan and Swales, 'Bewitchment of Christian Shaw', argue that the main authors were Andrew Turner, minister at Erskine, and James Brisbane, minister at Kilmacolm.

71 Grant also cited the trial of Aikenhead to show what happened when someone denied the existence of spirits and a devil who tormented sinners. *Witches of Renfrewshire*, p. 64.

72 On the authorship of this pamphlet see C. Larner, 'Two Late Scottish Witchcraft Tracts: *Witch-Craft Proven* and *The Tryal of Witchcraft*', in S. Anglo (ed.), *The Damned Art*, pp. 230–2.

73 *Witch-Craft Proven, Arreign'd and condemned in its Professors, Professions and Marks*, Glasgow, 1697, p. 2.

74 Ibid., p. 5.

75 *The Second Part of the Boy of Bilson, or a True and Particular Relation of the Impostor Susanna Fowles*, London, 1698.

76 The pamphlet, *The Bewitching of a Child in Ireland*, is no longer extant. It is described, however, in the late eighteenth-century edition and continuation of George Sinclair, *Satan's Invisible World Discovered*, Edinburgh, 1780, pp. 172–3. This edn of Sinclair also includes an account of the bewitching of Christian Shaw and that of Patrick Morton at Pittenweem in 1704.

77 For commentary on this trial see S.D. Seymour, *Irish Witchcraft and Demonology*, Baltimore, MD: Norman, Remington, 1913, pp. 194–9.

78 *A True and Full Relation of the Witches at Pittenweem*, Edinburgh, 1704.

79 I. Bostridge, *Witchcraft and its Transformations, c.1650–c.1750*, Oxford: Clarendon Press, 1997, pp. 24–8, develops connections between Aikenhead and the witch-hunt. See also the letter of Robert Wylie, minister of Hamilton, to the laird of Wishaw, 16 June 1697, defending both the execution of Aikenhead and the renewal of witch-hunting. NAS, GD 103/2/3/17/1.

80 R. Mandrou, *Magistrats et sorciers en France au XVIIe siècle*, Paris: Librairie Plon, 1968.

81 *The Manuscripts of the Duke of Roxburghe*, Historical Manuscripts Commission, *Fourteenth Report*, appendix III, London, 1894, p. 132.

82 *Witches of Renfrewshire*, p. 64. The phrase was taken from Cotton Mather, *Wonders of the Invisible World*, p. 5, who used it with reference to New England.

8   The decline and end of Scottish witch-hunting

1 A.F. Soman, 'Decriminalizing Witchcraft: Does the French Experience Furnish a European Model?', *Criminal Justice History* 10 (1989), 1–22, and B.P. Levack, 'The Decline and End of Witchcraft Prosecutions', in M. Gijswijt-Hofstra *et al.*, *Witchcraft and Magic in Europe*, London: Athlone Press, 1999, pp. 1–93.

2 R. Mandrou, *Magistrats et sorciers en France au XVIIe siècle*, Paris: Librairie Plon, 1968; H. Kneubühler, *Die Überwindung von Hexenwahn und Hexenprozess*, Diessenhofen: Verlag Rüegger, 1977; J.C.V. Johansen, 'Witchcraft, Sin and Repentance: The Decline of Danish Witchcraft Trials', *Acta Ethnographic* 37 (1991/2), 413–23; S. Lorenz and D.R. Bauer (eds), *Das Ende der Hexenverfolgung*, Stuttgart: Franz Steiner, 1995; J. Klaits, 'Witchcraft Trials and Absolute Monarchy in France', in R. Golden (ed.), *Church, State and Society under the Bourbon Kings of France*, Lawrence, KS: Coronado Press, 1982, pp. 148–72; E.W. Monter, *Witchcraft in France and Switzerland*, Ithaca, NY: Cornell University Press, 1976, pp. 37–41; A. Soman, 'The Parlement of Paris and the Great Witch Hunt (1565–1640)', *Sixteenth*

Century Journal 9 (1978), 31–44; G. Henningsen, *The Witches' Advocate: Basque Witchcraft and the Spanish Inquisition*, Reno, NV: University of Nevada Press, 1980; J. Sharpe, *Instruments of Darkness*, London: Hamish Hamilton, 1996, ch. 9.

3 See for example W.E.H. Lecky, *The History of the Rise and Influence of the Spirit of Rationalism in Europe*, New York: D. Appleton, 1910, ch. 1.

4 'Between 1680 and 1735 witch-belief disappeared almost without comment from the cognitive map of the ruling class.' Larner, *Enemies*, pp. 78–9. Even if we exclude the ministry from this class, there is no evidence of such a disappearance. On the persistence of Scottish witch beliefs and their association with a distinctive Scottish culture after the union of 1707 see I. Bostridge, 'Witchcraft Repealed', in J. Barry *et al.* (eds), *Witchcraft in Early Modern Europe*, Cambridge: Cambridge University Press, 1996, pp. 309–44.

5 The first national study of the decline of prosecutions, Mandrou, *Magistrats et sorciers*, focuses on the new jurisprudence of French judges, but that jurisprudence is viewed as part of a broader intellectual change. K. Thomas, *Religion and the Decline of Magic*, New York: Scribner, 1971, chs 20–2, identifies social and economic changes in the decline of English witchcraft prosecutions but gives equal weight to changes in mental attitudes.

6 E.W. Monter, 'Law, Medicine and the Acceptance of Witchcraft, 1560–1680', in E.W. Monter (ed.), *European Witchcraft*, New York: John Wiley, 1969, pp. 55–71.

7 Scot insisted in good Calvinist fashion that the age of miracles had passed and that a sovereign God would not permit human beings to exercise supernatural power, but he did not include the 'working of wonders by supernatural means' in his summary of the 'absurd and impossible crimes' attributed to witches. R. Scot, *The Discoverie of Witchcraft*, ed. M. Summers, London: John Rodker, 1930, pp. 7, 18–20, 89. Scot included these 'wonders' among the alleged crimes of witches that witch-hunters could not prove to be true. Ibid., p. 19.

8 For a full discussion of this problem see Levack, 'Decline and End of Witchcraft Prosecutions', pp. 33–40.

9 Mackenzie, *Laws*, pp. 80–108.

10 Mackenzie, *Pleadings*, pp. 185, 192.

11 JC 10/4, fols 63–81.

12 W. Forbes, *Institutes of the Laws of Scotland*, Edinburgh, 1730, p. 32. 'Nothing seems plainer to me than that there may be, and have been witches, and that perhaps such are now actually existing.'

13 Weyer, *De praestigiis daemonum*, book II, ch. 1; Scot, *Discoverie of Witches*, book VII, esp. ch. 1.

14 [Robert Filmer], *An Advertisement to the Jury-Men of England Touching Witches, together with a difference between an English and an Hebrew witch*, London, 1653.

15 B. Bekker, *The World Bewitched; or, an examination of the common opinion concerning spirits, their nature, power and operations*, London, 1695.

16 *Witchcraft Proven, Arreign'd and Condemn'd in its Professors, Professions and Marks*, Glasgow, 1697. For the biblicism of this work see C. Larner, 'Two Late Scottish Witchcraft Tracts: *Witchcraft Proven* and *The Tryal of Witchcraft*', in S. Anglo (ed.), *The Damned Art*, London: Routledge & Kegan Paul, 1976, pp. 236–7.

17 J. Paterson, *A Belief in Witchcraft Unsupported by Scripture*, Aberdeen, 1815. Paterson argues in the preface that the prevalent belief in witchcraft 'is alike repugnant to reason and inconsistent with he superintendance of Providence and mistakes certain passages of Scripture'. Paterson's book appeared more than 100 years after the publication of an English treatise that took this position, *The Impossibility of Witchcraft, plainly proving, from Scripture and Reason, that there never was a witch and that it is both irrational and impious to believe that there ever was*, London, 1712.

18 *RPCS*, 3rd ser., vol. 1, p. 198.

19 *RPCS*, 1st ser., vol. 5, pp. 409–10.

20 Mackenzie, *Laws*, p. 88.

21 Ibid. 'Nor have the panels any to plead for them and to take notice who are led as witnesses; so that many who are admitted are *testes inhabiles*, and suspect.'

22 *RPCS*, 2nd ser., vol. 2, pp. 437–8.

23 There were 133 cases in all. Of those whose outcomes are known, only 24 witches were executed, while 58 were acquitted. *Source-book, passim.*

24 NLS, MS 643, fol. 85; *A True and Full Relation of the Witches at Pittenweem*, Edinburgh, 1704, p. 12.

25 The justices ordered the release of five witches (Marie Innes, George Guislet, Marie Somervail, Andrew Laidlawe, and John Scot) on these grounds in 1670 and 1671. JC2/13, 3, 10, and 20 July; *Justiciary Cases*, vol. 2, pp. 56–7. Laidlawe had been released by the English commissioners in the 1650s on the same grounds, i.e. because 'nobody was insisting'. JC 26/38. In 1661 the laird of Newhall had acted himself to insist against Margaret Allen and also pay her maintenance in prison so that she could be brought to trial.

26 JC 2/14, fol. 181.

27 NAS, JC 2/15, fol. 103.

28 Mackenzie, *Laws*, pp. 89–90.

29 One effort to operate the system occurred in 1628. C. Rogers (ed.), *The Earl of Stirling's Original Register of Royal Letters*, Edinburgh, 1885, vol. 2, p. 377.

30 See for example, *RPCS*, 3rd ser., vol. 3, p. 45.

31 R. Chambers, *Domestic Annals of Scotland*, Edinburgh, 1858–61, vol. 3, p. 216.

32 [F. Spee], *Cautio Criminalis*, Rinteln, 1631; Augustin Nicolas, *Si la Torture est un moyen seur a vérifier les crimes sécrets: dissertation morale et juridique*, Amsterdam, 1682; M.J. Sassen, *De usu et abusu torturae*, 1697, 1726, 1735; Christian Thomasius, *De tortura ex fori Christianorum proscribenda*, Halle, 1705, idem, *De origine ac progressu processus inquisitorii contra sagas*, Halle, 1712; and idem, *Über di Hexenprozesse*, ed. R. Lieberwirth, Weimar, 1986.

33 See for example the action taken against the tutor and minister of Calder in Nov. 1644. *RPCS*, 2nd ser., vol. 8, p. 37.

34 *RPCS*, 3rd ser., vol. 1, pp. 188–9.

35 *RPCS*, 3rd ser., vol. 2, pp. 192–3, p. 614; vol. 5, p. 171.

36 *RPCS*, 3rd ser., vol. 6, p. 13. For the legal arguments in the prosecution of Liddell's tormentors, see the case of Liddell v. Rutherford in Lauder of Fountainhall, *Decisions*, vol. 1, pp. 15–16; G.F. Black, *A Calendar of Cases of Witchcraft in Scotland, 1510–1727*, New York: NY Public Library, 1971, p. 79.

37 JC 2/15, fol. 159.

38 7 Anne, c. 21, par. 8.

39 Sir George Mackenzie, *A Vindication of the Government of Scotland during the Reign of Charles II*, Edinburgh, 1691; 'A Discourse on the Four First Chapters of the Digest', BL, Sloane MS. 3828, fol. 127.

40 Mackenzie, *Laws*, p. 543. At no time during this period did the council recognize the right of the justices to administer torture. On the parlement of Paris see Soman, 'Decriminalizing Witchcraft', 1–10.

41 *RPCS*, 3rd ser, vol. 9, p. 66.

42 L.B. Taylor (ed.), *Aberdeen Council Letters*, vol. 4, London: Oxford University Press, 1954, pp. 393–4.

43 Ibid., p. 394.

44 Ibid., p. 398.

45 *RPCS*, 3rd ser., vol. 3, p. 45. Preston had to be present. For the Aberdeen council's discussion of the suitability of Preston see *Aberdeen Council Letters*, vol. 4, p. 403. For the inclusion of Preston in a later commission see *RPCS*, 3rd ser, vol. 5, p. 171.

46 *RPCS*, 3rd ser., vol. 3, pp. 211–12.

47 The council certainly could not have been referring to the most recent time it had received a commission, 25 Feb. 1669. That commission specifically prohibited them from using torture. See *RPCS*, 3rd ser., vol. 2, p. 614. The only precedent they could

have cited was the commission granted in 1649, which permitted 'any other form of probation'. *APS*, vol. 6, pt 2, p. 390.

48 *RPCS*, 3rd ser., vol. 3, p. 45.

49 *Witches of Renfrewshire*, p. 142.

50 JC 2/14, fols 181–2. The lawyers objected that the indictment was pretended; that justices of the peace had no authority to proceed against a person for witchcraft; that witnesses had not been examined in the presence of the panel or assize; that neither an informer nor procurator fiscal had pressed charges against her; and that she had not been given a list of the assizers and witnesses.

51 *RPCS*, 2nd ser., vol. 8, p. 37. This was in 1644.

52 Larner, *Enemies*, p. 117.

53 Mackenzie, *Laws*, pp. 86–7, Larner, *Enemies*, p. 177.

54 Larner, *Enemies*, p. 178.

55 Mackenzie, *Pleadings*, pp.187–8; Mackenzie, *Laws*, pp. 92–5.

56 JC 10/4, pt 2, pp. 18–32.

57 Ibid., p. 81.

58 *The Manuscripts of the Duke of Roxburghe*, Historical Manuscripts Commission, *Fourteenth Report*, appendix 3, London, 1894, p. 132.

59 This was especially true in France. See Levack, 'Decline and End of Witchcraft Prosecutions', p. 57.

60 *Aberdeen Council Letters*, vol. 4, pp. 406–7.

61 See Ch. 9.

62 On the murky history of this execution see E.J. Cowan and L. Hendersone, 'The Last of the Witches? The Survival of Scottish Witch Belief', *SWHC*, pp. 205–7.

63 Larner, *Enemies*, p. 78; E. Burt (ed.), *Letters from the North of Scotland*, Edinburgh, 1876, vol.1, pp. 242–3.

9 Witch-hunting and witch-murder in early eighteenth-century Scotland

1 Contemporary accounts of the murder varied considerably. This account is based on *An Account of an Horrid and Barbarous Murder in a Letter from a Gentleman in Fife to his Friend in Edinburgh*, 1705; *An Answer of a Letter from a Gentleman in Fife to a Nobleman*, 1705; *A Just Reproof to the False Reports, Bold, and unjust Calumnies Dropt in Two Late Pamphlets*, Edinburgh, 1705; and the report presented to the privy council on 14 Feb. 1705, PC1/53, pp. 358–9. It is uncertain why the murderers decided to press her to death in this way. It is unlikely that the two Englishmen in the crowd were aware of the English judicial procedure of *peine forte et dure*. It is more likely that the people in Pittenweem had learned of the pressing to death of Giles Corey at Salem in 1692, since accounts of the Salem witch-trials had circulated widely in Scotland. A third possibility is that the method was selected so that all the members of the crowd could add weights to the door, thus preventing the assignment of guilt for the crime to one person.

2 B. Baronowski, *Procesz czarownic w Polsce w XVII i XVIII wieku*, Lodzkie: Towarzystwo Naukowe, 1952, estimated that 5,000 Polish witches were killed in this way. His figures were highly inflated, but a significantly lower figure would still be exceptional by European standards. Baranowski lowered his estimates of the total number of Polish executions in 1963. See his afterward to K. Baschwitz, *Czarownice: Dzieje procesów o czary*, Warsaw: PWN, 1963, p. 430.

3 D. Cook (ed.), *Annals of Pittenweem ...1526–1793*, Anstruther, 1867, p. 128.

4 *An Answer of a Letter from a Gentleman in Fife to a Nobleman*, 1705, p. 3. C.K. Sharpe, *A Historical Account of the Belief in Witchcraft in Scotland*, London: Hamilton, Adams & Co., 1884, p. 175, refers to Morton as 'a fellow who pretended to take fits till he found them no longer profitable'.

5 *An Answer of a Letter from a Gentleman in Fife to a Nobleman*, 1705, p. 3. The author of *A Just Reproof to the False Reports and Unjust Calumnies Dropt in Two late Pamphlets*, Edinburgh,

1705, p. 19, admitted that the minister and the probationer took out the book when he saw that Morton had fallen into a convulsion, but read only two sentences 'for their own satisfaction' and then stopped. Cowper's sympathy for Morton may have been fostered by the fact that the boy and his father had often been employed by the church to do repairs. See for example CH2/832/3/13; CH2/833/3/237.

6 Deodat Lawson, *A Brief and True Narrative Of some Remarkable Passages Relating to sundry Persons Afflicted by Witchcraft*, Boston, 1692.

7 *The Surey Demoniack: or, An Account of Satan's Strange and Dreadful Actings in and about the Body of Richard Dugdale of Surey, near Lancashire*, London, 1697.

h See Zachary Taylor's attack on the dissenting Protestant ministers who gave credence to the possession as being guilty of popish superstition in Z. Taylor, *Popery, superstition, ignorance, and knavery, confes'd, and fully proved on the Surey dissenters from the second letter of an apostate friend to Zach. Taylor*, London, 1699.

9 *An Account of the Wicked and Terrible Confederacy of Betty Laing*, Edinburgh, 1704, p. 1, claims that Laing was very poor and made a living selling small wares but also admits that her husband was an honest person. In her petition to the privy council she refers to herself as the wife of William Brown, tailor and treasurer of the burgh. Cook, *Annals of Pittenweem*, p. 125.

10 *An Answer of a Letter from a Gentleman in Fife*, p. 3, notes that two of the witches were apprehended outside the jurisdiction of the burgh, one from Anstruther and one from the country six miles away.

11 St Andrews University Library, Minutes of St Andrews Presbytery, 1699–1705, CH2/1132/21, p. 292.

12 *Wicked and Terrible Confederacy of Betty Laing*, p. 1; PC1/53, p. 399.

13 *Endorism, or a Strange Relation of Dreamers or Spirits that Trouble the Minister's House of Kinross*, Edinburgh, 1718, Quoted in Sharpe, *Historical Account*, p. 117.

14 Cook, *Annals of Pittenweem*, p. 128. The act for wrongous imprisonment was passed in the ninth session of William III. In 1686 Horseburgh had accused Alexander before the session of calling her a witch and had refused to be reconciled with her despite the urging of the Episcopal minister, Mr Bruce.

15 CH2/1132/21, p. 295. Cornfoot apparently was not married.

16 CH2/1132/21, p. 294. See also CH2/833/3/239. In her interrogation by the presbytery Durkie testified that she said to Lawson, 'Oh, if I were a witch as you are.' CH2/1132/21, p. 295.

17 *Just Reproof*, p. 7.

18 *Annals of Pittenweem*, p. 11. Laing had been debarred from communion for using charms and for refusing to be reconciled to her neighbours. *Just Reproof*, p. 3; *Wicked and Terrible Confederacy of Betty Laing*, pp. 4–6; Sinclair, *Satan's Invisible World Discovered*, Edinburgh, 1780, pp. 171–2.

19 *Annals of Pittenweem*, p. 124.

20 CH2/833/3/27. Horseburgh contested the decision of the session to allow Griege and his wife sit in the front seats and her daughters and those of Alexander Atcheson, who was also away from Pittenweem, in the rear seats. It is noteworthy that the dispute arose because neither of the wives had been coming to church and thereby occupying the seats. One reason for assigning the rear seats to the young girls was 'as a means to keep them (that carry insolently) from making disturbances in the church'.

21 On wealthy Scottish witches see L. Yeoman, 'Hunting the Rich Witch in Scotland: High Status, Witch Suspects and their Persecutors, 1590–1650', *SWHC*, pp. 106–21.

22 H. Scott (ed.), *Fasti Ecclesiae Scoticanae*, vol. 5, p. 227.

23 CH2/833/3/225.

24 CH2/833/3/245.

25 CH2/833/3/247. The belated discovery that Varner was married, changing Courie's offence from fornication to adultery, strongly suggests that Varner was not a resident of the burgh.

26 CH2/833/3/249. On the kirk's treatment of rape as fornication see M. Todd, *The Culture of Protestantism in Early Modern Scotland*, New Haven: Yale University Press, 2002, pp. 296–7. Another example of this classification occurred in May 1705, when two residents of Pittenweem, John MacIntosh, a slatter, and George Lowrie, a mason, were cited for 'lying in the sin of fornication' with Jean Young, a worster from Anstruther, on the road from Anstruther to Pittenweem. Since MacIntosh forcibly took her off the highway, laid hands on her and threw her down before having intercourse with her, the offence was clearly rape. Despite the severity of the offence, to which the men confessed, the case was not referred to the civil magistrate. Lowrie was charged with twice profaning the Sabbath by lying in bed the whole day. CH2/833/3/249.

27 CH2/833/3/261.

28 M.B. Norton, *In the Devil's Snare: The Salem Witchcraft Crisis of 1692*, New York: Alfred A. Knopf, 2002.

29 For the actions taken by the burgh council during that witch-hunt see NLS, MS 683, fols 84–5.

30 R. Kieckhefer, *European Witch Trials*, London: Routledge & Kegan Paul, 1976.

31 *Account of the Wicked and Terrible Conspiracy*, p. 4, claims that the devil took the child on trips, including one to Norway, where her father, who was a seaman, was at the time.

32 The confessions were made by 29 May, when the kirk session recorded them. CH2/833/3/241.

33 *An Account of a Horrid and Barbarous Murder in a Letter from a Gentleman in Fife*, 1705, p. 2. Cornfoot later told two lawyers who visited her in prison that she had renounced her baptism only to the minister.

34 'She afterwards avowed and publicly told that what she had said to them of her having seen the devil, etc., was lies and untruths.' *Annals of Pittenweem*, p. 125.

35 *An Answer of a Letter from a Gentleman in Fife*, p. 2.

36 Folger Shakespeare Library, MS x.d.436 (58), 19 Nov. 1704.

37 *An Answer of a Letter from a Gentleman of Fife*, title-page, refers to 'the barbarous and illegal treatment of these poor women'.

38 CH2/833/3/241.

39 *Annals of Pittenweem*, p. 109.

40 St Andrews University Library, St Andrews Presbytery Records, vol. 4. CH2/1132/21, pp. 292–3.

41 Ibid., p. 293.

42 Ibid., p. 294.

43 Ibid., pp. 294–5.

44 Ibid., p. 297.

45 The three names given in the burgh records are Brown, Margaret Wallace, and Margaret Jack. *Annals of Pittenweem*, pp 11–14. The name of Margaret Wallace may have been intended to refer to Lillie Wallace. Margaret Jack's name does not appear in any of the proceedings or the pamphlets, whereas Horseburgh became a central figure in the witch-hunt. It is possible, however, that a woman named Margaret Jack was also accused and imprisoned. This would explain why *The True Relation* said that there were eight prisoners in all.

46 The meeting of the burgh council on 12 July appointed men to go to Edinburgh to consult with members of the commission of the general assembly and crave their concurrence of the lord advocate and Sir Robert Forbes, one of the clerks of the privy council, to help them secure the commission. The petition was apparently submitted a few days later and is referred to in the response of the privy council in *Annals of Pittenweem*, pp. 110–16. NLS, MS 683 fol. 85.

47 NAS, PC 1/53, register of the privy council, June 1703–April 1707, pp. 247–9. The burgh council was informed by the commissioners on 21 July that Rothes would take these persons off the magistrates' hands and transport them to Edinburgh. *Annals of Pittenweem*, p. 116.

48 *Annals of Pittenweem*, pp. 116–17. The five women were Adam, Laing, Horseburgh, Wallace, and Lawson. Cornfoot remained in prison.

49 PC1/53, p. 281.

50 *Answer of a Letter*, pp. 70–1. The payment of fines by acquitted witches was not unique to Scotland. In England, six witches acquitted by the assizes in Kent in 1653 had to pay fees before their release. Kent Archives Office, Q/SMc1/Maidstone Calendar, 4 Oct. 1653.

51 *Just Reproof*, p. 22. In 1644 Agnes Finnie complained to the privy council that her prosecutors would 'neither try her nor liberate her so that she is likely to die'. *Selected Justiciary Cases*, vol. 3, p. 628. In 1649 the presbytery of Dunfermline urgently petitioned parliament for a commission to try witches imprisoned in Inverkeithing because they were impoverished and could not pay for their maintenance. E. Henderson, *Annals of Dunfermline and Vicinity*, Edinburgh, 1879, p. 319. The danger facing the witches imprisoned at the town's expense in Aberdeen in 1669 was that if not tried promptly they would die because they were old. *Aberdeen Council Letters*, vol. 4, p. 394. The English response to the poverty of imprisoned witches was different from the Scottish. In 1645 the Suffolk quarter sessions taxed all the residents of Ipswich to provide for the witches who were too poor to pay any fees for their upkeep in gaol. The tax was justified on the ground that the witches 'were prosecuted by or with the consent and procurement of most of the inhabitants of the several parishes involved'. The action was taken because many of the witches had been acquitted 'by proclamation or by verdict'. Suffolk Record Office, B105/21/1, fol. 79r.

52 *An Account of a Horrid and Barbarous Murder*, pp. 2–3.

53 PC1/53, p. 359.

54 W. Blackstone, *Commentaries on the Laws of England*, vol. 4, 1769, Oxford: Clarendon Press, p. 60. Blackstone clearly regarded the repeal of the witchcraft statutes as an improvement in English law.

55 The effort to refute the sadducees began earlier, but it became a major philosophical and theological debate only in the late seventeenth century. For earlier references see King James, *Daemonolgie*, pp. 37–8, and Samuel Fairclough's sermon of 1645, in Samuel Clark, *The Lives of Sundry Eminent Persons in this Later Age*, London, 1683, p. 172.

56 Cotton Mather, *Wonders of the Invisible World*, Boston, 1693. The sermon, was published as a chapter in the book under the title 'A Discourse on the Wonders of the Invisible World'.

57 *A True Narrative of the Sufferings and Relief of a Young Girle*, Glasgow, 1698, preface, which claims that the possession of Christian Shaw proved the existence of God. The title of the London edn of the narrative of Shaw's possession was *Sadducismus Debellatus* (Sadducism Conquered). See also *Witch-Craft Proven, Arreign'd and Condemn'd in its Professors, Professions and Marks*, Glasgow, 1697.

58 Edinburgh, 1704. This was the first of the five pamphlets to be published about the Pittenweem episode and must have been written before the release of the five women on 12 Aug.

59 George Sinclair, *Satan's Invisible World Discovered; or, a choice collection of modern relations; proving evidently, against the atheists of this present age, that there are devils, spirits, witches ... To which is added, that marvellous history of Major Weir and his sister, the witches of Bargarran*, Edinburgh, 1780.

60 Folger Shakespeare Library, MS x.d. 436 (58).

61 White Kennet, *The Witchcraft of the Present Rebellion*, London, 1715.

62 Francis Hutchinson, *An Historical Essay concerning witchcraft*, London, 1718. Hutchinson argues that the English clergy had as little responsibility for witch-hunting as any group in England, despite the behaviour of some of them during Anne Wenham's trial in 1712.

63 The general assembly actually published procedures to be taken in bringing witches to trial. In 1708, in response to the events at Pittenweem, the assembly defined the function

of the kirk sessions, including its part in the trial of witches. The new rules, however, did not represent much of a change. *Acts of the General Assembly of the Church of Scotland, 1638–1842*, Edinburgh, 1843, pp. 7, 37.

64 *APS*, vol. 4, p. 434, c. 14.

65 *Annals of Pittenweem*, p. 110. The minister and elders also attended the meetings of the burgh council and were present on 1 June when the council appointed two of their members to travel to Edinburgh and ask the earl of Montcrieff to secure a local commission of justiciary.

66 See above, Ch. 1.

67 PC1/53, pp. 358–9. The four residents were John Ramsay, Andrew Flee, Alexander McGregor, and Peter Innes, a burgh officer. The four prisoners were Robert Alexander, John Findlay, David Jack, and Flee. In transcribing this report from the register of the privy council for inclusion in *Annals of Pittenweem*, David Cook omitted the names of all the town's residents who had not fled. *Annals of Pittenweem*, pp. 119–24.

68 PC1/53, p. 359. The five men named were the four prisoners listed above and Peter Innes, the officer.

69 *Annals of Pittenweem*, p. 124. The money to defray the expenses of the magistrates was to come from the 'grass, mails and malt money' of the town.

70 *An Answer of a Letter from a Gentleman in Fife*, p. 4; *Annals of Pittenweem*, p. 124 n.

71 PC1/53, p. 399.

72 *Annals of Pittenweem*, p. 127.

73 PC1/53, p. 399.

74 Ibid., p. 426. This order was dated 2 Oct. 1705.

75 In Nov. 1705 the bailies granted a bond under a great penalty to appear before the privy council in regard to Cornfoot's murder when required. The records of the town council indicate that the council agreed to relieve the bailies of that engagement. There was no further mention of the episode in the records of either the burgh council or the privy council.

76 CH2/833/3/249. This statement of disappointment formed part of a report given by the Pittenweem kirk session on 4 June 1705, objecting that the processes against the witches were never returned to the session after the presbytery of St Andrews had cited them.

77 *APS*, vol. 10, pp. 272–5.

78 *Annals of Pittenweem*, pp. 128–9.

79 Article 18 provided that the main Scottish criminal court, the court of justiciary, was to be preserved as it was then constituted, subject only to the regulation of the parliament of Great Britain.

80 JC26/86, D 228.

81 JC26/86, D 245.

82 JC26/88, D 346.

83 JC11/1; JC10/37.

84 7 Anne, c. 22.

85 *APS*, vol. 7, p. 415, c. 71.

86 7 Anne, c. 21, par. 8.

87 I. Bostridge, 'Witchcraft Repealed', in J. Barry *et al.* (eds), *Witchcraft in Early Modern Europe*, Cambridge: Cambridge University Press, 1996, pp. 321–9.

88 A. Carlyle, *Autobiography*, London, 1800, p. 10.

89 G.F. Black, *A Calendar of Cases of Witchcraft in Scotland, 1510–1727*, New York, 1938, p. 20.

Bibliography

Manuscripts

National Archives of Scotland, Edinburgh

CH2/84/2	Dalkeith kirk session records
CH2/121/7	Edinburgh presbytery records
CH2/197/1	Irvine Presbytery records
CH2/229/1	Kirkliston kirk session records
CH2/265/2	Synod of Merse and Teviotdale records
CH2/276/4	Newbattle kirk session records
CH2/283/2	Newton kirk session records
CH2/424/4	Dalkeith presbytery records
CH2/523/1	Iveresk kirk session records
CH2/832/3	Pittenweem kirk session records
GD 103/2/3/11	Petition against Christian Wilson,1661.
GD 103/2/3/17/1	Letter from Robert Wylie 1704
JC2	Justiciary court, books of adjournal
JC6/5	High court minute books 1655–59
JC10/2	Circuit court minute books, 1671
JC10/4	Circuit court minute books 1677–99
JC10/17	Circuit court minute books May 1656
JC 11/1	North circuit court minute books,1708–11
JC 26/2, 12, 13, 24–7, 38	Justiciary court processes
JC26/86, 88	Justiciary court process series D
JC10/37	Circuit court minute books, May 1709
JC40/11	Testimony of Andrew Reid, 1710
PA7/9/1	Supplementary parliamentary papers, 1661
PA7/23/1	Additional parliamentary papers
PA11/8,9	Registers of the committee of estates
PA12/5	Committee of estates warrant book, 1650
PC 1/53	Register of the privy council, June 1703–April 1707

National Library of Scotland

Advocates MS 25.3.15	Sir Thomas Hope on the Civil law
MS 683	Extracts from the records of the royal burgh of Pittenweem
Wodrow Fol. MS 28	Circuit court precognition 1699

St Andrews University Library, Special Collections

| CH2/1132/21 | St Andrews presbytery minutes |

Glasgow University Archives

| MS DC1/39 | Extracts from the records of the presbytery of Irvine, 1649–50 |

National Archives, Kew

SP 15/36/93	Examination of earl of Murray in the Star Chamber, 1607
SP 14/27/43	English description of Scottish criminal procedure, 1604
STAC 8/4/10	Prosecution of Anne and Brian Gunter in Star Chamber

British Library, London

Additional MS 12,497	Letter of James I to Salisbury 1605
Egerton MS 2879	Papers relating to the Alloa witches, 1658–9
Egerton MS 1048.	Paper concerning the union with Scotland in 1659
Harleian MS 4631	MS copy of James Kirkton's 'Secret and True History'
Sloane MS 3828	Sir George Mackenzie, 'A Discourse on the Four First Chapters of the Digest'

Berkshire Record Office, Reading

| D/P 86/1/1 | Parish register of North Moreton |

Kent Archives Office, Maidstone

| Q/SB4/54; Q/SMc1 | Quarter sessions records |
| Q/SB/1-4 | Session papers, 1640–1650 |

Suffolk Record Office

| B.105/2/1 | Quarter session orders |

Tyne and Wear Archives Service, Newcastle

| 589/4 | Newcastle Common Council Books, 1645–1650 |
| 540/1 | Quarter Sessions Order books, 1644–51 |

Beinecke Rare Book and Manuscript Library, Yale University, New Haven, CT

Osborn Shelves fb 224   Tract on the nature, extent and prosecution of witchcraft

Folger Shakespeare Library, Washington, DC

MS x.d. 436 (58)   Letter from Mr Miller, 1704

Huntington Library, San Marino, CA

Ellesmere MS. 5955/2   Depositions against Anne and Brian Gunter, 1607

Printed Primary Sources

Acts of the General Assembly of the Church of Scotland, 1638–1842, Edinburgh, 1843.

A Just Reproof to the False Reports, Bold, and Unjust Calumnies Dropt in Two Late Pamphlets, Edinburgh, 1705.

A Most Certain, Strange and True Discovery of a Witch, being taken by some of the Parliament forces, London, 1643.

An Account of an Horrid and Barbarous Murder in a Letter from a Gentleman in Fife, Edinburgh, 1705.

An Account of the Wicked and Terrible Confederacy of Betty Laing, Edinburgh, 1704.

An Answer of a Letter from a Gentleman of Fife to a nobleman, containing a brief account of the barbarous and illegal treatment of these poor women accused of witchcraft, 1705.

Anderson, W.J. (ed.), 'Narratives of the Scottish Reformation, III: Prefect Ballentine's Report, *circa* 1660: Part One', *Innes Review* 8 (1957), 39–66.

A Prodigious and Tragicall History of the Arraignment, Tryall, Confession, and Condemnation of Six Witches at Maidstone in Kent, London, 1652.

A Relation of the Diabolical Practices of above Twenty Wizards and Witches of the Sheriffdom of Renfrewshire, London, 1697.

A True Account of the Forms Us'd in Pursuits of Treason According to the Laws of Scotland, Edinburgh, 1691.

A True and Exact Relation of the Severall Informations, Examinations and Confessions of the Late Witches Arraigned and Executed in the county of Essex, London, 1645.

A True and Full Relation of the Witches at Pittenweem, Edinburgh, 1704.

A True Narrative of the Sufferings and Relief of a Young Girle, Edinburgh, 1698, reprinted in *A History of the Witches of Renfrewshire*, Paisley, 1877.

A Wonder, A Mercury without a Lye, London, 1648.

Bannatyne, Richard, *Memorials of Transactions in Scotland, AD 1559–1573*, ed. R. Pitairn, Edinburgh: Bannatyne Club, 1836.

Baxter, Richard, *The Certainty of the Worlds of Spirits*, London, 1691.

Bekker, Balthasar, *De Betoverde Weereld*, 4 vols, Amsterdam, 1691–3.

—— *The World Bewitched; or, an examination of the common opinion concerning spirits, their nature, power and operations*, London, 1695.

Bernard, Richard, *A Guide to Grand-Jury Men . . . in Cases of Witchcraft*, London, 1627.

Black, G.F. (ed.), *Some Unpublished Scottish Witchcraft Trials*, New York, 1941.

Boguet, Henri, *An Examen of Witches*, tr. E. Ashwin, London: John Rodker, 1929.

Burt, E. (ed.), *Letters from the North of Scotland*, Edinburgh, 1876.

Calendar of State Papers Domestic 1611–1618, London: Longmans, 1858.

Calendar of State Papers Relating to Scotland and Mary, Queen of Scots, 1547–1603, 13 vols, Edinburgh, 1898–1969.

Carlyle, A., *Autobiography*, London, 1800.

Clark, Samuel, *The Lives of Sundry Eminent Persons in this Later Age*, London, 1683.

Craig, Thomas, *De Unione Regnorum Britanniae Tractatus*, ed. S. Terry, Edinburgh: SHS, 1909.

Cook, D. (ed.), *Annals of Pittenweem … 1526–1793*, Anstruther, 1867.

Cotta, John, *The Triall of Witch-craft*, London, 1616.

Davenport, John, *The Witches of Huntingdon*, London, 1646.

[Des Niau], *The History of the Devils of Loudun: the Alleged Possession of the Ursuline Nuns and the Trial and Execution of Urbain Grandier*, tr. and ed. E. Goldsmid, Collectanea Adamantea, 21, Edinburgh, 1887.

Downame, John. *Annotations upon all the books of the Old and New Testament*, London, 1645.

Endorism, or a Strange Relation of Dreamers or Spirits that Trouble the Minister's House of Kinross, Edinburgh, 1718.

[Filmer, Robert], *An Advertisement to the Jury-Men of England, Touching Witches, together with A Difference between an English and an Hebrew Witch*, London, 1653.

Firth, C. H. (ed.), *Scotland and the Commonwealth*, Edinburgh: SHS 18, 1895.

—— *Scotland and the Protectorate*, Edinburgh: SHS, 1899.

Fontaine, J., *Discours des marques des sorciers*, Paris, 1611.

Forbes, William, *Institutes of the Laws of Scotland*, Edinburgh, 1730.

Gardiner, Ralph, *England's Grievance Discovered in Relation to the Coal Trade*, London, 1796.

Gardiner, S. R. (ed.), *Letters and Papers Illustrating the relations between Charles the Second and Scotland in 1650*, Edinburgh: SHS, 1894.

Gaskill, M. (ed.), *The Matthew Hopkins Trials* [*The English Witchcraft Trials, 1560–1736*, vol. 3], London: Pickering & Chatto, 2003.

Gaule, John, *Cases of Conscience touching Witches and Witchcraft*, London, 1646.

Gibson, M. (ed.), *Witchcraft and Society in England, 1550–1750*, Ithaca, NY: Cornell University Press, 2003.

Glanvill, Joseph, *Saducismus Triumphatus*, London, 1681.

Goodcole, Henry, *The Wonderful Discoverie of Elizabeth Sawyer a Witch, Late of Edmonton, her conviction and condemnation and death*, London, 1621.

Harsnett, Samuel, *A Declaration of Egregious Popish Impostures*, London, 1603.

Hemmingius, N., *Admonitio de superstitionibus magicis vitandis*, Copenhagen, 1580

Henderson, E. (ed.), *Extracts from the Kirk-Session Records of Dunfermline*, Edinburgh, 1865.

Hobbes, Thomas, *Leviathan*, ed. C.B. Macpherson, Harmondsworth: Penguin, 1968.

Holland, Henry, *A Treatise against Witchcraft*, Cambridge, 1590.

Homes, Nathaniel, *Daemonologie and Theologie*, London, 1650.

Hopkins, Matthew, *The Discovery of Witches*, London, 1647.

Hutchinson, Francis, *An Historical Essay Concerning Witchcraft*, London, 1718.

Jacobs, J. (ed.), *Epistolae Ho-Eliane: The Familiar Lettres of James Howell*, London, 1890.

Johnston, Robert, *Historia Rerum Britannicarum*, Amsterdam, 1655.

Jolly, T., *A Vindication of the Surey Demoniack*, London, 1698.

Jorden, Edward, *A Briefe Discourse of a Disease Called Suffocation of the Mother*, London, 1603.

—— *Discourse of Natural Baths*, 3rd edn, London, 1669.

Kennet, White, *The Witchcraft of the Present Rebellion*, London, 1715.

Kinloch, G.R. (ed.), *The Diary of Mr. John Lamont of Newton, 1649–71*, Edinburgh: Maitland Club, 1830.

Kirkton, James, *The Secret and True History of the Church of Scotland*, ed. C.K. Sharpe, Edinburgh, 1817.

Klingner, E., *Luther und der deutsche Volksaberglaube*, Berlin, 1912.

Laing, D. (ed.), *The Letters and Journals of Robert Baillie, A.M.*, Edinburgh: Bannatyne Club, 1841–2.

Lancre, Pierre de, *Tableau de l'inconstance des mauvais anges et demons*, Paris, 1613.

Larkin, F., and Hughes, P. (eds), *Stuart Royal Proclamations*, vol. 1, Oxford: Clarendon Press, 1973.

Lauder, Sir John, *Historical Notices of Scottish Affairs*, ed. J. Laing, Edinburgh: Bannatyne Club, 1848.

—— (ed.), *The Decisions of the Lords of Council and Session from June 6th 1678 to July 30th 1712*, Edinburgh, 1759–61.

The Lawes against Witches and Conjuration, London, 1645, title page.

Lawson, Deodat, *A Brief and True Narrative of Some Remarkable Passages relating to Sundry Persons Afflicted by Witchcraft*, Boston, 1693.

MacDonald, M. (ed.), *Witchcraft and Hysteria in Elizabethan London: Edward Jorden and the Mary Glover Case*, London: Routledge, 1990.

Mackenzie, Sir George, *A Vindication of the Government of Scotland*, Edinburgh, 1691.

—— *Jus Regium: or the just and solid foundations of monarchy in general*, London, 1684.

—— *Laws and Customes of Scotland in Matters Criminal*, Edinburgh, 1678.

—— *Pleadings in Some Remarkable Cases*, Edinburgh, 1672.

Mackie, J.D., and Dickinson, W.C., 'Relation of the Manner of Judicatores of Scotland', *SHR* 19 (1922), 254–72.

Mather, Cotton, *Memorable Providences Relating to Witchcrafts and Possessions*, Boston, 1689.

Mather, Increase, *Cases of Conscience Concerning Evil Spirits Personating Men*, Boston, 1693.

Melville, Sir James, *Memoirs of His Own Life by Sir James Melville of Halhill*, Edinburgh: Bannatyne Club, 1827.

Mercurius Politicus, 10 (10 Aug. 1650).

Michaelis, Sebastien, *Histoire admirable de la possession et conversion d'une pénitente séduite par un magicien*, Paris, 1614.

Mitchell, A., and Christie, J. (eds), *The Records of the Commissions of the General Assemblies of the Church of Scotland*, 3 vols, Edinburgh: SHS, 1892–1909.

Mora, G. (ed.), *Witches, Devils and Doctors in the Renaissance: Johann Weyer*, De Praestigiis daemonum, Binghamton, NY: Medieval and Renaissance Texts and Studies, 73, 1991.

More, George, *A True Discourse concerning the certain possession and dispossession of 7 persons in one family in Lancashire*, 1600.

More, Henry, *An Antidote Against Atheism*, London, 1655.

Neilson, G. (ed.), 'A Sermon on Witchcraft in 1697', *SHR* 7 (1910), 390–9.

Nicoll, J., *A Diary of Public Transactions and Other Occurrences, chiefly in Scotland*, Edinburgh, 1836.

Normand, L. and Roberts, G. (eds), *Witchcraft in Early Modern Scotland: James VI's Demonology and the North Berwick Witches*, Exeter: Exeter University Press, 2000.

Nicolas, Augustin, *Si la torture est un moyen seur a vérifier les crimes sécrets: dissertation morale et juridique*, Amsterdam, 1682.

Paterson, James, *A Belief in Witchcraft Unsupported by Scripture*, Aberdeen, 1815.

Perkins, William, *A Discourse of the Damned Art of Witchcraft*, Cambridge, 1608.

Perrault, François, *The Devill of Mascon, or, a true relation of the chiefe things which an unclean spirit did, and said at Mascon*, Oxford, 1658.

Pitcairn, R. (ed.), *Criminal Trials in Scotland*, 3 vols, Edinburgh: William Tait, 1833.

Potts, Thomas, *A Wonderfull Discoverie of Witches in the Countie of Lancaster*, London, 1613.

Prynne, W., *Diotrephes Catechised: Or Sixteen Important Questions touching the Ecclesiastical Jurisdiction*, London, 1646.

Reid, A.G. (ed.), *The Diary of Andrew Hay of Craignethan 1659–1660*, Edinburgh: SHS, 1901.

Roberts, Alexander, *A Treatise of Witchcraft*, London, 1616.

Rogers, C. (ed.), *The Earl of Stirling's Original Register of Royal Letters*, 2 vols, Edinburgh, 1885.

Rutt, J.T. (ed.), *Diary of Thomas Burton, Esq., Member of Parliaments of Oliver and Richard Cromwell from 1656 to 1659*, London, 1828.

Saducismus Debellatus, London, 1698.

Sassen, J., *De usu et abusu torturae*, 1697, 1726, 1735.

Scot, Reginald, *The Discoverie of Witchcraft*, ed. M. Summers, London: John Rodker, 1930.

Scott, Sir Walter, *Letters on Demonology and Witchcraft*, London: G. Routledge, 1884.

Scott-Montcrieff, W.G. (ed.), *The Records of the Proceedings of the Justiciary Court, Edinburgh, 1661–1678*, vol. 1, Edinburgh: SHS, 1905.

Sinclair, George, *Satan's Invisible World Discovered*, Edinburgh, 1685.

—— *Satan's Invisible World Discovered … To which is added …the witches of Bargarran …*, Edinburgh, 1780.

Smith, J.I. (ed.), *Selected Justiciary Cases, 1624–1650*, vols 2–3, Edinburgh: Stair Society, 1972, 1974.

[Spee, Friedrich], *Cautio Criminalis*, Rinteln, 1631.

Stevenson, D. (ed.), *The Government of Scotland under the Covenanters, 1637–1651*, Edinburgh: SHS, 1982.

Summers, M. (ed.), The *Malleus Maleficarum of Heinrich Kramer and James Sprenger*, London: John Rodker, 1928.

Taylor, L.B. (ed.), *Aberdeen Council Letters*, 4 vols, London: Oxford University Press, 1954.

Taylor, Zachary, *Popery, superstition, ignorance, and knavery, confess'd, and fully proved on the Surey dissenters from the second letter of an apostate friend to Zach. Taylor*, London, 1699.

—— *The Surey Impostor*, London, 1697.

The Book of the General Laws and Liberties concerning the Inhabitants of the Massachusets, Cambridge, MA, 1648.

The Examination, Confession, Triall, and Execution of Joane Williford, Joan Cariden, and Jane Holt: who were executed at Feversham in Kent, London, 1645.

The History of the Witches of Renfrewshire, Paisley: Alex Gardner, 1877.

The Impossibility of Witchcraft, plainly proving, from Scripture and reason, that there never was a witch and that it is both irrational and impious to believe that there ever was, London, 1712.

The Manuscripts of the Duke of Roxburghe, Historical Manuscripts Commission, *Fourteenth Report*, appendix III, London, 1894.

The Parliaments Post, 13(3) (29 July–5 Aug. 1645).

The Register of the Privy Council of Scotland, 38 vols, Edinburgh 1877– .

The Second Part of the Boy of Bilson, or a True and Particular Relation of the Impostor Susanna Fowles, London, 1698.

The Surey Demoniack: or, An Account of Satan's Strange and Dreadful Actings in and about the Body of Richard Dugdale of Surey, near Lancashire, London, 1697.

Thomasius, Christian, *De origine ac progressu processus inquisitorii contra sagas*, Halle, 1712.

—— *De tortura ex fori Christianorum proscribenda*, Halle, 1705.

—— *Über die Hexenprozesse*, ed. R. Lieberwirth, Weimar, 1986.

Trial, Confession and Execution of Isobel Inch, John Stewart, Margaret Barclay and Isobel Crawford for Witchcraft at Irvine. Anno 1618, Ardrossan and Saltcoates, 1855.

Two Terrible Sea-Fights … Likewise The Tryal of Six Witches at Edenborough in Scotland, London, 1652.

Whitelocke, Bulstrode, *Memorials of the English Affairs*, London, 1652.

Witchcraft Proven, Arreign'd and Condemn'd in its Professors, Professions and Marks, Glasgow, 1697.

Secondary sources

Baker, J.H., 'Criminal Courts and Procedure at Common Law, 1550–1800', in J.S. Cockburn (ed.), *Crime in England, 1550–1800*, Princeton: Princeton University Press, 1977.

Baronowski, B., *Process czarownic w Polsce w XVII i XVIII wieku*, Lodz, 1952.

Baschwitz, K., *Czarownice: Dzieje procesów o czary*, Warsaw, 1963.

Baxter, C., 'Johann Weyer's *De Praestigiis daemonum*: Unsystematic Psychopathology', in S. Anglo (ed.), *The Damned Art: Essays in the Literature of Witchcraft*, London: Routledge & Kegan Paul, 1977, pp. 53–75.

Behringer, W., 'Das "Reichskhündig Exempel" von Trier: Zur paradigmatischen Rolle einer Hexenverfolgung in Deutschland', in G. Franz and F. Irsigler (eds), *Hexenglaube und Hexenprozesse in Raum Rhein-Mosel-Saar*, Trier: Paulinus Verlag, 1995, pp. 435–47.

—— 'Machiavellianism', in R. Golden (ed.), *Encyclopedia of Witchcraft: The Western Tradition*, Santa Barbara, CA: ABC-Clio, 2004, vol. 3, pp. 688–90.

—— 'Weather, Hunger and Fear: Origins of the European Witch-hunts in Climate, Society and Mentality', *German History* 13 (1995), 351–77.

—— *Witches and Witch-hunts: A Global History*, Cambridge: Polity Press, 2004.

Black, G.F., *A Calendar of Cases of Witchcraft in Scotland, 1510–1727*, New York: New York Public Library, 1938.

Boyer, P. and Nissenbaum, S., *Salem Possessed: The Social Origins of Witchcraft*, Cambridge, MA: Harvard University Press, 1974.

Bostridge, I., *Witchcraft and its Transformations, c.1650–c.1750*, Oxford: Clarendon Press, 1997.

—— 'Witchcraft Repealed', in J. Barry, M. Hester and G. Roberts (eds), *Witchcraft in Early Modern Europe*, Cambridge: Cambridge University Press, 1996, pp. 309–44.

Braddick, M.J., *State Formation in Early Modern England, c.1550–c.1700*, Cambridge: Cambridge University Press, 2000.

Brand, J., *The History and Antiquities of the Town and County of the Town of Newcastle upon Tyne*, London, 1789.

Carlton, C., *Going to the Wars: The Experience of the British Civil Wars, 1638–1651*, London, 1992.

Calderwood, David, *The History of the Kirk of Scotland*, 8 vols, Edinburgh: Wodrow Society, 1842–9.

Certeau, M. *The Possession at Loudun*, tr. M.B. Smith, Chicago: University of Chicago Press, 1996.

Chajes, J.H., 'Judgments Sweetened: Possession and Exorcism in Early Modern Jewish Culture', *Journal of Early Modern History* 1 (1997), 124–69.

Chambers, R., *Domestic Annals of Scotland: From the Reformation to the Revolution*, 3 vols, Edinburgh: W. & R. Chambers, 1858–61.

Charcot, J., *Lectures on the Diseases of the Nervous System*, 3 vols, tr. G. Sigerson, London: New Sydenham Society, 1877–9.

Clark, S., 'Inversion, Misrule and the Meaning of Witchcraft', *Past and Present* 87 (1980), 110–27.

—— 'King James's *Daemonologie*: Witchcraft and Kingship', in S. Anglo (ed.). *The Damned Art: Essays in the Literature of Witchcraft*, London: Routledge & Kegan Paul, 1977, pp. 156–81.

—— 'Protestant Demonology: Sin, Superstition, and Society (c.1520–c.1630), in B. Ankarloo and G. Henningsen (eds), *Early Modern European Witchcraft: Centres and Peripheries*, Oxford: Clarendon Press, 1990, pp. 45–81.

—— *Thinking with Demons: The Idea of Witchcraft in Early Modern Europe*, Oxford: Clarendon Press, 1997.

Cockburn, J.S., *A History of English Assizes, 1558–1714*, Cambridge: Cambridge University Press, 1972.

Cowan, E.J., 'The Darker Vision of the Scottish Renaissance: The Devil and Francis Stewart', in I.B. Cowan and D. Shaw (eds), *The Renaissance and Reformation in Scotland*, Edinburgh: Scottish Academic Press, 1983, pp. 125–40.

—— and Hendersone, L., 'The Last of the Witches? The Survival of Scottish Witch Belief', *SWHC*, pp. 198–217.

Cowan, I.B., *The Scottish Covenanters, 1660–1688*, London: V. Gollancz, 1976.

Dalyell, J., *The Darker Superstitions of Scotland*, Edinburgh: Waugh & Innes, 1834.

Davies, G., and Hardacre, P., 'The Restoration of the Scottish Episcopacy, 1660–1661', *Journal of British Studies* 1 (1962), 45–50.

Decker, R., *Die Hexen und ihre Henker*, Freiburg: Herder, 1994.

Demos, J., 'Underlying Themes in the Witchcraft of Seventeenth-Century New England', *American Historical Review* 75 (1970), 1311–26.

Dillinger, J., *Böse Leute: Hexenverfolgungen in Schwäbisch-Österreich und Kurtrier im Vergleich*, Trier: Spee, 1999.

Dow, F.D., *Cromwellian Scotland*, Edinburgh: John Donald, 1979.

Durston, G., *Witchcraft and Witch Trials: A History of English Witchcraft and its Legal Perspectives, 1542 to 1736*, Chichester: Barry Rose Law Publishers, 2000.

Elmer, P., 'Towards a Politics of Witchcraft in Early Modern England', in S. Clark (ed.), *Languages of Witchcraft: Narrative, Ideology and Meaning in Early Modern Culture*, Basingstoke: Macmillan, 2001, pp. 101–18.

Ewen, C.L., *Witchcraft and Demonianism*, London: Heath Cranton, 1933.

—— *Witchcraft in the Star Chamber*, privately printed, 1936.

—— *Witch Hunting and Witch Trials*, London: Kegan Paul, 1929.

Ferber, S., *Demonic Possession and Exorcism in Early Modern France*, London: Routledge, 2004.

Gaskill, M., *Witchfinders: A Seventeenth-Century English Tragedy*, Cambridge, MA: Harvard University Press, 2005.

Gilmore, J., 'Witchcraft and the Church of Scotland', unpublished Ph.D. thesis, University of Glasgow, 1948.

Gleason, J.H., *The Justices of the Peace in England, 1558 to 1640*, Oxford: Clarendon Press, 1969.

Goodare, J., *State and Society in Early Modern Scotland*, Oxford: Oxford University Press, 1999.

—— 'The Framework for Scottish Witch-hunting in the 1590s', *SHR* 81 (2002), 240–50.

—— 'The Scottish Witchcraft Act', *Church History* 74 (2004), 39–67.

—— 'The Scottish Witchcraft Panic of 1597', *SWHC*, pp. 51–72.

—— (ed.), *The Scottish Witch-hunt in Context*, Manchester: Manchester University Press, 2002.

—— 'Witch-hunting and the Scottish State', *SWHC*, pp. 122–45.

Goodare, J., Miller, J., Martin, L. and Yeoman, L. 'The survey of Scottish Witchcraft, 1563–1736', www.arts.ed.ac.uk/witches/.

Godbeer, R., *The Devil's Dominion: Magic and Religion in Early New England*, Cambridge: Cambridge University Press, 1992.

Gorski, P.S., *The Disciplinary Revolution: Calvinism and the Rise of the State in Early Modern Europe*, Chicago: Chicago University Press, 2003.

Graham, M.F., 'Social Discipline in Scotland, 1560–1610', in R.A. Mentzer (ed.), *Sin and the Calvinists: Morals Control and the Consistory in the Reformed Tradition*, Kirksville, MO: Sixteenth Century Journal, 1994, pp. 129–57.

Greenblatt, S., *Shakespearean Negotiations*, Berkeley, CA: University of California Press, 1988.

Harley, D., 'Explaining Salem: Calvinist Psychology and the Diagnosis of Possession', *American Historical Review* 101 (1996), 307–30.

Henderson, E., *Annals of Dunfermline and Vicinity*, Glasgow, 1879.

Henningsen, G., *The Witches' Advocate: Basque Witchcraft and the Spanish Inquisition*, Reno, NV: University of Nevada Press, 1980.

Hindle, S., *The State and Social Change in Early Modern England, 1550–1640*, London: Palgrave, 2000.

Holmes, C., 'Popular Culture? Witches, Magistrates and Divines in Early Modern England', in S.L. Kaplan (ed.), *Understanding Popular Culture*, New York: Mouton, 1984, pp. 85–111.

Howell, R., *Newcastle upon Tyne and the Puritan Revolution*, Oxford: Clarendon Press, 1967.

Jackson, C., 'Judicial Torture, the Liberties of the Subject, and Anglo-Scottish Relations, 1660–1690', in T.C. Smout (ed.), *Anglo-Scottish Relations from 1603 to 1900*, Oxford: Proceedings of the British Academy, 2005, pp. 75–101.

Johansen, J.C.V., 'Witchcraft, Sin and Repentance: The Decline of Danish Witchcraft Trials', *Acta Ethnographica* 37 (1991/2), 413–23.

Johnstone, N., *The Devil and Demonism in Early Modern England*, Cambridge: Cambridge University Press, 2000.

Kantorowiz, E., *The King's Two Bodies*, Princeton: Princeton University Press, 1957.

Karlsen, C., *The Devil in the Shape of a Woman*, New York: W.W. Norton, 1987.

Kieckhefer, R., *European Witch Trials: Their Foundations in Popular and Learned Cultures, 1300–1500*, London: Routledge & Kegan Paul, 1976.

Kittredge, G.L., *Witchcraft in Old and New England*, Cambridge, MA: Harvard University Press, 1929.

Klaits, J., 'Witchcraft Trials and Absolute Monarchy in France', in R. Golden (ed.), *Church, State and Society under the Bourbon Kings of France*, Lawrence, KS: Coronado Press, 1982, pp. 148–72.

Kneubühler, H., *Die Überwindung von Hexenwahn und Hexenprozess*, Diessenhofen: Rüegger, 1977.

Lamont, W., *Godly Rule: Politics and Religion 1603–60*, London: Macmillan, 1969.

Langbein, J., *Prosecuting Crime in the Renaissance*, Cambridge, MA: Harvard University Press, 1974.

—— 'The Criminal Trial before the Lawyers', *University of Chicago Law Review* 45 (1978), 307–16.

—— *Torture and the Law of Proof*, Chicago: Chicago University Press, 1976.

Larner, C., *Enemies of God: The Witch-hunt in Scotland*, Baltimore, MD: Johns Hopkins University Press, 1981.

—— 'Two Late Scottish Witchcraft Tracts: *Witchcraft Proven* and *The Tryal of Witchcraft*', in S. Anglo (ed.), *The Damned Art: Essays in the Literature of Witchcraft*, London: Routledge & Kegan Paul, 1977, pp. 227–45.

—— *Witchcraft and Religion: The Politics of Popular Belief*, Oxford: Basil Blackwell, 1984.

—— Lee, C.H. and McLachlan, H.V., *A Source-book of Scottish Witchcraft*, Glasgow: Department of Sociology, University of Glasgow, 1977.

Lecky, W.E.H., *The History of the Rise and Influence of the Spirit of Rationalism in Europe*, New York: D. Appleton, 1910.

Lee, M., Jr., *Government by Pen: Scotland under James VI and I*, Urbana, IL: University of Illinois Press, 1980.

—— *The Cabal*, Urbana, IL: Illinois University Press, 1965.

Legge, F., 'Witchcraft in Scotland', *The Scottish Review* 18 (1891), 257–88.

Leutenbauer, S., *Hexerei- und Zaubereidelikt in der Literatur von 1450 bis 1550*, Berlin: Schweizer, 1972.

Levack, B.P., 'Judicial Torture in Scotland during the Age of Mackenzie', in *Miscellany* IV, Edinburgh: Stair Society, 2002, vol. 49, pp.185–98.

—— 'Possession, Witchcraft and the Law in Jacobean England', *Washington and Lee Law Review* 52 (1996), 1613–40.

—— *The Civil Lawyers in England, 1603–1641: A Political Study*, Oxford: Clarendon Press, 1973.

—— 'The Decline and End of Witchcraft Prosecutions', in M. Gijswijt-Hofstra, B.P. Levack and R. Porter, *Witchcraft and Magic in Europe: The Eighteenth and Nineteenth Centuries*, London: Athlone Press, 1999, pp. 1–93.

—— *The Witch-hunt in Early Modern Europe*, 3rd edn, London: Longman, 2006.

Lorenz, S. and Bauer, D.R. (eds), *Das Ende der Hexenverfolgung*, Stuttgart: Franz Steiner, 1995.

Macdonald, S., 'In Search of the Devil in Fife Witchcraft Cases, 1560–1705', *SWHC*, pp. 33–50.

—— *The Witches of Fife: Witch-hunting in a Scottish Shire, 1560–1710*, East Linton: Tuckwell, 2002.

—— 'Torture and the Scottish Witch-hunt: A Re-examination', *Scottish Tradition* 27 (2002), 95–114.

McDonald, S.W., 'The Devil's Mark and the Witch-Prickers of Scotland', *Journal of the Royal Society of Medicine* 90 (1997), 507–10.

—— Thom, A. and Thom, A., 'The Bargarran Witchcraft Trial: A Psychiatric Assessment', *Scottish Medical Journal* 41 (1996), 152–8.

Macfarlane, A., *Witchcraft in Tudor and Stuart England: A Regional and Comparative Study*, New York: Harper & Row, 1970.

McLachlan, H., and Swales, K., 'The Bewitchment of Christian Shaw: A Reassessment of the Famous Paisley Witchcraft Case of 1697', in Y.G. Brown and R. Ferguson (eds), *Twisted Sisters: Women, Crime and Deviance in Scotland since 1400*, East Linton: Tuckwell Press, 2002, pp. 54–83.

Mandrou, R., *Magistrats et sorciers en France au XVIIe siècle*, Paris: Librairie Plon, 1968.

Mathieson, W.L., *Politics and Religion*, Glasgow, 1902.

Maxwell Stuart, P.G., *An Abundance of Witches: The Great Scottish Witch-hunt*, Stroud: Tempus, 2005.

—— *Satan's Conspiracy: Magic and Witchcraft in Sixteenth-Century Scotland*, East Linton: Tuckwell Press, 2001.

Melville, R.D., 'The Use and Form of Judicial Torture in Scotland', *SHR* 2 (1905), 225–48.

Midelfort, H.C.E., *A History of Madness in Sixteenth-Century Germany*, Stanford, CA: Stanford University Press, 1999.

—— 'Catholic and Lutheran Reactions to Demon Possession in the Late Seventeenth Century: Two Case Histories', *Daphnis* 15 (1986), 623–48.

—— 'The Devil and the German People: Reflections on the Popularity of Demon Possession in Sixteenth-Century Germany', in S. Ozment (ed.), *Religion and Culture in the Renaissance and Reformation*, Kirksville, MO: Sixteenth Century Essays and Studies, 11, 1989, pp. 99–119.

—— *Witch-hunting in Southwestern Germany, 1562–1684*, Stanford, CA: Stanford University Press, 1972.

Miller, J., 'Devices and Directions: Folk Healing Aspects of Witchcraft Practice in Seventeenth-Century Scotland', *SWHC*, pp. 90–105.

Monter, E. W., 'Law, Medicine and the Acceptance of Witchcraft, 1560–1680', in E.W. Monter (ed.), *European Witchcraft*, New York: John Wiley, 1969, pp. 55–71.

—— 'The Catholic Salem; or, How the Devil Destroyed a Saint's Parish (Mattaincourt 1627–1631)', in W. Behringer and J. Sharpe (eds), *Witchcraft in Context*, Manchester: Manchester University Press, forthcoming.

—— *Witchcraft in France and Switzerland: The Borderlands during the Reformation*, Ithaca, NY: Cornell University Press, 1976.

Moore, J., and Silverthorne, M., 'Protestant Theologies, Limited Sovereignties: Natural Law and Conditions of Union in the German Empire, the Netherlands and Great Britain', in J. Robertson (ed.), *A Union for Empire: Political Thought and the Union of 1707*, Cambridge: Cambridge University Press, 1995, pp. 171–97.

Muchembled, R., *Popular Culture and Elite Culture in France, 1400–1750*, tr. L. Cochrane, Baton Rouge, LA: Louisiana State University Press, 1978.

—— 'The Witches of the Cambrésis: The Acculturation of the Rural World in the Sixteenth and Seventeenth Centuries', in J. Obelkevich (ed.), *Religion and the People, 800–1700*, Chapel Hill, NC: North Carolina University Press, 1979, pp. 221–76.

Neil, W.N., 'The Professional Pricker and his Test for Witchcraft', *SHR* 19 (1922), 205–13.

Newman, B., 'Possessed by the Spirit: Devout Women, Demoniacs, and the Apostolic Life in the Thirteenth Century', *Speculum* 73 (1998), 733–70.

Nischan, B., 'The Exorcism Controversy and Baptism in the Late Reformation', *Sixteenth Century Journal* 18 (1987), 31–51.

Norton, M.B., *In the Devil's Snare: The Salem Witchcraft Crisis of 1692*, New York: Alfred A. Knopf, 2002.

Oldridge, D., *The Devil in Early Modern England*, Stroud: Sutton, 2000.

Olli, S., 'The Devil's Pact: A Male Strategy', in O. Davies and W. de Blécourt (eds), *Beyond the Witch Trials: Witchcraft and Magic in Enlightenment Europe*, Manchester: Manchester University Press, pp. 100–16.

Orr, D.A., *Treason and the State: Law, Politics, and Ideology in the English Civil War*, Cambridge: Cambridge University Press, 2002.

Paterson, J., *History of the County of Ayr*, Ayr, 1847.

Paul, H.N., *The Royal Play of Macbeth*, New York: Macmillan, 1950.

Pócs, É., 'Possession Phenomena, Possession Systems: Some East-Central European Examples', in G. Klaniczay and E. Pócs (eds), *Communicating with the Spirits*, Budapest: Central European University Press, 2005, pp. 84–151.

Purkiss, D., *The English Civil War: A People's History*, London: HarperPress, 2006.

Radford, G.H., 'Thomas Larkham', *Reports and Transactions of the Devonshire Association*, 24 (1892), pp. 96–146.

Rapley, R., *A Case of Witchcraft: The Trial of Urbain Grandier*, Montreal: McGill-Queen's University Press, 1998.

Richardson, M.A., *The Local Historian's Table*, London, 1841.

Ross, W., *Aberdour and Inchcolme*, Edinburgh, 1885.

Scott, H. (ed.), *Fasti Ecclesiae Scoticanae*, Edinburgh, 1925.

Seymour, S. D., *Irish Witchcraft and Demonology*, Baltimore, MD: Norman, Remington, 1913.

Sharpe, C.K., *A Historical Account of the Belief in Witchcraft in Scotland*, London: Hamilton, Adams & Co., 1884.

Sharpe, J., *Instruments of Darkness: Witchcraft in England, 1550–1750*, London: Hamish Hamilton, 1996.

—— 'The Devil in East Anglia', in J. Barry, M. Hester and G. Roberts (eds), *Witchcraft in Early Modern Europe*, Cambridge: Cambridge University Press, 1996, pp. 237–54.

—— 'Witch-hunting and Witch Historiography: Some Anglo-Scottish Comparisons', *SWHC*, pp. 182–97.

Sluhovsky, M., 'The Devil in the Convent', *American Historical Review* 107 (2002), 1379–411.

Skeel, C.A.J., *The Council in the Marches of Wales*, London: H. Rees, 1904.

Smith, J.I., 'Criminal Procedure', in *An Introduction to Scottish Legal History*, Edinburgh: Stair Society, 1958, pp. 426–48.

Smith, L.M., 'Scotland and Cromwell: A Study in Early Modern Government', unpublished D.Phil. thesis, University of Oxford, 1979.

Soman, A.F., 'Decriminalizing Witchcraft: Does the French Experience Furnish a European Model?', *Criminal Justice History* 11 (1989), 1–22.

—— 'The Parlement of Paris and the Great Witch Hunt (1565–1640)', *Sixteenth-Century Journal* 9 (1978), 31–44.

Stafford, H., 'Notes on Scottish Witchcraft Cases, 1590–91', in N. Downs (ed.), *Essays in Honor of Conyers Read*, Chicago: University of Chicago Press, 1953, pp. 96–118, 278–84.

Stephen, W., *History of Inverkeithing and Rosyth*, Aberdeen: G. & W. Fraser, 1921.

Thomas, K. *Religion and the Decline of Magic*, New York: Scribner, 1971.

Todd, M., *The Culture of Protestantism in Early Modern Scotland*, New Haven: Yale University Press, 2002.

Trevor Roper, H.R., 'Scotland and the Puritan Revolution', in *Religion, the Reformation and Social Change*, New York: Harper & Row, 1967.

Tyler, P., 'The Church Courts at York and Witchcraft Prosecutions 1567–1640', *Northern History* 4 (1969), 84–110.

Waite, G., *Heresy, Magic and Witchcraft in Early Modern Europe*, Basingstoke: Palgrave, 2003.

Walker, D.P., *Unclean Spirits: Possession and Exorcism in France and England in the Late Sixteenth and Early Seventeenth Centuries*, London and Philadelphia: University of Pennsylvania Press, 1981.

Wasser, M.B., 'The Western Witch-hunt of 1697–1700: The Last Major Witch-hunt in Scotland', *SWHC*, pp. 146–65.

—— and Yeoman, L., 'The Trial of Geillis Johnstone for Witchcraft, 1614', *Miscellany XIII*, Edinburgh: SHS, 2004, pp. 83–114.

Willock, I.D., *The Origins and Development of the Jury in Scotland*, Edinburgh: Stair Society, 1966.

Wormald, J., 'The Witches, the Devil and the King', in D.T. Brotherstone and D. Ditchburn (eds), *Freedom and Authority: Scotland c.1050–c.1650*, East Linton: Tuckwell, 2000, pp. 165–80.

Worobec, C., *Possessed: Women, Witches, and Demons in Imperial Russia*, Dekalb, IL: Northern Illinois University Press, 2001.

Yeoman, L., 'Hunting the Rich Witch in Scotland: High Status Witchcraft Suspects and their Persecutors, 1590–1650', *SWHC*, pp. 106–21.

—— 'The Devil as Doctor: Witchcraft, Wodrow and the Wider World', *Scottish Archives* 1 (1995), 93–105.

Young, John R., 'The Scottish Parliament and Witch-hunting in Scotland under the Covenanters', *Parliaments, Estates and Representation* 26 (2006), 53–65.

—— *The Scottish Parliament, 1639–1661: A Political and Constitutional Analysis*, Edinburgh: John Donald, 1996.

Index